VARIATION AND DISCHARGE
OF LAND OBLIGATIONS

AUSTRALIA
LBC Information Services
Sydney

CANADA and USA
Carswell
Toronto

NEW ZEALAND
Brooker's
Auckland

VARIATION AND DISCHARGE OF LAND OBLIGATIONS

by

Sir Crispin Agnew of Lochnaw, Bt., Q.C.

EDINBURGH
W. GREEN/Sweet & Maxwell
1999

First published 1999

Published in 1999 by W. Green & Son Limited
21 Alva Street
Edinburgh EH2 4PS

Computerset by LBJ Typesetting Ltd
of Kingsclere

Printed in Great Britain by
Redwood Books
Trowbridge, Wiltshire

No natural forests were destroyed to make this product;
only farmed timber was used and replanted

A CIP catalogue record of this book is available from the British Library

ISBN 0 414 01226 7

PREFACE

The jurisdiction given to the Lands Tribunal for Scotland by the Conveyancing and Feudal Reform (Scotland) Act 1970 to vary or discharge a land obligation is an important and under-used one. Unfortunately, the majority of the Lands Tribunal cases in the exercise of this jurisdiction are unreported and little has been written in explanation of the wide powers that the tribunal has to vary and discharge land obligations.

Having an interest in all aspects of land law, I have always thought that feudal obligations and conditions, real burdens and conditions in conveyances give a very good insight into the social development of Scotland and its people. The types of feudal conditions and real burdens and conditions to be found in feu charters, contracts and dispositions reflect the changing concerns, interests and ambitions of those with an interest in land. It is from a reading of some of the more obscure and interesting conditions (payment of a silver penny Scots or the obligation to provide a galley with oarsmen or just to preserve the view) that my interest in the jurisdiction given to the Lands Tribunal has developed.

It is hoped that this book will provide a fairly full introduction to the law and procedures connected with applying to the Lands Tribunal for variation or discharge of land obligations. As we live in a time where land law reform is at the top of the agenda and as the Scottish Law Commission is already recommending revisions to this jurisdiction, no doubt there will be changes in the law in the new millennium.

Also included are chapters on the creation, closure or variation of public footpaths by local authorities and on rectifying land certificates under the Land Registration (Scotland) Act 1979, which are analogous jurisdictions to that exercised by the Lands Tribunal in varying and discharging land obligations.

I would like to thank all the staff at W. Green for their patience and help with the manuscript; Neil Tannock, Principal Clerk to the Lands Tribunal, for his help; Ann Lanzl, who read the manuscript and made helpful corrections; and my family, who had to put up with "I'm sorry, I'm writing my book and cannot take you" sailing or climbing or swimming or riding.

I have tried to state the law at September 30, 1998 with a note of some later cases.

Crispin Agnew of Lochnaw

v

CONTENTS

TABLE OF CASES

TABLE OF STATUTES

TABLE OF STATUTORY INSTRUMENTS

ABBREVIATIONS

Gordon   William M. Gordon, *Scottish Land Law* (W. Green, 1989)

Halliday   John M. Halliday, *Conveyancing Law and Practice in Scotland* (2nd ed. by Iain J.S. Talman, W. Green, 1997)

Halliday   *Conveyancing Legislation and Practice*, Report by a
Report   Committee appointed by the Secretary of State for Scotland, Cmnd 3118 (1966)

Scammell   Ernest Scammell, *Land Covenants* (Butterworths, 1996)

1925 Act   Law of Property Act 1925

1967 Act   Countryside (Scotland) Act 1967

1970 Act   Conveyancing and Feudal Reform (Scotland) Act 1970

1979 Act   Land Registration (Scotland) Act 1979

1971 Rules   Rules of the Lands Tribunal for Scotland 1971 (S.I. 1971 No. 218)

CHAPTER 1

INTRODUCTION

Historical aspects

Prior to the passing of the Conveyancing and Feudal Reform **1–01**
(Scotland) Act 1970,[1] which conferred jurisdiction on the Lands
Tribunal for Scotland to vary or discharge a land obligation, real
burdens and conditions, positive and negative servitudes and other
binding land obligations were enforceable in their terms, even if
the purpose of the obligation was obsolete or no longer reasonable.

If a real burden, condition or servitude was to become unenforceable, this could be only by operation of law, where loss of the
right to enforce usually occurred through: (1) express consent or
deed of waiver; (2) acquiescence or implied consent; (3) loss of
interest to enforce; (4) the long negative prescriptive period; (5)
consolidation of the *dominium directum* with the *dominium utile*; or
(6) compulsory purchase.[2]

The Halliday Report[3]

A committee chaired by Professor John M. Halliday was com- **1–02**
missioned to consider appropriate feudal reform. One aspect
considered by the committee was the variation and discharge of
conditions and servitudes affecting land. As a result of that part of
the report, Part I of the 1970 Act was passed. This Part established
the Lands Tribunal for Scotland, with jurisdiction to vary or
discharge what were called "land obligations".

The Halliday Report identified that:

"25. One of the major problems which affects any system of
landownership is to secure that land conditions, created within

[1] "the 1970 Act".
[2] See William M. Gordon, *Scottish Land Law* (W. Green, 1989) ("Gordon"),
Chaps 21–24; John M. Halliday, *Conveyancing Law and Practice in Scotland* (2nd
ed. by Iain J. S. Talman, W. Green, 1997) ("Halliday"), Vol. 2, paras 34-42 to 34-62
(real burdens and conditions) and 35-26 to 35-34 (servitudes); and *Stair Memorial
Encyclopaedia*, Vol. 18, paras 426–437 (real burdens) and 470–476 (servitudes).
[3] *Conveyancing Legislation and Practice*, Report by a Committee appointed by the
Secretary of State for Scotland Cmnd 3118 (1996) ("the Halliday Report").

1

the structure of a permanent or long-term holding, can be modified to changed circumstances so that proper developments are not unreasonably impeded. . . . The person entitled to the benefit of a land condition or servitude . . . may be willing to modify it on reasonable terms, but he may not, or indeed he may be unwilling to modify it at all, and in that case desirable redevelopment may either be prevented or be hindered by excessive consideration demanded for the modification. The problem is already evident in older urban areas where redevelopment is taking place and will arise in due course in newer areas. The existing procedures for compulsory acquisition, which provide no more than a partial solution since they are available only to particular bodies, are more appropriate to large scale developments and are slow and cumbersome. We consider that special judicial machinery should be provided in Scotland for the variation and discharge of land conditions."

1–03   The report recommended:

"Jurisdiction and procedure

26. We set out what we regard as the essential features of the jurisdiction and procedure of the judicial body to which this task would be entrusted, as follows:

(1) Where a person is desirous of using or developing his property in a manner prohibited or restricted by a land condition or servitude and (a) the person or persons entitled to enforce the condition or servitude or any of them cannot be ascertained by reasonable enquiry, or (b) the persons so entitled are numerous, or (c) a person so entitled has refused to vary or discharge the condition or servitude so as to permit the desired use or development, or (d) there has been failure to reach agreement as to the terms upon which such variation or discharge will be granted, then the judicial body may, on application by the person desiring such variation or discharge, vary or discharge the condition or servitude if it is satisfied

  (i) that by reason of changes in the character of the property or the neighbourhood or other circumstances which it may deem material, the condition or servitude has become obsolete or inappropriate or of little practical value to the person or persons entitled to enforce it, or

  (ii) that the use or development of the property for which variation or discharge of the condition or servitude is desired is reasonable and that any substantial loss or damage which such variation or discharge may cause to any person who was entitled to enforce the condition or servitude can adequately be compensated by a payment of money.

(2) Where variation or discharge of a condition or servitude is so authorised the judicial body may award such compensation as it may consider appropriate to any person who was entitled to enforce such condition or servitude.

(3) On points of law the decision of the body should be subject to appeal to the Court of Session but no further; on all other matters the decision of the body should be final.

(4) The procedure should be speedy and inexpensive.

(5) Notice of the application for variation or discharge of a land condition or servitude should require to be served on any person having a legal right to enforce it and on any 'affected proprietor', the definition whereof might be modelled with suitable adaptations on that contained in Regulation 6 of the Building (Scotland) Act 1959 (Procedure) Regulations 1964.

(6) The proceedings of the body should be public and its decisions should be available, for reporting.

(7) An extract of any decision varying or discharging a land condition or servitude should be recorded in the Register of Sasines in order to be effective in a question with third parties."

From these recommendations, sections 1 and 2 of the 1970 Act **1–04** were born. In the years 1987–97 there were on average about 72 applications a year to the tribunal for variation or discharge of a land obligation. In the period 1971–86 the indications were that application levels were similar, but slightly lower, perhaps because of a lack of awareness of the tribunal's powers. Of the 40 most recent applications dealt with by the tribunal in the period mid-1997 to mid-1998, 20 were opposed and 20 unopposed, with 34 applications granted. The six refused applications were opposed applications. In the period 1990–97 the overall success rate in applications to the tribunal, including unopposed applications granted, was 89.8 per cent. Taking the last 20 applications to be dealt with to mid-1998, the average time taken to dispose of an opposed application was 37 weeks and an unopposed application 14 weeks.

The time taken to dispose of applications was often lengthened if the application was incomplete or parties requested extensions of time or were unavailable for a suggested hearing date. As the tribunal has a duty to investigate the title so that service can be effected on all benefited and affected proprietors, it is essential that it has sufficient information to achieve this result speedily if delay is to be avoided.[4]

The English position

1–05   In England certain of the Official Arbiters appointed under the Acquisition of Land (Assessment of Compensation) Act 1919[5] were, and later, from 1950, the Lands Tribunal was, given jurisdiction under section 84 of the Law of Property Act 1925[6] to vary or discharge restrictions, affecting freehold land arising under covenant or otherwise. The original grounds for variation or discharge were:

> "84.—(1) The Authority hereinafter defined shall (without prejudice to any concurrent jurisdiction of the court) have power from time to time, on the application of any person interested in any freehold land affected by any restriction arising under covenant or otherwise as to the user thereof or the building thereon, by order wholly or partially to discharge or modify any such restriction (subject or not to the payment by the applicant of compensation to any person suffering loss in consequence of the order) on being satisfied—
>
> (a) that by reason of changes in the character of the property or the neighbourhood or other circumstances of the case which the Authority may deem material, the restriction ought to be deemed obsolete, or that the continued existence thereof would impede the reasonable user of the land for public or private purposes without securing practical benefits to other persons, or, as the case may be, would unless modified so impede such user; or
>
> (b) that the persons of full age and capacity for the time being or from time to time entitled to the benefit of the restriction, whether in respect of estates in fee simple or any lesser estates or interests in the property to which the benefit of the restriction is annexed, have agreed, either expressly or by implication, by their acts or omissions, to the same being discharged or modified; or
>
> (c) that the proposed discharge or modification will not injure the persons entitled to the benefit of the restriction.

---

[4] Lands Tribunal statistics provided to the Scottish Law Commission.
[5] Law of Property Act 1925, s. 10.
[6] 15 & 16 Geo. 5, c. 20 ("the 1925 Act").

Provided that no compensation shall be payable in respect of the discharge or modification of a restriction by reason of any advantage thereby accruing to the owner of the land affected by the restriction, unless the person entitled to the benefit of the restriction also suffers loss in consequence of the discharge or modification, nor shall any compensation be payable in excess of such loss; but this provision shall not affect any right to compensation where the person claiming the compensation proves that by reason of the imposition of the restriction, the amount of the consideration paid for the acquisition of the land was reduced."

This jurisdiction was substantially extended in 1969 by the amendment of section 84 by the Law of Property Act 1969.[7]

While the jurisdiction under the 1970 Act is substantially similar **1–06** to the jurisdiction under the 1925 Act, there are significant differences in the wording of the statutes, which will be considered in relation to the relevant sections of the 1970 Act. Reliance on English authorities in applications under the 1970 Act therefore have to be treated with caution and the differences between the two statutes clearly understood.

For a consideration of the law in England relating to section 84 of the Law of Property Act 1925, reference should be made to *inter alia*: the introduction to Vol. 7 of the *Property and Compensation Reports; Halsbury's Encyclopaedia of the Laws of England,*[8] Vol. 16, paras 803–814; and *Land Covenants* by Ernest Scammell, Chaps 14–21, which is probably the most recent and detailed work on the subject.[9] The majority of English law reports regarding modification and discharge of restrictive covenants are to be found in the *Property and Compensation Reports*, with useful summaries of Lands Tribunal decisions to be found in the annual *Current Law Yearbooks* under "Real Property and Conveyancing".

The future

The Scottish Law Commission is actively involved in considering **1–07** reform of the law relating to real burdens. This was dealt with initially in Discussion Paper No. 93, *Property Law, Abolition of the Feudal System.*[10] A further discussion paper, No. 106, *Real Burdens*, was published in October 1998.

---

[7] See App. 2: 1925 Act, s. 84 (as now amended).
[8] (4th ed. (reissue), Butterworths, 1992).
[9] (Butterworths, 1996), "Scammell".
[10] (July 1991).

The object of land reform is to abolish the feudal system. The effect of this will be to abolish the position of the superior in relation to land and the superior's current right to enforce land obligations contained in any feu charter or disposition. This will have a radical effect on the definition of "benefited proprietor"[11] and will restrict the enforceability of land obligations to a much narrower class of persons.

In Discussion Paper No. 93 the Scottish Law Commission proposed that the conditions should be enforceable either by proprietors, who qualify by virtue of owning land in the proximity of the burdened land and who can demonstrate that failure to comply with the conditions would be detrimental to them, or by the disponers and their successors, who can establish the necessary title and interest.[12] Proprietors benefiting from a common part or service might also have a right to enforce service conditions.

It was suggested that the Lands Tribunal for Scotland might be the only jurisdiction in which there could be enforcement of any land condition, with power to the tribunal to award compensation in lieu of enforcement.[13]

The Commission also suggested that the jurisdiction of the tribunal should be extended to enable consideration to be given to the variation or discharge of all real burdens and land conditions. Further, the tribunal should be given jurisdiction, on application by the Keeper of the Registers or a burdened proprietor, to declare that land conditions or real burdens were obsolete or unenforceable.[14]

1–08   The reforms suggested and put forward for comment by Discussion Paper No. 106 are more radical. The proposals refer to "community" and "neighbourhood" burdens, with a suggestion that conservation burdens should be introduced. Consideration is also given to varying the rules regarding the right to enforce real burdens and for registration of the right to enforce, where there is only an implied right at present.

In relation to the variation and discharge of land obligations by the Lands Tribunal the proposals include:

> (1) that, as a general rule, expenses should follow success, which is contrary to the present rule (that there are usually no expenses due to or by either party), where the benefited proprietor's opposition is reasonable[15] and that any fee

---

[11] See below, para. 4–04.
[12] Discussion Paper No. 93, p. 165.
[13] *ibid.* p. 167.
[14] *ibid.*
[15] See below, para. 8–11.

should be payable by an objector. These suggestions are designed to discourage speculative objections to applications[16];

(2) that unopposed applications should be granted as of right[17];

(3) that the grounds for variation will require to be reformulated to take account of the abolition of feudal burdens and the increasing prominence of community burdens. The tentative suggestion is that there should be only one ground for variation or discharge, namely that the tribunal should vary or discharge a real burden "if satisfied that it is reasonable to do so", having regard to factors listed in the legislation. The suggested factors include changes in the character of the dominant and servient tenements and neighbourhood since the burden was first created; the benefit the burden confers on the property owned by the objector; the extent to which the burden impedes the enjoyment of the servient property; whether compliance is impractical or unreasonable; the age of the burden; in the case of a community burden, the effect of the proposed change on the community as a whole; and any other material circumstances[18];

(4) that reasonableness of the proposed use, a section 1(3)(c) factor, should not be included in the list of factors and in particular that the tribunal should not be concerned with planning and other regulatory matters[19];

(5) that the rule that no application should be made within two years of the creation of the real burden should be abolished[20];

(6) the Commission invites views on whether the burden of proof should be on the applicant or the objector[21];

(7) that applications for the variation or discharge of neighbourhood or community burdens should be brought by the owner of the particular property or, where it relates to the whole community, should be brought by owners representing more than 10 per cent of the land owned[22];

---

[16] Discussion Paper No. 106, p. 139, proposal 25.

[17] *ibid.* p. 140, proposal 26.

[18] *ibid.* p. 154, proposal 27.

[19] *ibid.* p. 155, paras 6.43–6.45.

[20] *ibid.* p. 154, proposal 28; see 1970 Act, s. 2(5).

[21] Discussion Paper No. 106, p. 159, proposal 30.

[22] *ibid.* p. 160, proposal 31. The latter provision will obviate the problem raised in *Mrs Young*, 1978 S.L.T. (Lands Tr.) 28 where garden maintenance obligations could not be varied because some of the burdened proprietors refused to consent.

(8) that the special status of affected proprietor should be discontinued because the burdens, after the abolition of the feudal system, will in general be enforceable by the neighbours[23];

(9) that the tribunal, in addition to its power to vary or discharge a real burden, should have the power to declare whether a burden affects the land, the extent and effect of the burden and to determine the identity of the dominant tenements[24];

(10) the Commission seeks views on whether or not the tribunal should be given a role in enforcing real burdens or whether the courts should be able to vary or discharge real burdens in the course of other (*e.g.* enforcement) proceedings[25];

(11) the Commission seeks views on whether or not the tribunal should be able to vary or discharge planning or conservation burdens.[26]

It remains to be seen what legislation will in fact be enacted, but it is clear that the abolition of the feudal system will have a major impact on land obligations, particularly where they are enforceable only by the superior.

Similar jurisdictions

1–09   The sheriff is given a very similar jurisdiction, under section 54(3) of the Housing (Scotland) Act 1987, to vary the terms and conditions of a lease. The section provides that on summary application by a landlord or the tenant of a secure tenancy:

"Where—

(a) a landlord wishes to vary the terms of conditions of a secure tenancy, but the tenant refuses or fails to agree the variation; or

(b) the tenant wishes to vary any term of a secure tenancy which restricts his use of enjoyment of the house on the grounds that—

(i) by reasons of changes in the character of the house or of the neighbourhood or other circumstances which

---

[23] Discussion Paper No. 106, p. 161, proposal 32.

[24] *ibid*. p. 166, proposal 34. This will end the artificial situation where the tribunal explicates its jurisdiction in effect finding that there is or is not a valid land obligation, but its decision is not *res judicata* of the matter; see below, para. 3–23.

[25] Discussion Paper No. 106, p. 168, proposal 35.

[26] *ibid*. p. 169, proposal 36.

the sheriff may deem material, the term is or has become unreasonable or inappropriate; or

(ii) the term is unduly burdensome compared with any benefit which would result from its performance; or

(iii) the existence of the term impedes some reasonable use of the house,

but the landlord refuses or fails to agree the variation."

There do not appear to be any reported decisions on this subsection.

CHAPTER 2

THE LANDS TRIBUNAL FOR SCOTLAND

Origins

2–01   The Lands Tribunal for Scotland[1] was established in 1971 under the Lands Tribunal Act 1949,[2] specifically to deal with the discharge and variation of land obligations under the Conveyancing and Feudal Reform (Scotland) Act 1970 ("the 1970 Act"). This was contrary to the recommendations of the Halliday Report, which had doubted "whether the expense of establishing and maintaining a Lands Tribunal for Scotland would be justified. In our view the judicial functions which we have indicated should be discharged by a new division of the Scottish Land Court".[3]

Address

2–02   The address of the Lands Tribunal is:
    The Lands Tribunal for Scotland
    1 Grosvenor Crescent
    Edinburgh
    EH12 5ER (DX ED259)
    Tel: 0131-225 7996
    Fax: 0131-226 4812

Members of the tribunal

2–03   The President of the Lands Tribunal for Scotland, who has to be suitably qualified by holding judicial office or having experience as an advocate or solicitor, is also Chairman of the Scottish Land Court. A deputy President, similarly qualified, may be appointed. The other members of the tribunal are persons with experience in

---

[1] The Lands Tribunal for Scotland is a tribunal subject to the Tribunals and Inquiries Act 1992; see s. 1 and Sched. 1, Pt II, No. 54.

[2] Lands Tribunal Act (Appointed Day) (Scotland) Order 1971 (S.I. 1971 No. 215).

[3] Halliday Report, para. 27.

valuation of land, appointed after consultation with the Scottish Branch of the Royal Institution of Chartered Surveyors.[4]

The jurisdiction of the Lands Tribunal may be exercised by one or more of its members.[5]

If it appears to the President that any case before the tribunal calls for special knowledge and that it would be desirable for the tribunal to sit with an assessor or assessors, the President may direct that the tribunal shall hear the case with the aid of such assessor or assessors as the President may, after consulting with such persons, if any, as he may think fit, appoint.[6]

Role of the tribunal

The tribunal is not a court of law.[7] The members of the tribunal **2–04** are expected to bring their general expertise and knowledge to bear on consideration of any application and, in general, evidence will not require to be led to establish matters which should be within their general expertise.[8] If the tribunal intends to rely on any specific knowledge or valuation evidence known to the members, this requires to be disclosed to the parties for their comment.[9]

Rule-making power

The Lord Advocate may make rules for regulating procedure **2–05** before the Lands Tribunal for Scotland,[10] subject to the specific powers and directions contained in section 3 of the Lands Tribunal Act 1949.

The current rules are the Lands Tribunal for Scotland Rules 1971 ("the 1971 rules").[11] These rules "are enabling rather than detailed so as to facilitate the carrying out of the tribunal's diverse jurisdictions and to keep it accessible to unrepresented party litigants".[12]

Where a person fails, without reasonable excuse, to comply with any rule requiring him to attend to give evidence and produce

[4] Lands Tribunal Act 1949, s. 2(1), (2) and (3).
[5] *ibid.* s. 3(1).
[6] Lands Tribunal for Scotland Rules 1971 (S.I. 1971 No. 218), r. 29.
[7] *Murray v. MacKinlay*, July 29, 1976; LTS/APP/1/138.
[8] See, *e.g. Pagliocca v. City of Glasgow District Licensing Board*, 1995 S.L.T. 180; *Crofton Investment Trust Ltd v. Greater London Rent Assessment Committee* [1967] 2 Q.B. 955.
[9] *Freeland v. City of Glasgow District Licensing Board*, 1979 S.C. 226; *Fountain Forestry Holdings Ltd v. Sparkes*, 1989 S.L.T. 853 and *Pagliocca v. City of Glasgow District Licensing Board*, above.
[10] Lands Tribunal Act 1949, s. 3(6) and (11)(b).
[11] S.I. 1971 No. 218; see App. 7.
[12] *Stair Memorial Encyclopaedia*, Vol. 6, para. 1147.

documents, he shall be guilty of an offence and liable on summary conviction to a fine at level 3 or imprisonment for a term not exceeding three months, or both.[13]

Representation before the tribunal

2–06   In any proceedings before the tribunal any party to the proceedings may appear in person or be represented by counsel or a solicitor or, with the leave of the tribunal, by any other person.[14]

Where parties are not represented by counsel or a solicitor the tribunal has:

> "accepted that being a Tribunal and not a Court of Law, we should be willing to exercise a quasi-administrative function where parties are not represented by Counsel or Agents so that where possible we may help parties to a practical solution of their problems."[15]

although in that case "where such good offices are clearly not being encouraged" the tribunal said that it could only deal with the application on its legal merits.

Similarly, the tribunal has indicated that it is not imperative for objectors to lead the evidence of professional witnesses in order to establish the fact of a reduction in value where this is fully obvious from other evidence and inspection, particularly where levels of value are low.[16]

It is important to note that an affected person has to attend in person or be represented at a hearing, because the tribunal cannot take into account any written representations without their being spoken to at the hearing,[17] unless consent has been given for the case to be disposed of without a hearing.[18]

Legal aid

2–07   Legal aid is available in respect of applications to the tribunal.[19]

---

[13] Lands Tribunal Act 1949, s. 3(6)(c) and (12)(c).

[14] 1971 Rules, r. 23.

[15] *Murray v. MacKinlay*, July 29, 1976; LTS/APP/1/138.

[16] *Ness v. Shannon*, 1978 S.L.T. (Lands Tr.) 13 at 16.

[17] 1970 Act, s. 2(2); *Scott v. Wilson*, 1993 S.L.T. (Lands Tr.) 51. This is consistent with r. 24, that if a party fails to appear or be represented, the tribunal may dispose of the application in his absence.

[18] 1971 Rules, r. 31.

[19] Legal Aid (Scotland) Act 1986, Sched. 2, Pt 1, para. 1. See *MacDonald v. Stornoway Trust*, 1989 S.L.T. 87.

Procedure

An application under section 1 of the 1970 Act is made to the   **2–08**
tribunal on Form 1.[20] The tribunal will intimate the application to
the other burdened and benefited proprietors and to affected
persons or arrange for its advertisement. The tribunal undertakes
the necessary investigation into title to establish who are the
benefited or affected proprietors, but it is for the applicant to
provide such material as is available to him to assist the tribunal
with this task.[21]

Procedure, including adjustment, amendment, etc., is regulated
by the tribunal as it thinks fit.[22] This is usually done informally by
correspondence with the tribunal staff, particularly if a party is
unrepresented.[23]

The tribunal may, on the motion of any party to the proceedings
or at its own hand, by notice given in writing, require a party to
furnish further particulars of his case in writing.[24] An applicant is
advised:

> "2. At any hearing (usually held near the subjects) relating to
> this application you will be required to adhere to the case set
> out . . . [in the application] . . . unless the Tribunal considers
> that the introduction of new material would not prejudice the
> interests of other parties."[25]

The tribunal does not subject pleadings to the detailed scrutiny
of court pleadings. The pleadings are required merely to focus the
main issues beforehand by giving each side fair notice of the
other's case.[26] As the tribunal has said in *Co-operative Wholesale
Society v. Usher's Brewery*,[27] failure to give adequate notice is
sometimes not cost-effective. It said:

> "The pleadings in this case (comprising the application, the
> objections thereto and the applicants' answers to the
> objections) failed to give proper notice either (a) of the main
> grounds upon which the application was based under
> s. 1 (3) (a), (b) and (c) of the 1970 Act; and (b) the subsection
> under which and the main grounds on which compensation

[20] 1971 Rules, r. 3, Form 1. See App. 8. See also below, para. 4–07.
[21] 1971 Rules, r. 4. See below, para. 4–08.
[22] 1971 Rules, r. 20.
[23] *Stair Memorial Encyclopaedia*, Vol. 6, para. 1148.
[24] 1971 Rules, r. 25(1)(a).
[25] *ibid*. Form 1, n. 2.
[26] *Walton's Exrs v. Farquharson of Invercauld*, January 26, 1978; LTS/LO/1977/7.
[27] 1975 S.L.T. (Lands Tr.) 9 at 11.

was to be claimed in the event of a discharge. The Tribunal have no wish to encourage meticulous detail and the close scrutiny of pleadings which one finds in court actions—for we must, as a Tribunal, remain readily accessible to the layman. Nevertheless, it is an illusion to suppose that informality involving complete surprise saves time and expense. It may do the precise reverse if, as here, the pleadings fail to focus beforehand the main issues between the parties."

The tribunal may determine that the pleadings in the application are irrelevant and dismiss the application,[28] although it should generally be slow to dismiss an application for lack of evidence or specification.[29]

The tribunal may order a record to be made up.[30]

The tribunal may, on such terms as to expenses or otherwise as it thinks fit, extend any time appointed by, or specified by, it in terms of the 1971 Rules, notwithstanding that the time may have expired.[31]

If it is necessary to ask the tribunal to extend a time-limit this may be done by a simple letter stating the reasons for the request. This is intimated to the other parties for their consent but, if opposed a hearing will be fixed.[32]

Motions and hearings

2–09   Where a motion is lodged or an application made to the tribunal for a step in procedure, such as an extension of a time-limit or to sist an application, the tribunal will fix a hearing. There is a hearing fee for such motions.

The hearing

2–10   Unless a shorter time is agreed, the parties must be given at least 21 days' notice of the date, time and place of a hearing.[33] A hearing is usually fixed to take place at a venue near to the land or premises to which the application relates,[34] although if there is a

---

[28] *James Miller & Partners Ltd v. Hunt*, 1974 S.L.T. (Lands Tr.) 9 at 10.
[29] *Stair Memorial Encyclopaedia*, Vol. 6, para. 1152.
[30] 1971 Rules, r. 25(1)(b).
[31] *ibid.* r. 28(a).
[32] *Guidance Notes for Prospective Applicants*.
[33] 1971 Rules, r. 21(1).
[34] See 1971 Rules, r. 25(1), proviso (i): restriction on power to order attendance of witnesses residing more than 10 miles distant, unless reasonable expenses are tendered or paid.

debate, and/or counsel are involved, the tribunal may sit in Edinburgh.

The tribunal may, by notice in writing, require that documents to be put in evidence are lodged by a date before the hearing.[35] This is usually 14 days before the hearing.

The tribunal may, by notice in writing, require a list of comparables to be founded upon at any hearing to be lodged together with copies for the other parties.[36] The tribunal usually requires that these be lodged 28 days before a hearing. After receipt of the lists, the Clerk to the tribunal will simultaneously release to each party a copy of the list lodged by the opposing party.[37]

The tribunal requests that at least five days prior to the hearing, parties lodge a list specifying the full names, occupations, qualifications and addresses of any witnesses and a list of cases or statutes that might be referred to during the hearing. Neither list is made available to the other party.[38]

The tribunal may, on such terms as to expenses or otherwise as it thinks fit, postpone or adjourn any hearing.[39]

The tribunal requires to sit in public.[40] Usually a legally qualified chairman and a member with surveying expertise sit where questions of law and valuation are intermixed. Where there is a debate on legal issues, a legally qualified member may sit alone. In simpler cases a single member (lawyer or surveyor) will sit alone. In complex cases, or those where the tribunal is considering reviewing an earlier decision of a single member, a full tribunal will probably be convened.[41]

If, after due notice, a party or his representative fails to appear **2–11** at the hearing, the tribunal may dispose of the application in the absence of the party or his representative or it may adjourn the hearing. Where an application is so disposed of, the tribunal may, on an application made within seven days of the disposal, if satisfied that there was sufficient reason for such absence, set aside the decision on such terms as to expenses or otherwise as it thinks fit.[42]

The tribunal, with the consent of all parties whom it considers to have an interest in the application, may dispose of an application

[35] 1971 Rules, r. 25(2).
[36] *ibid.*
[37] *Guidance Notes for Prospective Applicants.*
[38] *ibid.*
[39] 1971 Rules, r. 28(b).
[40] *ibid.* r. 21(2).
[41] *Stair Memorial Encyclopaedia*, Vol. 6, para. 1140. *Robertson v. Church of Scotland General Trustees*, 1976 S.L.T. (Lands Tr.) 11 at 12, regarding reviewing its own decisions.
[42] 1971 Rules, r. 24.

without an oral hearing.[43] Where there is such a disposal, affected parties would not require to attend and be heard.[44]

Claims for compensation

2–12   Although the Rules make no particular provision for the lodgment of claims for compensation, the usual tribunal procedure is to provide, in the letter which notifies parties of the date of the hearing, that claims for compensation under section 1(4) of the 1970 Act, with details of any comparables, are to be lodged with the tribunal and intimated to the other parties more than 14 days prior to date of the hearing. In exceptional circumstances the tribunal may allow claims to be lodged at a later date.[45]

Evidence and witnesses

2–13   Evidence may be given orally or, if the parties consent or the tribunal so orders, by affidavit, but the tribunal may at any stage of the proceedings require the personal attendance of any deponent for examination and cross-examination.[46] Witnesses are generally put on oath.[47]

Rule 24A[48] would appear to be at variance with section 2 of the Civil Evidence (Scotland) Act 1988 (Admissibility of hearsay).[49] In *Glaser v. Glaser*[50] the Court of Session held that the court had no discretion to refuse to admit in evidence any written statement admissible under section 2 of the 1988 Act. If the tribunal is bound to admit written statements or affidavits, the consent or order provisions of rule 24A would appear to be at variance with the provisions of the 1988 Act. Similarly, if written statement evidence is admissible under the 1988 Act, it would have to be considered, whether or not a party required to attend for examination and cross-examination.

---

[43] Lands Tribunal Act 1949, s. 3(6A); 1971 Rules, r. 31; see, *e.g. Schrader v. Lady Saltoun*, May 30, 1995; LTS/LO/94/55.

[44] See *Scott v. Wilson's Trs.*, 1993 S.L.T. (Lands Tr.) 51.

[45] *e.g. Bearsden & Milngavie District Council v. The Liverpool Victoria Society*, August 2, 1990; LTS/LO/1989/76 (accepted three days before hearing, with consent), *Sillars' Exrs v. Farrimond*, May 8, 1991; LTS/LO/1989/25.

[46] 1971 Rules, r. 24A; see *Stair Memorial Encyclopaedia*, Vol. 6, para. 1152; and *Cameron v. Stirling*, 1988 S.L.T. (Lands Tr.) 18 at 19F, where evidence of benefited proprietor given by affidavit, but tribunal ordered cross-examination at her home.

[47] 1971 Rules, r. 23; *Stair Memorial Encyclopaedia*, Vol. 6, para. 1151.

[48] Inserted by S.I. 1985 No. 581.

[49] Applies to the Lands Tribunal: s. 9(c) of the Civil Evidence (Scotland) Act 1988 ("civil proceedings").

[50] 1997 S.L.T. 456.

The tribunal "does not regard itself as legally bound to follow all the strict rules of evidence applicable in the Scottish Courts".[51] This rule is probably now of less relevance following the abolition of the requirement for corroboration in civil matters and the allowance of hearsay evidence.[52] Where issues of credibility arise the position is different.

"As a valuation tribunal we are not legally obliged to have regard only to direct evidence. Nevertheless, when, as here, an issue of credibility is involved, we choose as a matter of practice to disregard all evidence not directly spoken to or agreed; and also to prefer evidence which is properly corroborated."[53]

As the surveyor members are experts, background or general evidence of valuation matters need not be led before the tribunal. While the expert members will take into account their own general expertise and general knowledge, particularly of valuation, if they are to have regard to a particular piece of information (*e.g.* the value of a comparable not mentioned by either party), that information should be put to the parties for comment.[54] The tribunal will usually inspect the subjects and form its own opinion.[55]

As the tribunal is required by the statute to reach a decision on certain matters, while it determines issues by the evidence led before it, it may require to undertake its own investigation by asking questions of the parties and their witnesses in order to elicit the necessary information. The tribunal should generally be slow to dismiss an application for lack of evidence or specification.[56]

As a matter of practice, the tribunal will usually allow an expert witness to read from a written statement as his evidence-in-chief, which is handed to the tribunal at the commencement of his evidence, after which cross-examination and re-examination follow. Sufficient copies of such a statement should be available for each member of the tribunal sitting and for the opposing parties.[57]

---

[51] *Stair Memorial Encyclopaedia*, Vol. 6, para. 1152. See *Douglas v. Provident Clothing Supply Co. Ltd*, 1969 S.C. 32, *per* the Lord President, at 36, where he said of an industrial tribunal, "This is not an ordinary litigation in a court of law, but an inquiry under a statute where the rules in relation to evidence are much looser than in an ordinary action in a court of law."
[52] Civil Evidence (Scotland) Act 1988, ss. 1 and 2.
[53] *Gibbon v. Inland Revenue*, 1980 S.L.T. (Lands Tr.) 3 at 5.
[54] *Fountain Forestry Holdings Ltd v. Sparkes*, 1989 S.L.T. 853.
[55] *Stair Memorial Encyclopaedia*, Vol. 6, para. 1152.
[56] *ibid.*
[57] *ibid.; Guidance Notes for Prospective Applicants.*

Production and recovery of documents

2–14   The tribunal may grant a commission and diligence for the recovery of documents or provide such other means for recovery:

> "as could be granted or provided by the Court of Session in a cause depending before them, such recovery being effected, where commission and diligence has been granted, by execution thereof or in that or any other case in any manner which recovery could be provided for by the Court of Session in such a cause".[58]

The Court of Session rules relating to applications for commission and diligence for the recovery of documents or for orders under section 1 of the Administration of Justice (Scotland) Act 1972 are found in rule 35.2 of the Rules of the Court of Session 1994.[59]

The tribunal has no power to require the production of any book or document which a witness, on grounds of privilege or confidentiality, would be entitled to refuse to produce in any proceedings in a court of law.[60]

The tribunal has no power to order a person to attend for the production of any document at any place more than 10 miles from the place at which he resides unless the necessary expenses are paid or tendered to him by the party at whose instance his attendance is required or by the tribunal, as the case may be.[61]

The tribunal may, by notice in writing, order any party who intends to use or put in evidence any documents or to rely for valuation purposes on any comparables, to produce the documents or to produce a list of comparable before the proof or hearing.[62] The normal practice is for the tribunal to issue an order requiring production of such documents 14 days, and lists of comparables 28 days, before any such hearing.

Site visit

2–15   The tribunal usually requires to carry out a site inspection of the relevant location. This may be either accompanied or unaccompanied. Where the site visit is accompanied parties may draw the

---

[58] 1971 Rules, r. 25(1)(c). See s. 3(6)(c) of the Lands Tribunal Act 1949 which provides for a rule to be made "for granting to any person such recovery of documents as might be granted by the Court of Session".
[59] See App. 11, r. 35.2 and notes thereto.
[60] 1971 Rules, r. 25(1), proviso (ii).
[61] *ibid.* proviso (i).
[62] *ibid.* r. 25(2)

tribunal's attention to any matter they deem appropriate. No new evidence may be given at a site visit.[63]

The decision

Where there is a difference of opinion among members of the **2–16** tribunal, the decision will be taken by a majority vote and, in the event of an equality of votes, the person presiding has a second or casting vote.[64]

The decision has to be given in writing and requires to include a statement of the tribunal's reasons for its decision.[65] A copy of the decision has to be sent by the tribunal to all parties to the proceedings.[66]

Where an amount of compensation awarded depends upon a decision of the tribunal on a question of law which is in dispute, the tribunal is required to state in its award the alternative amount, if any, which it would have awarded if it had decided otherwise on the question of law.[67]

The tribunal may correct an accidental or arithmetical error in any decision if, before making the correction, it gives notice to all parties to the proceedings of its intention to make the correction.[68] Where a correction is made under rule 32(4) or for the purpose of giving effect to any decision of the Court of Session in a case stated for its opinion, the tribunal is required to send a copy of the corrected decision to all parties to the proceedings.[69]

An order of the tribunal given under section 1 of the 1970 Act takes effect in accordance with rule 5 of the 1971 Rules.[70]

Judicial precedent

The tribunal considers itself bound by decisions of the Inner **2–17** House of the Court of Session and of the House of Lords in Scottish cases.[71] It is less clear whether the tribunal is bound by the decision of a Lord Ordinary in the Outer House but, following the

---

[63] *Guidance Notes for Prospective Applicants.*
[64] Lands Tribunal Act. 1949, s. 3(b).
[65] 1971 Rules, r. 32(1).
[66] *ibid.* r. 32(3).
[67] *ibid.* r. 32(2).
[68] *ibid.* r. 32(4).
[69] *ibid.* r. 32(5).
[70] See rule 5 of the 1971 Rules, made under s. 2(3) of the 1970 Act, and also para. 8–09 below.
[71] *Stair Memorial Encyclopaedia*, Vol. 22, para. 324.

sheriff court rule, the tribunal is probably not bound, albeit that the decisions will be persuasive.[72]

In *Ness v. Shannon*[73] the tribunal followed a decision of the Lands Valuation Appeal Court,[74] although the LVAC is probably not a "superior court" to the tribunal, except perhaps in rating matters.

The tribunal has regard to decisions of the Lands Tribunals of England and Northern Ireland[75] as persuasive authority, where the statutory provisions are the same.[76] While frequently referred to in relation to the similar jurisdictions under section 1 of the 1970 Act and section 84 of the 1925 Act, English and Northern Irish decisions must be treated with caution, as the statutory provisions are significantly different.

In construing statutory provisions the tribunal will have regard to reports,[77] Law Commission Reports and now, no doubt, Ministerial statements.[78]

Tribunal's power to review own decisions

2–18   While the tribunal will in general, for the sake of consistency, follow its own legal decisions, in certain circumstances it will reconsider an earlier decision. The tribunal is not bound by its earlier decisions, although it is reluctant to depart from a decision reached by a full tribunal.

The tribunal has outlined the circumstances in which it might review one of its own decisions. It said[79]:

> "We have to indicate at this stage that this Tribunal, for the sake of consistency, feels that it should endeavour to follow its own legal decisions—especially where reached (as in *McVey*) by a large tribunal. Only where a legal decision has been given by a small tribunal might we exceptionally be persuaded—following the practice of the Court of Session—to convene a fuller tribunal to review it."

---

[72] *Stair Memorial Encyclopaedia*, Vol. 22, para. 298.

[73] 1978 S.L.T. (Lands Tr.) 13.

[74] *Ferguson v. Glasgow Assessor*, 1977 S.L.T. 142.

[75] *Smith v. Strathclyde Regional Council*, 1992 S.L.T. (Lands Tr.) 2 at 6, considering *McGonigal v. Department of Environment for Northern Ireland* [1976] R.V.R. 56.

[76] See English and Northern Irish tribunal cases referred to in this book.

[77] Halliday Report, considered in *Keith v. Texaco Ltd*, 1977 S.L.T. (Lands Tr.) 16 at 23.

[78] *Pepper v. Hart* [1993] A.C. 593.

[79] *Robertson v. Church of Scotland General Trustees*, 1976 S.L.T. (Lands Tr.) 11 at 12.

Review of Lands Tribunal decision

Apart from its own power to review its earlier decisions, there **2–19** are two means whereby the decision of the tribunal may be brought under review. It is important to note that it is only on a point of law that the tribunal's decision may be reviewed. The first means is by a case stated on a question of law for the opinion of the Court of Session, during the course of proceedings before the tribunal. A stated case will be appropriate if, during the course of proceedings, a difficult question of law arises which requires to be resolved before the tribunal can give a decision. Until relatively recently, it was thought that review by stated case was the only means of review. As a result, all the earlier references to the Court of Session were by way of stated case.[80] The second means is by appeal to the Court of Session on a question of law, following the issue of the tribunal's decision. Appeal is now the more common way of proceeding to bring a decision of the tribunal under review.

Question of law

There is a right of appeal only on a question of law. If the court **2–20** determines that the appeal or stated case does not relate to a question of law, the appeal will be dismissed[81] or the court will refuse to answer the questions stated.

While a detailed consideration of what is and what is not a question of law is beyond the scope of this book, the following is given for guidance.[82] While some of the examples (breach of natural justice; strict application of a policy; failure to give adequate reasons) raise questions of law, it is unlikely that a professional tribunal such as the Lands Tribunal for Scotland would fall into such error.

The court will not interfere with the tribunal's decision:

"where there was no question of the tribunal taking into account irrelevant considerations, failing to take into account a relevant one, misdirecting themselves on a question of law

---

[80] *e.g. Murrayfield Ice Rink Ltd v. Scottish Rugby Union*, 1973 S.C. 20; *Keith v. Texaco Ltd*, 1977 S.L.T. (Lands Tr.) 16 at 22.

[81] *Re Purkiss' Application* [1962] 1 W.L.R. 902, *per* Evershed MR at 909: "In all those circumstances it seems to me to be impossible to say in this court that there is a question of law for this court to decide and it seems to me that the present appeal must fail."

[82] See, generally, Walker, *Civil Remedies*, pp. 166–169; de Smith, Woolf and Jowell, *Judicial Review of Administrative Action* (5th ed.).

or reaching a conclusion which was unreasonable on the facts before them".[83]

As there are no examples of the Court of Session upholding an appeal against a decision of the tribunal under section 1 of the 1970 Act, the Scottish case references give examples of the grounds upon which the challenge was made, albeit unsuccessfully.

In general, a question or point of law includes:

(1) whether the tribunal acted within its jurisdiction or refused to act in circumstances where it had jurisdiction[84];

(2) whether the tribunal applied the statutory provisions, case law and E.U. law properly[85];

(3) whether the evidence before the tribunal entitled it to make the findings that it made[86];

(4) whether the tribunal had regard to material which it ought not to have taken into account[87]; or failed to take into account material that it ought to have considered[88];

---

[83] *Anderson v. Trotter*, 1999 S.L.T. 442.

[84] *e.g.* purported to act where there was no land obligation: see *Re Purkiss' Application* [1962] 1 W.L.R. 902 and *Shepherd Homes Ltd v. Sandham* [1971] Ch. 340.

[85] *Murrayfield Ice Rink Ltd v. Scottish Rugby Union*, 1973 S.C. 21 (proper construction of s. 1(3)(b) and whether it included both positive and negative obligations); *George T. Fraser v. Aberdeen Harbour Board*, 1985 S.L.T. 384 (whether qualification of "tenant" that assignees were not permitted "except with the consent in writing of the [landlord]" in long lease was a land obligation); *Anderson v. Trotter*, 1998 G.W.D. 28–1438, 2nd Div. (misconstruction of the proper approach to the definition of "neighbourhood" in s. 1(3)(a) of 1970 Act); *Ridley v. Taylor* [1965] 1 W.L.R. 611 (construction of s. 84(1)(c) of 1925 Act).

[86] *Murrayfield Ice Rink Ltd v. Scottish Rugby Union*, above (whether tribunal entitled to reach the decision it did on the facts found); *MacDonald v. Stornoway Trust*, 1987 S.L.T. 240 (whether evidence entitled tribunal to find that obligation was not unduly burdensome and did not impede some reasonable use); *Driscoll v. Church Commissioners for England* [1957] 1 Q.B. 330 at 340 ("It is also well established that the question whether an inference drawn from primary facts is a legitimate inference is also a question of law"); *Gee v. National Trust for Places of Historic Interest and Natural Beauty* [1966] 1 W.L.R. 170 (tribunal's discretion purportedly exercised on the basis of two factors not proved by admissible evidence).

[87] *Murrayfield Ice Rink Ltd v. Scottish Rugby Union*, above (whether tribunal entitled to take into account amenity in considering s. 1(3)(b) and (c)); *MacDonald v. Stornoway Trust*, above (whether tribunal entitled to have regard to commercial viability of applicant's proposals and/or the form of landownership and constitution of the Stornoway Trust); *Cressell v. Proctor* [1968] W.L.R. 906 (regard had to fact that purchase price less because of covenant or that if he succeeded the applicant would make a large profit).

[88] *Cumbernauld Development Corporation v. County Properties and Developments Ltd*, 1996 S.L.T. 1106 at 1109K (failure to take account of a material consideration).

(5) where the tribunal has a discretion, whether the discretion was exercised reasonably[89] or whether it failed to exercise a discretion at all[90];

(6) whether the tribunal acted with procedural fairness or in breach of natural justice[91];

(7) whether the tribunal applied a policy rigidly[92];

(8) whether the tribunal acted *Wednesbury*[93] unreasonably in reaching its decision[94];

[89] *Smith v. Strathkelvin District Council*, 1997 S.C. 98 (*sub nom. Smith v. East Dunbartonshire Council*, 1997 S.L.T. 997).

[90] *Gee v. National Trust for Places of Historic Interest and Natural Beauty* [1966] 1 W.L.R. 170.

[91] *Barrs v. British Wool Marketing Board*, 1957 S.C. 72; *Cigaro (Glasgow) Ltd v. City of Glasgow District Licensing Board*, 1982 S.C. 104; *JAE (Glasgow) Ltd v. City of Glasgow Licensing Board*, 1994 S.L.T. 1164 (requirement for procedural fairness and to deal equally between parties); *Freeland v. City of Glasgow District Licensing Board*, 1979 S.C. 226 and *Fountain Forestry Holdings Ltd v. Sparkes*, 1989 S.L.T. 853 (requirement that if tribunal intends to take into account particular facts or valuations within its own knowledge, parties should be given an opportunity to comment on those facts); and see *Gilbert v. Spoor* [1983] Ch. 27, where it was said that "This was not a case where the Tribunal took a point of its own" without giving parties an opportunity to comment on the point; *Smith v. Strathkelvin District Council*, 1997 S.C. 98 where the court held that the fact that the Chairman of the tribunal connected to the solicitor for a party through an association as consultant with a firm in which the solicitor's brothers were partners was so tenuous as not to be a breach of natural justice of the type *auctor in rem suam*, and *Barrs*, above, where having an official who was involved in the application in with the board while considering the decision was criticised, *i.e.* justice must not only be done, but be seen to be done.

[92] See *Re Findlay* [1985] 1 A.C. 318 and *Elder v. Ross & Cromarty District Licensing Board*, 1990 S.L.T. 307, which summarise the basis upon which a policy may be applied. In *Elder* it was said: "The principles which are established, in my opinion, may be summarised in this way. Where a statutory body having discretionary power is required to consider numerous applications there is no objection to it announcing that it proposes to follow a certain general policy in examining such applications. Indeed, in certain circumstances it may be desirable to achieve a degree of consistency in dealing with applications of similar character. Moreover, there is nothing wrong with policies being made public so that applicants may know what to expect. However, such a declared policy may be objectionable if certain conditions are not fulfilled. A policy must be based on grounds which relate to and are not inconsistent with or destructive of the purposes of the statutory provisions under which the discretion is operated. Moreover, the policy must not be so rigidly formulated that, if applied, the statutory body is thereby disabled from exercising the discretion entrusted to it. Finally, the individual circumstances of each application must be considered in each case, whatever the policy may be. It is not permissible for a body exercising a statutory discretion to refuse to apply its mind to that application on account of an apparent conflict with policy".

[93] *Associated Provincial Picture Houses Ltd v. Wednesbury Corporation* [1948] 1 K.B. 223.

[94] *Smith v. Strathkelvin District Council*, 1997 S.C. 98 at 102F "The question for us is therefore whether . . . no reasonable Tribunal would have granted the council's application".

(9) whether the tribunal failed to give adequate reasons.[95]

The stated case

2–21   Section 11(3)[96] of the Tribunals and Inquiries Act 1992 provides that Rules of Court may be made authorising or requiring the Lands Tribunal for Scotland to state a case for the opinion of the Court of Session on "any question of law arising in the proceedings".

"(A)rising in the proceedings", means that the stated case has to be requested prior to the issue of a decision by the tribunal. Any party minded to request a stated case should consider asking the tribunal either to issue a draft decision or to apply for the case prior to the issue of any decision. It is too late to ask for a stated case after the decision is issued.[97] Where a decision has been issued, the appropriate procedure is to appeal the decision.[98]

Rule 41.39[99] provides that the tribunal may state a case for the opinion of the Court of Session.[1] Where the tribunal decides to state a case at its own instance, the decision has to be intimated to all the parties and once the case has been settled five copies have to be sent to each party and the original and six copies transmitted to the Deputy Principal Clerk with four copies of any relevant productions.[2]

An application may be made by any party to the proceedings for the tribunal to state a case for the opinion of the Court of Session. The procedures for a party to apply for a stated case, applying to the court where a tribunal refuses to state a case and the procedures for dealing with a stated case are set out in rules 41.4–41.17 of the Rules of the Court of Session 1994, to which reference should be made.[3]

---

[95] *Albyn Properties v. Knox*, 1977 S.C. 108, *per* the Lord President at 112, commenting on the obligation to give reasons under the Tribunals and Inquiries Act 1971 (now 1993), which applies to the Lands Tribunal: "The statutory obligation to give reasons is designed not merely to inform the parties of the result of the committee's deliberations but to make clear to them and to this court the basis on which their decision was reached, and that they have reached their result in conformity with the requirements of the statutory provisions and the principles of natural justice. In order to make clear the basis of their decision a committee must state: (i) what facts they found to be admitted or proved; (ii) whether and to what extent the submissions of parties were accepted as convincing or not; and (iii) by what method or methods of valuation applied to the facts found their determination was arrived at. In short they must explain how their figures of fair rent were fixed."

[96] As modified by Tribunals and Inquiries Act 1992, s. 11(7)(a)(ii) and (b)(ii).

[97] *Fairlie Yacht Slip Ltd v. Lumsden*, 1977 S.L.T. (Notes) 41.

[98] See para. 2–22 below.

[99] Rules of the Court of Session, 1994: App. 9.

[1] r. 41.40 applies or modifies rr. 41.4–41.7 (stated case procedure) to apply to a case stated by the tribunal at its own instance.

[2] r. 41.42(2) and (3) amending r. 41.9 of the Rules of the Court of Session.

[3] App. 9.

The application is made by minute sent to the Clerk to the tribunal, before the decision of the tribunal is made, setting out the question on which the case is applied for.[4] A copy of the minute requires to be sent to every other party to the proceedings and on receipt of that minute any other party has 14 days in which to lodge with the clerk a minute setting out any additional question that is proposed for the case.[5]

On the expiry of the above time-limits, the tribunal may decide either to state a case or to refuse to state a case if it is of the opinion that the proposed question: (1) does not arise; (2) does not require to be decided for the purposes of the appeal; (3) is frivolous; or (4) if the application is made before the facts have been ascertained, and the tribunal is of the opinion that it is necessary to determine the facts before the application is disposed of, to defer the application for consideration until the facts have been ascertained.[6] The decision made has to be intimated to the parties.[7]

Where the tribunal refuses to state a case, the party whose application was refused may, within 14 days after the date on which the refusal was intimated, lodge in the General Department an application by note to the Inner House for an order to require the other parties to show cause why a case should not be stated, stating briefly the grounds upon which the application is made.[8]

Appeal to the Court of Session

A party to proceedings before the Lands Tribunal, if "dissatisfied in point of law with a decision of the Tribunal", may appeal to the Court of Session.[9]   2–22

The tribunal's practice is that where an appeal is marked, the applicant should enrol a motion in the tribunal to sist the tribunal application. Notwithstanding that an appeal has been taken, the Lands Tribunal remains seised of the application, for the purposes of dealing with a motion for expenses. The benefit of this procedure is that any decision on expenses could be appealed and the appeal conjoined with the main appeal.[10]

The appeal must be lodged with the General Department of the Court of Session within 42 days of the date on which the decision

---

[4] Rules of the Court of Session, r. 41.5.
[5] *ibid.* r. 41.6.
[6] *ibid.* r. 41.7(1).
[7] *ibid.* r. 41.7(2).
[8] *ibid.* r. 41.8.
[9] Tribunals and Inquiries Act 1992, s. 11(1) and (7)(b)(ii).
[10] *MRS Hamilton Ltd v. Keeper of the Registers*, August 27, 1998; LTS/LR/1997/4–8.

or, if later, the reasons, were intimated to the appellant.[11] This time-limit is inconsistent with rule 5(1)(a) which provides that an order, in certain circumstances, is to take effect 21 days after the date on which the order is made. Where an order is to take effect within 21 days, a prospective appellant would be wise to appeal within the 21 days.

The appeal requires to be presented[12] in Form 41.19, in which the decision is either set out or appended to the appeal. The appeal requires to set out, in brief numbered propositions, the grounds of appeal, which have to be sufficiently detailed to give fair advanced notice of the points to be taken on appeal.[13]

Appeals to the Court of Session proceed under rules 41.18–41.22 of the Rules of the Court of Session, to which reference should be made.[14]

Appeal to the House of Lords

2–23   There is a right of appeal to the House of Lords against a decision of the Court of Session, both on a stated case and on appeal from the Lands Tribunal, with the leave of the House of Lords or the Court of Session. Such leave may be given on such terms as to costs or otherwise as the Court of Session or the House of Lords may determine.[15]

Disposal of an appeal

2–24   There remains the question of what is a proper disposal of an appeal to the Court of Session, and possibly the House of Lords, if the appeal is successful.

As the tribunal is vested with a discretion in relation to applications, it would seem that the proper disposal of an appeal would be to remit the application to the tribunal for reconsideration, or perhaps rehearing by the same or another tribunal, if there remains a decision to be made in the exercise of the discretion after the decision in the appeal.[16]

---

[11] Rules of the Court of Session 1994, r. 41.20(1)(b).

[12] *ibid.* r. 41.19

[13] *ibid.* r. 41.19(1)(e); see *City of Glasgow District Council v. Secretary of State of Scotland (No. 1)*, 1993 S.L.T. 198 at 204 E–G.

[14] See App. 10.

[15] Tribunals and Inquiries Act 1992, s. 11(7)(d).

[16] *Jones v. Rhys-Jones* (1974) 30 P. & C.R. 451; see the reasoning in *Matchurban v. Kyle & Carrick District Council*, 1995 S.L.T. 505, a licensing case: "Parliament has decided that the decision on matters of this kind should be taken by the local licensing authority and there would need to be compelling reasons for removing from such an authority the responsibility for taking such decisions."

If the outcome of the appeal is in effect that the tribunal had to grant or refuse the application or the opinion of the court is such that it indicates that the tribunal would have granted, or refused, the application, but for the error into which it fell, the court should probably remit to the tribunal with a direction to grant or refuse the application, as appropriate.[17]

This question does not arise in stated case procedure because the case is stated before a decision is made by the tribunal. After the question of law has been answered by the Court of Session, the tribunal requires to reach its decision in conformity with the answer given.

---

[17] See *Re Wickins' Application* (1962) 183 E.G. 541 and *Gee v. National Trust for Places of Historic Interest and Natural Beauty* [1966] 1 W.L.R. 170.

CHAPTER 3

JURISDICTION OF THE LANDS TRIBUNAL FOR SCOTLAND

General

3–01 The jurisdiction of the Lands Tribunal for Scotland to vary or discharge a "land obligation" is entirely statutory. It is therefore important to have regard to both the statutory definition of "land obligation",[1] which is not necessarily co-extensive with the more familiar terms used in a conveyance of real burdens or real conditions or servitudes, and to the statutory exclusions from the jurisdiction.[2]

The term "land obligation" would appear to have been adopted by the English Law Commission.[3] The Halliday Report[4] uses the terms "land conditions", which is more akin to the recognised Scottish terminology.

It should be noted that the jurisdiction applies "without prejudice to any other method of variation or discharge". Other methods by which land obligations can become unenforceable or extinguished through operation of law usually occur through: (1) express consent or deed of waiver; (2) acquiescence or implied consent; (3) loss of interest to enforce; (4) the long negative prescriptive period; (5) consolidation of the *dominium directum* with the *dominium utile*; or (6) compulsory purchase.[5]

---

[1] 1970 Act, s. 1(2).

[2] *ibid.* s. 1(1) and Sched. 1.

[3] *Transfer of Land. The Law of Positive and Restrictive Covenants. Report on Restrictive Covenants* (Law Com. No. 11, 1967), paras 27 *et seq.* See Gordon, p. 691.

[4] Chap. III, para. 25, p. 17.

[5] 1970 Act, s. 1(1). Other methods of variation or discharge are dealt with in Gordon, Chaps 21–24; Halliday, Vol. 2, paras 34-42 to 34-62 (real burdens and conditions) and paras 35-26 to 35-34 (servitudes); and *Stair Memorial Encyclopaedia*, Vol. 18, paras 426–437 (real burdens) and 470–476 (servitudes).

Contracting out

It is not competent to contract out of the jurisdiction of the   **3–02**
tribunal to vary or discharge a land obligation. Section 7 of the
1970 Act provides:

> "Any agreement or other provision, however constituted, shall
> be void in so far as it purports to exclude or limit the
> operation of any enactment contained in section 1 to 6 of this
> Act."

The same conclusion has been reached in England in relation to
the provisions of section 84 of the 1925 Act, without there being a
similar statutory prohibition against contracting out on the ground
"that the right was conferred upon landowners not merely for their
own personal benefit but also for the public good in ensuring that
land was not frozen in a time warp".[6]

Scope of the jurisdiction

The tribunal's function is a judicial one, to determine whether or   **3–03**
not the applicant has satisfied the onus of bringing himself within
one of the statutory grounds for variation or discharge given in
section 1(3)(a)–(c) of the 1970 Act. The tribunal has explained the
jurisdiction thus[7]:

> "[The applicant] must discharge the onus of showing that its
> continuing enforcement has become unreasonable in terms of
> one or more of subs. (a), (b) or (c) of s. 1 (3) of the 1970 Act.
> For these are the only statutory grounds upon which this
> tribunal is empowered to grant relief, due generally to mater-
> ial change of circumstances rendering the obligation unreason-
> able or inappropriate; or because it is unduly burdensome
> compared with any corresponding benefit; or because it
> impedes some reasonable use of the land.
>   The tribunal's function is thus a judicial one of determining
> whether an applicant has succeeded on the evidence in
> bringing his case within any of the three statutory grounds—
> otherwise the benefited proprietor is entitled to continue to
> enforce the title conditions against the burdened proprietor.
> As was observed in relation to the equivalent English legisla-
> tion by Lord Evershed M.R. in *Re Ghey and Galton's
> Application*[8] at p. 659: 'what has to be done, if an applicant is

---

[6] Scammell, p. 319.
[7] *MacDonald v. Stornoway Trust*, 1987 S.L.T. 240 at 241 B–D.
[8] [1956] 2 Q.B. 650.

to succeed, is something far more than to show that to an impartial planner the applicant's proposal might be called, as such, a good and reasonable thing: he must affirmatively prove that one or other of the grounds for the jurisdiction has been established; and, unless that is so, the person who has the proprietary right, as covenantee, of controlling the development of the property as he desires and protecting his own proprietary interest, is entitled to continue to enjoy that proprietary right'.

The tribunal's judicial function thus differs from the purely administrative one exercised by a building control committee when granting warrant for building alterations in accordance with the Building (Scotland) Regulations; or, likewise, a planning committee in deciding whether planning permission for a proposed development should be granted. For they can only refuse permission on proper planning grounds which take no account of local proprietary rights."

The tribunal does not have jurisdiction to vary or discharge a land obligation when an application is made to it under other statutory procedures. For example, in *Walker v. Strathclyde Regional Council*,[9] in an application by a tenant to buy under the Housing (Scotland) Act 1987, the council sought a discharge of the right of reversion in favour of the superior as a prelude to grant of the application to purchase. The tribunal refused this motion on the ground that it had no jurisdiction under the 1987 Act to vary or discharge a land obligation.[10]

Retrospective applications

3–04   The tribunal has jurisdiction to consider retrospective applications, where there has been an antecedent breach of the land obligation, because there still exists an enforceable land obligation. The tribunal will ignore all alterations to the status quo ante in considering whether or not to grant a discharge or variation, because it would be inappropriate for an applicant to benefit from self-created changes in breach of his land obligation.[11]

---

[9] 1990 S.L.T. (Lands Tr.) 17.
[10] *ibid.* at 18L.
[11] *Bruce v. Modern Homes Investment Co. Ltd*, 1978 S.L.T. (Lands Tr.) 34 at 36; *Harris v. Douglass*, 1993 S.L.T. (Lands Tr.) 56 at 58A; *Eadie v. Nenadic*, May 28, 1996; LTS/LO/1995/11.

The proper attitude to such an application:

"where an applicant has anticipated a tribunal order by constructing or starting to construct a building in contravention of his title conditions—is to deal with the application without regard to the presence of the new building or partially-completed building and to ignore all alterations of the status quo ante in deciding whether any of the conditions of s. 1 (3) of the 1970 Act have been satisfied. To do otherwise would enable applicants to benefit from self-created changes in breach of their land obligations. If therefore the tribunal are not satisfied that any of the conditions of s. 1 (3) have been fulfilled then the application must be refused. Consequently an applicant who is so ill-advised as to anticipate a tribunal order may find himself in the position of having no title clearance to enable the house to be sold. In the present case the completion and sale of no. 23 Blackford Hill Grove has since the tribunal application thus been brought to a halt. ... We therefore ask ourselves the question; should the application be granted in the absence of the almost completed house?"[12]

In *Anderson v. Trotter*[13] the tribunal commented on *Bruce*, saying:

"*Bruce* however establishes only that applicants are not barred by their antecedent breach from applying to the tribunal under section 1; and cannot take any advantage from the fact that they themselves have brought about a chance in breach of the very obligation they now seek to have varied or discharged. It remains the case that, as the tribunal in Bruce went on to say, 'if . . . the tribunal are not satisfied that any of the conditions of section 1(3) have been fulfilled then the application must be refused.' Moreover it seems to us that the proposition put forward on the objectors' behalf in reference to *Bruce*, namely that nothing done by the applicants in breach of their obligations should be allowed to detract from the objectors' position, is equally sound. In our opinion it would clearly be wrong to allow the shortcomings of the applicants' former solicitors, or indeed the serious consequences for the applicants if the order they seek is not granted, to deflect us in any way from giving due consideration to the objections which have been put to us."

---

[12] *Bruce v. Modern Homes Investment Co Ltd*, above, at 36.
[13] August 12, 1997; LTS/LO/1996/46.

In the exercise of its general discretion in deciding whether or not to grant the application, the tribunal may well take into account the applicant's attitude to the breach. In *Anderson v. Trotter*[14] the tribunal was asked to have regard to the fact that it was said that the applicants had deliberately flouted the obligation to use the house as a dwelling-house, when they established their nursery. The tribunal, commenting on *Bruce*, said that in that case the applicant was:

> "under the impression that the superiors were prepared to grant him a minute of waiver. It may therefore be open to question what attitude the tribunal would have adopted if the evidence had shown that Mr Bruce had deliberately flouted the prohibitions in his title".

A similar approach has been adopted in England, where in *Re Bradley Clare Estates Ltd's Application*[15] the tribunal said:

> "If I had decided this matter under paragraph (aa) alone and not under paragraph (a) I would have seriously had to consider whether I ought to refuse to exercise the discretion of the Lands Tribunal in favour of the applicants on the ground that they have partially erected a building in breach of covenant and that they have continued to cause or permit the work to be carried out on that building (notwithstanding a warning I gave during the hearing) and continued to do so whilst I was inspecting the land . . . However, since I have also decided under paragraph (a) that the restrictions ought to be deemed obsolete it appears to me that it is right that I should exercise the discretion of the Lands Tribunal in favour of the applicants."

In some cases the tribunal will impose a condition on the applicant to reflect the works that have been undertaken.[16] In other cases the application has been refused notwithstanding that the work has been completed.[17]

Where there has been an antecedent breach the tribunal will in fact have regard to evidence of the situation as it exists in

---

[14] August 12, 1997; LTS/LO/1996/46.

[15] (1988) 55 P. & C.R. 126 at 132.

[16] *Bruce v. Modern Homes Investment Co Ltd*, above, at 36—condition to undertake remedial work to render a retaining wall safe, in circumstances where, had there been no work, the tribunal would have directed the new house to be sited differently.

[17] *Orsi v. McCallum*, 1980 S.L.T. (Lands Tr.) 2 (ashbin completed on access, which it was sought to vary).

determining whether or not a variation or discharge will in fact damage the amenity or otherwise affect neighbouring properties.[18]

Concurrent tribunal application and irritancy

There have been a number of cases where a superior has raised **3–05** irritancy proceedings in the ordinary courts against the vassal, who has then subsequently applied to the tribunal for a variation or discharge of the land obligation in respect of which the irritancy is sought. No case has yet determined whether or not a subsequent discharge or variation of a land obligation will nullify a prior irritancy application, where the variation or discharge takes effect prior to a decision in the case.[19]

> "It remains an open question—and one that it is for the courts alone to decide—whether decree of declarator of irritancy should be granted in respect of a past breach of land obligations where a discharge order of the lands tribunal has intervened."[20]

The tribunal's view is that:

> "If . . . the applicants were to succeed in discharging the onus upon them of proving that any of the conditions of s. 1 (3) of the 1970 Act have been satisfied, the resultant variation order could in our view be a factor which might weigh with the court when deciding whether or not to grant decree of declarator of irritancy. If, on the other hand, the tribunal were to refuse the application after an inquiry then the way would be clearer for the court. It is not of course for this tribunal to comment upon the extent of the court's jurisdiction nor how this might be exercised in the light of the 1970 Act and tribunal orders made thereunder. We cannot however overlook the possibility that if the tribunal were now to sist the present application to await the outcome of the court action it might form a precedent in other similar cases. The Lord Ordinary might well take the view that he first wished to know whether the land obligations

[18] *Bruce v. Modern Homes Investment Co Ltd*, above; *Anderson v. Trotter*, August 12, 1997; LTS/LO/1996/46.

[19] See *James Miller & Partners Ltd v. Hunt*, 1974 S.L.T. (Lands Tr.) 9; *Highland Regional Council v. Macdonald-Buchanan*, 1977 S.L.T. (Lands Tr.) 37; *Ross and Cromarty District Council v. Ullapool Property Co. Ltd*, 1983 S.L.T. (Lands Tr.) 9; *British Steel plc v. Kaye*, 1991 S.L.T. (Lands Tr.) 7.

[20] *Bruce v. Modern Homes Investment Co. Ltd*, 1978 S.L.T. (Lands Tr.) at 36; see *British Steel plc v. Kaye*, above, where it was commented that it is still an open question.

in question were variable under the 1970 Act and therefore continue the case so he could see the tribunal's decision before dealing with the matter."[21]

A conventional irritancy in a feu contract may be purged at any time prior to decree.[22] The court also has a discretion as to whether or not to allow purgation.[23] There may be a question whether a variation or discharge amounts to a purging of the irritancy or whether the court should exercise its discretion in circumstances where the tribunal has varied or discharged the land obligation. The tribunal has suggested that:

"It is for the courts to decide whether decree of declarator of irritancy should be granted or not in the new context of the 1970 Act where a defaulting party has obtained from the tribunal an order varying or discharging the land obligation in question as from the effective date of their order—from which date in terms of s. 1 (6) the irritancy clause will only be effective (if at all) 'in so far as it would have been effective if the obligation had to that extent been varied or discharged by the person entitled to enforce the obligation'. It may thus still be open to a defaulting burdened proprietor confronted by an action of decree of declarator of irritancy and removing to persuade the court that a tribunal order is equivalent to a waiver by the benefited proprietor; or the equivalent of purgation; or that it would be oppressive in the face of such an order to grant decree."[24]

The tribunal will not usually extend time-limits which have expired, in order to avoid an irritancy, although it may extend a time-limit which has not yet expired.[25] In circumstances where the time-limit has expired any alleviating circumstances should be brought to the attention of the court in any motion seeking further time to purge an irritancy. [26]

The situation may be different with a lease, where a conventional irritancy cannot be purged.[27] In such a case, where the irritancy has been invoked, it may well be too late because the court has no discretion.[28]

---

[21] *Ross and Cromarty District Council v. Ullapool Property Co. Ltd*, above, at 11.

[22] *Anderson v. Valentine*, 1957 S.L.T. 57.

[23] *Precision Relays Ltd v. Beaton*, 1980 S.L.T. 20.

[24] *Highland Regional Council v. MacDonald-Buchanan*, 1977 S.L.T. (Lands Tr.) 37 at 39.

[25] *Avonside Homes Ltd v. Fyfie*, November 9, 1978; LTS/LO/1977/22.

[26] *Nicholson v. Campbell's Trs*, 1980 S.L.T. (Lands Tr.) 10 at 13.

[27] *C.I.N. Properties Ltd v. Dollar Land (Cumbernauld) Ltd*, 1992 S.C.(H.L.) 108.

[28] See *British Steel plc v. Kaye*, 1991 S.L.T. (Lands Tr.) 7 and *Anderson v. Valentine*, above.

The tribunal has held that notwithstanding such an action it retains a jurisdiction to vary or discharge such an obligation because it subsists pending a decision by the court on the irritancy. It has described the role of the concurrent jurisdictions thus:

> "Despite the wording of a conventional clause of irritancy this does not of course have the effect of terminating the feu until decree of declarator of irritancy has been pronounced, extracted and recorded. Accordingly there is now a still subsisting feu burdened by land obligations in respect of which it is still competent for this tribunal to grant a variation order provided that any of the conditions contained in s. 1 (3) (a), (b) or (c) of the 1970 Act are proved to have been satisfied. Such a variation order, however, can only be effective in terms of s. 1 (6) of the 1970 Act from the date it is made and from which date also the irritancy clause, in relation to any act or omission occurring after that date, only attaches to the land obligations as so varied. The 1970 Act is not in our opinion sufficiently worded to enable a tribunal order to operate retrospectively by superseding prior irritancies. It is of course entirely for the courts and not for this tribunal to say what is the effect, when it comes to granting decree of declarator of irritancy, of a tribunal order discharging or varying the very land obligation which is alleged to have been broken and in respect of which purgation might reasonably have been allowed."[29]

There is a similar approach in England, where Lord Denning, in **3–06** *Driscoll v. Church Commissioners for England*,[30] said of an argument by counsel that an action of forfeiture precluded an application to the tribunal:

> "Counsel said that the issue of a writ for forfeiture is an unequivocal election by the landlords to determine the leases, and in consequence the leases had gone and the covenants had gone, and that there was nothing left to modify. I do not agree with that argument, for this reason, that, although a writ is an unequivocal election, nevertheless, until the action is finally determined in favour of the landlord, the covenant does not cease to be potentially good."

It is not competent to raise irritancy proceedings in respect of a **3–07** breach of a land obligation, where the land obligation has been

---

[29] *Ross and Cromarty District Council v. Ullapool Property Co. Ltd*, 1983 S.L.T. (Lands Tr.) 9 at 10. See also *James Miller & Partners Ltd v. Hunt*, 1974 (Lands Tr.) 9.
[30] [1957] 1 Q.B. 330, *per* Lord Denning at 339.

varied or discharged by the tribunal prior to the raising of the irritancy action.[31]

In *Volante v. Lord Burton*[32] the applicants had built a house in breach of a restriction. They applied to the tribunal for a discharge of the obligation. The superior raised irritancy proceedings in the Court of Session. The tribunal sisted the application because one of the issues in the Court of Session action was whether or not there was a subsisting land obligation which needed to be determined before it could be said that the tribunal had jurisdiction.

3–08   In England the situation is dealt with by section 84(9) of the 1925 Act which provides:

> "Where any proceedings by action or otherwise are taken to enforce a restrictive covenant, any person against whom the proceedings are taken, may in such proceedings apply to the Court for an order giving leave to apply to the Lands Tribunal under this section, and staying the proceedings in the meantime."

The proper approach to such an application has been set out in *Richardson v. Jackson*[33] where it was held that:

> "Where proceedings are taken to enforce a restrictive covenant and the defendant applies to the court under the Law of Property Act, 1925, s. 84 (9), for leave to apply to the Lands Tribunal to modify the covenant and for an order staying the proceedings pending the result of the application to the tribunal, the court should not make an order under s. 84 (9) if it is clear on the evidence that the application to the tribunal would not be successful, but if it appears that the defendant would have some chance of obtaining from the tribunal the modification which he seeks, and if the application under s. 84 (9) has been made promptly, the court should, normally, make the order which is asked for, as the modification of covenants is not within its power, and, therefore, it would seem unfair to deprive the defendant of his chance to obtain the modification from the tribunal."[34]

3–09   While there is no statutory procedure for sisting an action of irritancy or other enforcement of a land obligation, it would seem

---

[31] *Fraser v. Church of Scotland General Trustees*, 1986 S.L.T. 692 at 695F. See *Church of Scotland General Trustees v. Fraser*, January 8, 1985; LTS/LO/1984/24.

[32] October 18, 1976; LTS/APP/1/135, commented on in *Ross and Cromarty District Council v. Ullapool Property Co Ltd*, 1983 S.L.T. (Lands Tr.) 9 at 11.

[33] [1954] 1 W.L.R. 447; followed in *Shepherd Homes Ltd v. Sandham* [1971] Ch. 340 at 352F.

[34] *Richardson v. Jackson* [1954] 1 All E.R. 437 (headnote).

reasonable that a Scottish court should apply a similar discretion to an application to sist, pending an application to the Lands Tribunal.

Land obligations that may be varied or discharged

The Lands Tribunal may discharge any land obligation "however 3–10 constituted, and whether subsisting at the commencement of this Act or constituted thereafter".[35] This provision permits the Act to have retrospective effect with regard to any land obligation constituted and subsisting at the commencement of the Act.[36]

The words "however constituted" were included to cover those servitudes which are not recorded in the Register of Sasines or Land Register[37] because they have been constituted by prescription[38] or by implied grant[39] or created under statutory powers.[40]

The tribunal probably has jurisdiction to vary a land obligation imposed by a private Act of Parliament or a provisional order under the Private Legislation Procedure (Scotland) Act 1936.[41]

Where the land obligation is contained in a general deed of 3–11 conditions incorporated by reference in subsequent conveyances, the tribunal varies the condition in the subsequent conveyance as it relates to the particular subjects, but does not vary the deed of conditions itself.[42]

The tribunal may vary or discharge a land obligation in a long registered lease because a lease is an interest in land that may be registered in the Register of Sasines.[43] It has been suggested that it

[35] 1970 Act, s. 1(1).
[36] Commencement date for ss. 1 and 2 was March 1, 1971 (s. 54(2)(b)); Conveyancing and Feudal Reform (Scotland) Act 1970 (Commencement) Order 1971 (S.I. 1971 No. 199).
[37] Halliday Report, Chap. III, p. 17, para. 25.
[38] Positive servitudes created by possession under s. 3(2) of the Prescription and Limitation (Scotland) Act 1973.
[39] Gordon, paras 24-34 to 24-41.
[40] *ibid.* para. 24-04. Whether or not statutorily created servitudes or wayleaves fall within the jurisdiction of the Lands Tribunal depends on whether the obligation is imposed by the statute or under enabling powers under statute (*Macdonald, Applicant,* 1973 S.L.T. (Lands Tr.) 26).
[41] *Westminster City Council v. Duke of Westminster* [1991] 4 All E.R. 136, *per* Harman J. at 146j.
[42] *Bachoo v. George Wimpey & Co. Ltd,* 1977 S.L.T. (Lands Tr.) 2 at 3, where an applicant was burdened by a general deed of conditions recorded by Wimpey under s. 32 of the Conveyancing (Scotland) Act 1874 prior to selling houses from their development.
[43] 1970 Act, s. 2(6). See *e.g. McQuiban v. Eagle Star Insurance Co.,* 1972 S.L.T. (Lands Tr.) 39; *East Kilbride Development Corporation v. The Norwich Union Life Insurance Society,* March 29, 1995; LTS/LO/1993/34.

should be more difficult to persuade the tribunal to exercise its discretion in leasehold than in freehold cases.[44]

3–12   In England, the Lands Tribunal has considered applications to discharge an agricultural occupancy condition[45] and a condition that the roof space was not used for habitation,[46] imposed under section 52 of the Town and Country Planning Act 1971. Such a condition is not a land obligation in Scotland because it is not an obligation relating to land enforceable by a proprietor of an interest in land.[47] The tribunal in Scotland does not have a jurisdiction to discharge such a condition because there is no benefited proprietor.

3–13   It is doubtful whether a conservation agreement entered into by the National Trust for Scotland under section 7 of the National Trust for Scotland Order Confirmation Act 1938[48] is a land obligation that may be discharged or varied by the tribunal. While there is a burdened proprietor, there is no benefited proprietor, because the National Trust for Scotland will not be enforcing the obligation as "the proprietor of an interest in land by virtue of being such proprietor".[49]

3–14   The situation is different in England, where it has been held that a restrictive covenant agreed with the National Trust may be varied by the Land Tribunal. This is because of the different provisions of section 84(1)(c) of the 1925 Act which allow a discharge if it "will not injure the persons entitled to the benefit of the restriction". The National Trust was entitled to the benefit of the restriction,

---

[44] *Ridley v. Taylor* [1965] 1 W.L.R. 611, *per* Harman L.J. at 618.

[45] *Re Quarterly's Application* (1989) 58 P. & C.R. 518 (application refused on merits).

[46] *Re Poulton's Application* (1992) 65 P. & C.R. 319 (application granted).

[47] 1970 Act, s. 1(2).

[48] 2 & 3 Geo. 6, c. LV. Section 7 provides: "Where any person is willing to agree his interest in the land enables him to bind it be made subject either permanently or for a specified period to conditions restricting the planning development or use thereof being conditions which are in conformity with the purposes of the National Trust for Scotland as defined by, the Order of 1935 and this Order the National Trust for Scotland may if it thinks fit enter into an agreement with such person to that effect and if the agreement shall have been recorded in the appropriate register of sasines the National Trust for Scotland shall have power to enforce such agreement against persons deriving title to the land from the person with whom it was entered into: Provided that no such agreement shall at any time be enforceable against a third party who shall have in bona fide onerously acquired right (whether completed by infeftment or not) to the land prior to the agreement being recorded as aforesaid or against any persons deriving title from such third party."

[49] 1970 Act, s. 1(2).

and in addition although this was not a ground of the decision, under section 7 of the National Trust Act 1937, the National Trust was entitled to enforce agreed covenants in like manner as if it "were possessed of or entitled to or interested in adjacent land".[50]

The tribunal cannot discharge a spent land obligation merely as **3–15** a means of clearing the land title. Where a pre-emption clause was spent, because the superior had declined the offer first time round, the tribunal refused to "discharge" the obligation so as to clear the register of the obligation.[51]

"Land obligations"

The essential requisite for conferring jurisdiction on the Lands **3–16** Tribunal is that there should be a land obligation capable of being varied or discharged. Where a land obligation has already been varied by minute of waiver, the tribunal is concerned with the obligation as varied and not with the original obligation.[52] Land obligations are defined statutorily by section 1(2) of the 1970 Act. The definition is:

"a land obligation is an obligation relating to land which is enforceable by a proprietor of an interest in land, by virtue of his being such proprietor, and which is binding upon a proprietor of another interest in that land, or of an interest in other land, by virtue of being such a proprietor".

The important points to note are:

(1) the obligation must relate to land;
(2) it must be enforceable by a proprietor, by virtue of his being proprietor of an "interest in land";
(3) it must be binding upon the proprietor of another interest in that land or other land, by virtue of his being proprietor.

As the tribunal has said:

"it is first necessary . . . to observe that a land obligation in terms of s. 1 (2) of the 1970 Act is an obligation relating to land which is enforceable by a proprietor of an interest in land, by virtue of his being such proprietor ('the benefited proprietor') and which is binding upon a proprietor of another

---

[50] *Gee v. National Trust for Places of Historic Interest and Natural Beauty* [1966] 1 W.L.R. 170.
[51] *Geddes v. Cluny Trs*, January 25, 1993; LTS/LO/1992/23.
[52] *Alexandra Workwear Ltd v. Lothian Regional Councils*, October 21, 1992; LTS/LO/1991/62.

interest in the land, or of an interest in other land, by virtue of his being such proprietor ('the burdened proprietor'). A clear distinction is therefore drawn between land and an interest in land".[53]

It can therefore be seen that the statutory scheme is restricted to a discharge or variation of a land obligation which is enforceable by the proprietor of one interest in land against another proprietor of another interest in land, where their rights in respect of the land obligation arise from their ownership of the particular interest. The scheme is not concerned with the variation of any personal obligation which might exist between proprietors of land or which might exist between other persons and a proprietor of land, unless it falls within the definition.

A "land obligation" includes:

"a future or contingent obligation, an obligation to defray or contribute towards some costs, an obligation to refrain from doing something, and an obligation to permit or suffer something to be done or maintained".[54]

The definition includes an obligation to "defray or contribute towards some costs".[55] This was probably included because doubt has been expressed as to whether or not such an obligation can be a real burden where it is for an indefinite sum. This is because such an obligation does not necessarily affect the subject itself.[56]

An obligation to refrain from "doing something" will in general be a negative servitude, which can only be constituted by recorded deed.[57] The Lands Tribunal has held that its jurisdiction includes a power to vary an obligation whose performance only required compliance with the obligation.[58]

The Halliday Report[59] used the term "land conditions" as meaning:

---

[53] *Grampian Regional Council v. Viscount Cowdray*, 1985 S.L.T. (Lands Tr.) 6 at 7.

[54] 1970 Act, s. 1(2).

[55] *ibid.*

[56] *Corporation of Tailors of Aberdeen v. Coutts* (1840) 1 Rob. 296; *Stair Memorial Encyclopaedia*, Vol. 18, para. 418.

[57] See, *e.g. Hunter v. Fox*, 1964 S.C. (H.L.) 95: reservation providing that the disponee "shall not plant or allow to grow any shrubs, trees or other plants or build any erections" which would exclude the view of the sea.

[58] *McQuiban v. Eagle Star Insurance Co.*, 1972 S.L.T. (Lands Tr.) 39: an obligation not to dispose of a 99-year tack in parcels.

[59] Chap. III, p. 17, para. 25.

> "such conditions, restrictions, provisions, limitations, obliga-
> tions, stipulations, servitudes and real burdens of a continuing
> nature affecting land as are created by any deed recorded in
> the Register of Sasines or by any registerable lease, which has
> not been so recorded, but excluding reservations or exceptions
> from land. Servitudes affecting land otherwise created present
> similar problems".

The recommendation was that a judicial body should be established "having power to vary or discharge land conditions and
servitudes".[60]

This definition means that "land obligation" includes real burdens and conditions, servitudes[61] and other conditions inherent in a
feudal grant. It has been construed to include land obligations:
(1) contained in a deed of conditions incorporated by reference
into a feu disposition, although it is only the obligation in relation
to the subsequent conveyance that can be varied or discharged[62];
(2) a right of pre-emption conferred upon proprietors as such[63];
(3) an expired time-limit in which to build houses remains a
subsisting and enforceable land obligation because the ordinary
courts could enforce such an obligation by an action *ad factum
praestandum* or by irritancy or allow additional time for the
building, although it is unlikely that the tribunal will vary or
discharge an expired time-limit[64]; (4) an obligation in a 99-year
lease that the subjects would be disposed of only in whole and not
in parcels[65]; (5) a temporary obligation, being a right of pre-
emption personal against the original purchasers, provided that it

---

[60] Halliday Report, p. 18.
[61] *Devlin v. Conn*, 1972 S.L.T. (Lands Tr.) 11: discharge of servitude right of
access reserved in a disposition.
[62] *Bachoo v. George Wimpey & Co. Ltd*, 1977 S.L.T. (Lands Tr.) 2.
[63] *Macdonald, Applicant*, 1973 S.L.T. (Lands Tr.) 26; *Walton's Exr v. Farquharson
of Invercauld*, January 26, 1978; LTS/LO/1977/8, where the tribunal allowed a proof
before answer regarding change of circumstances to consider whether there had
been a material change under s. 1(3)(a) to allow it to vary the pre-emption price;
Macdonald v. Begg, August 24, 1979; LTS/LO/1978/29 (pre-emption discharged
under s. 1(3)(b) as benefited proprietor not willing to indicate whether he intended
to operate it or not, when given the offer); *Banff and Buchan District Council v. Earl
of Seafield's Estate*, 1988 S.L.T. (Lands Tr.) 21.
[64] *James Miller & Partners Ltd v. Hunt*, 1974 S.L.T. (Lands Tr.) 9; *Nicolson v.
Campbell's Trs*, 1981 S.L.T. (Lands Tr.) 10, where extension of time-limit after it
had expired was refused; *Avonside Homes Ltd v. Fyvie*, November 9, 1978; LTS/
LO/1977/12, where an unexpired time-limit was extended by two years.
[65] *McQuiban v. Eagle Star Insurance Co.*, 1972 S.L.T. (Lands Tr.) 39.

related to an interest in land[66]; (6) a personal covenant, provided that it restricted the use of land, even if it would not bind singular successors[67]; and (7) obligations to maintain trees or an avenue of trees.[68]

3–17   A trust obligation in a feu disposition is not a land obligation. Where subjects were "granted in trust always for the ends, uses and purposes after mentioned", being use as church subjects, the tribunal held that these were not land obligations because they were enforceable by the beneficiaries of the trust and not by anyone with an interest in land.[69]

It has been held that land obligations do not include irritancy clauses because they are an "irritant or resolutive clause or other condition relating to the enforcement of the obligation" in terms of section 1(6),[70] or land obligations imposed directly by Act of Parliament, as opposed to those imposed under enabling powers.[71]

A qualification of a land obligation is not itself a land obligation which is capable of discharge or variation. In *Reid v. Stafford*[72] the feuar's disposition provided that "the vassal . . . and the Superior's other feuars shall be entitled, but only with the consent in writing of the superior . . . , to enforce against each other *hinc inde* the conditions and restrictions expressed in their Feu Contracts".

On an application to discharge the words requiring the superior's consent, the Lands Tribunal held that the application was incompetent because the words did not constitute a separate land obligation but were simply a qualification attached to a separate right, and the applicant was a conditionally benefited, rather than a burdened, proprietor. The tribunal said:

> "the qualification requiring the superior's consent to the exercise of a right cannot in our view be construed as a separate real burden. Nor does it satisfy in itself the necessary legal requirements. While land obligations attaching to land

---

[66] *Walton's Exr v. Farquharson of Invercauld*, above.

[67] See *Shepherd Homes Ltd v. Sandham* [1971] Ch. 340 (a covenant not to erect fences said to be personal).

[68] *Henderson v. Mansell*, November 9, 1993; LTS/LO/1992/41.

[69] *Church of Scotland General Trs v. Fraser*, January 8, 1985; LTS/LO/1984/24. See *Fraser v. Church of Scotland General Trs*, 1986 S.L.T. 692 regarding concurrent irritancy action.

[70] *Highland Regional Council v. MacDonald-Buchanan*, 1977 S.L.T. (Lands Tr.) 37 at 39; *Nicolson v. Campbell's Trs*, 1981 S.L.T. (Lands Tr.) 10.

[71] *Macdonald, Applicant*, above.

[72] 1979 S.L.T. (Lands Tr.) 16.

are given a somewhat wider definition under s. 1 (2) of the 1970 Act when read with s. 1 (6), the words of qualification, if constituting a separate land obligation, would invert the position of burdened and benefited proprietor. This is clearly not intended from the context of clause ninth which was intended rather to confer a qualified right upon co-feuars as benefited proprietors. The words are thus a restriction upon the land obligation and not a direct restriction on the land. In contrast clause second relating to building imposes burdens upon the vassal, as burdened proprietor, one of which is to obtain the superior's consent to plans. Under clause ninth however the words of qualification operate as a power of veto over the exercise of a jus quaesitum tertio in which the applicant is a conditional benefited rather than a burdened proprietor; and it is, of course, only as a burdened proprietor that he can apply to this tribunal for a variation or discharge order under s. 1 (3)".[73]

A similar approach was taken in *Mackay v. Burton*[74] where the Lands Tribunal held that the grant of a right of access for agricultural purposes was the grant of a restricted right and not the grant of a right, burdened by the restriction on the type of use to which the access might be put. The applicant was the person in right of the access, who argued that the servitude was a separate interest in land, burdened by the restriction on the type of access. The Lands Tribunal went on to say:

"Accordingly, if this right of access is properly to be regarded as one the extent of which is limited, rather than one which is in itself limitless in extent and which is then made subject to a restriction on the use which the applicants may make of it, that being a restriction which can then be treated as a separate land obligation, it follows that there is here no obligation which the tribunal may competently vary on an application by the persons who enjoy the benefit of the right of access."[75]

This is in accordance with the approach in *Murrayfield Ice Rink Ltd v. SRU*[76] where there was a proposal to develop the ice rink as a supermarket, but one of the difficulties was that the parking

[73] 1979 S.L.T. (Lands Tr.) 16 at 18.
[74] 1994 S.L.T. (Lands Tr.) 35 at 38C.
[75] *ibid*. at 38E–F.
[76] 1972 S.L.T. (Lands Tr.) 20 at 24.

rights were on the superiors' (the SRU's) land and the Lands Tribunal commented that it:

> "cannot, of course, vary the car parking rights which are a burden not on the applicants but on the superiors' land and are declared not to run with the land".

In *George T. Fraser Ltd v. Aberdeen Harbour Board*[77] the First Division refused an appeal against the Lands Tribunal's decision that a clause designating the tenant under a long lease was not a land obligation. The applicants under a lease "let to the tenant, exclusive of assignees, legal and voluntary, and sub-tenants, except with the consent in writing" applied to have the obligation varied by the addition of the words "which consent will not be unreasonably withheld". The court held that this was not a land obligation because the relevant obligation must have a direct relationship to the land. The Lands Tribunal did not have power to interfere with the operative words of a lease, which defined who might be the tenant, because these related to "the relationship between the respective proprietors of the interests in it [the land] or the identity of those proprietors".[78]

3–18   The Lands Tribunal does not have jurisdiction to discharge a land obligation which has been extinguished by, for example, a consolidation of the feu and superiority or perhaps a loss of interest to enforce, nor to discharge a spent obligation in order to clear the record.[79] In such circumstances there is no remaining benefited proprietor to enforce the obligation.[80]

A similar approach is taken in England, where the jurisdiction is "by order wholly or partially to discharge or modify" a restriction arising under a covenant over "any freehold land affected".[81] In *Re Purkiss's Application*[82] it was said:

> "If, therefore, the applicant's land was held not to be affected by any restriction, or if, to take an extreme case as here suggested, it was the right answer to say that there was no building scheme and no suggestion of restriction had been put

---

[77] 1985 S.L.T. 384, IH.

[78] 1985 S.L.T. 384, *per* Lord Stott at 387; at 385, the Lands Tribunal is quoted as saying that it did not have power to vary a destination in a conveyance.

[79] *Geddes v. Cluny Trs*, January 25, 1993; LTS/LO/1992/23, where the tribunal refused to "discharge" a pre-emption clause, which the superior had already declined to operate, on the ground that it was spent and it had no jurisdiction to grant a "discharge" simply to clear the record.

[80] *McCarthy & Stone (Developments) Ltd v. Smith*, 1995 S.L.T. (Lands Tr.) 19.

[81] 1925 Act, s. 84(1).

[82] [1962] 1 W.L.R. 902, *per* the Master of the Rolls at 908.

forward, then the premise on which the tribunal's jurisdiction rested had gone altogether."

While the onus is on the applicant to show that, on a balance of probabilities, the obligation remains enforceable by someone even if that person cannot be readily identified,[83] the Lands Tribunal will probably assume that there is a benefited proprietor entitled to enforce the obligation unless the contrary is clearly shown. The tribunal has been enjoined by the Court of Appeal in all but the simplest cases to assume that there are persons entitled to enforce the restriction complained of or alternatively to hand the matter over for a decision by the court.[84] In *Re Coulsdon and Purley UDC's Application*[85] the Lands Tribunal said that there is a presumption, in the absence of the contrary being established, that a restriction remains operative, but that was an assumption and not a determination.

If a land obligation remains on the face of the title, which is no longer enforceable, the proper procedure where the title remains on the Sasine register would be to seek a declarator that it is no longer enforceable or where it is on the Land Register to appeal to the Lands Tribunal under sections 9(1) and 25(1) of the Land Registration (Scotland) Act 1979, seeking a rectification of the register by cancelling those obligations.[86]

Where an application is made by a number of, but not all, the burdened proprietors for the variation of a common land obligation, the Lands Tribunal does not have power to override the minority and increase a burden on the non-consenting proprietors. Where 93 out of 120 burdened proprietors sought a variation of the land obligation regulating the upkeep of the *pro indiviso* owned central gardens in which each feu contract restricted the annual contribution to £2, the Lands Tribunal held that the application was incompetent without the consent of all the burdened proprietors.[87]

[83] *cf. R. v. Westminster City Council and the London Electricity Board* (1989) 59 P. & C.R. 51 where, in a judicial review, the court concluded that on a balance of probabilities the covenant remained enforceable even though despite strenuous efforts no one was discovered who might enforce it.

[84] *R. v. Westminster City Council and the London Electricity Board*, above, at 57, a judicial review case, citing *Re Purkiss's Application* [1962] 1 W.L.R. 902.

[85] (1951) 7 P. & C.R. 16; *cf. R. v. Westminster City Council and the London Electricity Board*, above, a judicial review case.

[86] *McCarthy & Stone (Developments) Ltd v. Smith*, 1995 S.L.T. (Lands Tr.) 19 at 21L; *Brookfield Developments Ltd v. Keeper of the Registers of Scotland*, 1989 S.L.T. (Lands Tr.) 105.

[87] *Mrs Young, Applicant*, 1978 S.L.T. (Lands Tr.) 28.

The fact that the Keeper of the Registers might have determined to include a land obligation in the burdens section of a land certificate does not "convert a burden which should have been excluded because it was in truth no longer subsisting into a subsisting one".[88]

It is not competent to vary a land obligation by suspending it temporarily.[89]

Interest in land

3–19   In order to have title and interest to apply for a discharge or variation of a land obligation, the applicant has to show that he is the proprietor of an "interest in land" bound by an obligation and that the respondent, even if he cannot be readily identified, is also proprietor of an "interest in land", entitled to enforce the obligation.

There is no statutory definition of "land" in the 1970 Act, but "interest in land" is defined by section 2(6) to mean:

> "any estate or interest in land which is capable of being owned or held as a separate interest and to which a title may be recorded in the Register of Sasines".[90]

Note that it is "capable of being owned" and which "may be recorded", so that the interest does not have to be owned as a separate interest and it does not have to be recorded in the Register of Sasines at the time the jurisdiction of the Land Tribunal is invoked.

Regard must therefore be had to the earlier conveyancing statutes to see what estates or interests in land may be recorded in the Register of Sasines.

Section 2 of the Titles to Land Consolidation (Scotland) Act 1868 defines "lands" as extending to and including "all heritable subjects, [securities][91] and rights". Section 2 of the Conveyancing (Scotland) Act 1874 defines "Land" or "Lands" to "include all subjects of heritable property which are or may be held of a superior according to feudal tenure, or which prior to the commencement of this Act have been or might have been held by burgage tenure, or by tenure of booking" and "Estate in land"

---

[88] *Brookfield Developments Ltd v. Keeper of the Registers of Scotland*, above, at 110J.

[89] *Nicolson v. Campbell's Trs*, 1981 S.L.T. (Lands Tr.) 10.

[90] This includes the Land Register: Land Registration (Scotland) Act 1979, s. 29(2).

[91] Deleted by Conveyancing (Scotland) Act 1924, s. 2(1).

means "any interest in land, whether in fee, liferent, [or security],[92] and whether beneficial or in trust, or any real burden on land, and shall include an estate of superiority".

In general the land variation provisions are invoked by a vassal against a superior or by neighbouring proprietors, under the burden of a land obligation, and by tenants against landlords, under a long lease. Usually there is little difficulty in determining that a particular land obligation falls within the jurisdiction of the Lands Tribunal, but there are marginal cases.

While an applicant might be the burdened proprietor under an obligation, he will have no interest to make the application if the discharge is sought for the benefit of some other party who does not have an interest in the land in question. In *Henderson v. Mansell*[93] a builder who owned nearby land obtained planning permission, subject to a condition that a road junction was realigned so as to make a safer bellmouth, with a clear line of sight where it entered the main road. The house at the corner was subject to land obligations that a tree on the road edge of the garden should be maintained as part of an avenue of trees and that the garden wall and metal railing should be maintained. The owner of the house, who had been offered a sum of money to allow the tree to be removed and the garden wall and metal railing to be set back, sought a discharge or variation of the land obligation. The tribunal held that the applicant did not have a genuine motive or interest in pursuing the application because he was not going to be the user of the land in question. The tribunal said:

> "If the application is intended ultimately to benefit some person other than the applicant that could, in certain circumstances, be a proper and legitimate use of the section 1 procedures: if the objective of the application is, as here, to benefit someone who is, or will be, the proprietor of land other than the application subjects (or, possibly, subjects immediately adjacent to or connected therewith). We have come to the view that Parliament never intended section 1 of the 1970 Act to be used for the purposes of an application such as this."

Additional or substitutional provisions

The power to vary or discharge a land obligation "includes **3–20** power to add or substitute any such provision . . . as appears to the Lands Tribunal to be reasonable as the result of the variation or

[92] Deleted by Conveyancing (Scotland) Act 1924, s. 2(1).
[93] November 9, 1993; LTS/LO/1992/41.

discharge of the obligation and as may be accepted by the applicant".[94]

This jurisdiction extends only to imposing additional or subsitutional provisions on the applicant's land and with his agreement. It is not competent for the tribunal to impose conditions on neighbouring land. In *Irving v. John Dickie & Sons Ltd*[95] the tribunal, in varying a right of access, held it to be incompetent to impose a maintenance and costs sharing regime on all the proprietors entitled to share in the access as an additional or substitutional provision.[96]

Statutory exclusions

3–21   Section 1(1) provides that:

> "the provisions of the said sections shall not apply in relation to an obligation specified or referred to in Schedule 1 of this Act".

Schedule 1 to the 1970 Act provides for "Land Obligations not subject to variation or discharge under section 1". The difficulty with the heading to Schedule 1 is that it is not clear whether the Schedule excluded what might otherwise be a land obligation, or whether in some cases the exclusion is for the avoidance of doubt. Paragraph 5 excludes obligations in leases of agricultural holdings, small landholdings and crofts, all of which are usually leases from year to year running on tacit relocation, which are not registrable in the Register of Sasines.

The Schedule provides:

> "1. An obligation to pay feu duty, ground annual, rent, skat, dry multure, teind, stipend, standard charge or other payment of a like nature, or an obligation of relief relating to any such payment.
> 2. An obligation, however constituted, relating to the right to work minerals or to any ancillary right in relation to minerals

---

[94] 1970 Act, s. 1(5). See para 8–04. It should be noted that s. 84(1C) of the 1925 Act provides that "the power . . . to modify a restriction includes power to add such further provisions", so that the Lands Tribunal of England appears not to have power to impose a substitutional provision when it discharges a restrictive covenant. In *Re Forrestmore Properties Ltd's Application* (1980) 41 P. & C.R. 390 the tribunal indicated that unless the applicants were willing to accept a modified restriction, the application would be refused and, in *Re Cox's Application* (1985) 51 P. & C.R. 335, the tribunal purported to impose a substitutional provision when it granted a discharge. These decisions have been criticised in Scammell at p. 363, n. 12.

[95] August 31, 1995; LTS/LO/94/17.

[96] See also *Murrayfield Ice Rink Ltd v. SRU*, 1972 S.L.T. (Lands Tr.) 20.

within the meaning of section 2 of the Mines (Working Facilities and Support) Act 1966.[97]

3. An obligation imposed by or on behalf of the Crown[98] for the protection of any royal park,[99] garden or palace.[1]

4. An obligation created or imposed—

(i) for naval, military or air force purposes;

(ii) for civil aviation purposes under the powers conferred by section 19 or 23 of the Civil Aviation Act 1949 or any enactment replaced thereby.[2]

Provided that this paragraph—

(i) shall exclude the application of section 1 of this Act to an obligation falling within sub-paragraph (i) above, and not created or imposed in connection with the use of any land as an aerodrome, only so long as the obligation is enforceable by or on behalf of the Crown; and

(ii) shall exclude the application of section 1 of this Act to an obligation falling within sub-paragraph (ii) above, or created or imposed in connection with the use of any land as an aerodrome, only so long as the

---

[97] s. 2(1) of the Mines (Working Facilities and Support) Act 1966 provides:

"In this Act 'ancillary right' means, in relation to minerals, any facility, right or privilege and, in particular, but without prejudice to the generality of the foregoing provisions of this subsection, that expression shall include—

(a) a right to let down the surface;

(b) a right of air-way, shaft-way or surface or underground wayleave, or other right for the purpose of access to or conveyance of minerals (otherwise than by means of a pipe) or the ventilation or drainage of the mines;

(c) a right to use and occupy the surface for the erection of washeries, coke ovens, railways, by-product works or brick making or other works, or of dwellings for persons employed in connection with the working of the minerals or with any such works as aforesaid;

(d) a right to obtain a supply of water or other substances in connection with the working of minerals;

(e) a right to dispose of water or other liquid matter obtained from mines or any by-product works."

[98] See s. 51 ("Application to Crown") includes land held of the Prince of Scotland.

[99] See *Officers of State v. Earl of Haddington* (1830) 8 S. 867; (1831) 5 W. & S. 570, re Holyrood Park.

[1] There may be a question whether "palace" includes a royal palace now conveyed to a hereditary keeper, *e.g.* Falkland Palace or Dunfermline Palace

[2] Civil Aviation Act 1982, s. 30 (replacing s. 19) and ss. 41–43 (replacing s. 23) in modified form.

obligation is enforceable by or on behalf of the Crown
or any public or international authority.

5. An obligation created or imposed in or in relation to a
lease of—

(a) an agricultural holding, within the meaning of the Agricultural Holdings (Scotland) Act [1991];

(b) a holding within the meaning of the Small Landholders
(Scotland) Acts 1886 to 1931[3]; or

(c) a croft, within the meaning of the Crofters (Scotland) Act
[1993]."

No application for variation may be brought under section 1, in
respect of any new land obligation "first created . . . in a conveyance, deed, instrument or writing . . . until the expiry of two
years from the date of its creation".[4] While an application may be
brought after two years, the tribunal is reluctant to discharge a
recently created obligation, particularly where the parties to the
application are the original parties to the contract.[5]

The tribunal has held that it has no power to vary a land
obligation imposed by a statute, as opposed to a land obligation
imposed under enabling powers given by statute. In *Macdonald,
Applicant* the tribunal held:

"The Tribunal is therefore driven to the conclusion that the
words 'any land obligation however constituted' in s. 1(1) of
the 1970 Act are intended to be confined to private land
obligations including, however, those constituted under statutory enabling powers. These may be obligations created by
conveyance, deed, instrument or writing as mentioned in
s. 2(5); but may also be land obligations constituted by
implication or prescription as in the case of servitudes. We
consider that this was probably why the words 'however
constituted' were inserted in s. 1(2) and not to cover land
obligations directly imposed by the legislature."[6]

This is consistent with *Re Elan & Co Ltd's Application*[7] where the
tribunal, in considering a restrictive covenant, ultimately held not

[3] A smallholding under the Small Holdings Act 1892 is not included: *Macdonald,
Applicant*, 1973 S.L.T. (Lands Tr.) 26.

[4] s. 2(5). See s. 53(4): "conveyance", "deed" and "instrument" are defined by
reference to s. 3 of the Titles to Land Consolidation (Scotland) Act 1868, s. 3 of the
Conveyancing (Scotland) Act 1874 and s. 2 of the Conveyancing (Scotland) Act
1924. *Watters v. Motherwell District Council*, 1991 S.L.T. (Lands Tr.) 2 (the two years
run from the date of the delivery of the disposition).

[5] See below, para. 5–11.

[6] 1973 S.L.T. (Lands Tr.) 26 at 29.

[7] (1962) 14 P. & C.R. 230.

to have been imposed by a private Act of Parliament, referred to certain exclusions of jurisdiction and commented:

"All these exclusions, however, relate to restrictions imposed by statute, and it might be argued whether these wide powers would entitle the Tribunal to make an order which would, in effect, amend or repeal a statutory provision."

Notwithstanding the doubts expressed in *Re Elan & Co Ltd's Application*, it would appear that the tribunal has power to discharge or vary an obligation imposed by a private Act of Parliament or provisional order.[8]

Limits of jurisdiction

The Lands Tribunal's prime jurisdiction under section 1(3) of the 1970 Act is restricted to pronouncing an order to "vary or discharge the obligation wholly or in part" with the subsidiary powers conferred by section 1(5). **3–22**

The Lands Tribunal does not have power "to grant an applicant new rights. Their jurisdiction is merely to vary or discharge burdens upon rights already granted."[9] While the case was decided on different grounds, in *Mackay v. Burton*[10] the Lands Tribunal recognised that if it granted an order varying a servitude right of access for agricultural purposes to a general right of access, it would be granting the applicant increased rights, and opined that this was not the intention of the Act.

Determining jurisdiction

Before the Lands Tribunal will entertain an application it has to be "prima facie satisfied that they have statutory jurisdiction over an enforceable land obligation".[11] **3–23**

The tribunal does not have a declaratory power to declare that a land obligation is unenforceable, but the tribunal:

"sometimes have to explicate their statutory jurisdiction under s 1 of the 1970 Act by deciding whether they are confronted by an enforceable land obligation which they can then vary or discharge".[12]

---

[8] *Westminster City Council v. Duke of Westminster* [1991] 4 All E.R. 136, *per* Harman J. at 146j.

[9] *George T. Fraser Ltd v. Aberdeen Harbour Board*, 1985 S.L.T. 384, IH, *per* the Lord President at 386.

[10] 1994 S.L.T. (Lands Tr.) 35 at 38H.

[11] *Bachoo v. George Wimpey & Co. Ltd*, 1977 S.L.T. (Lands Tr.) 2 at 4.

[12] *Brookfield Developments Ltd v. Keeper of the Registers of Scotland*, 1989 S.L.T. (Lands Tr.) 105 at 109A–B.; *McCarthy & Stone (Developments) Ltd v. Smith*, 1995 S.L.T. (Lands Tr.) 19 at 26C–D and H–J.

The tribunal has determined that a ground annual which had been redeemed was no longer an enforceable land obligation[13]; that a purported restriction in a feu charter of 1807 was not an enforceable land obligation because it had never entered the record[14]; and that on a proper construction of the land obligation it did not prevent the development proposed and accordingly variation was not required.[15]

An application requesting the tribunal to make a provision in the variation that office use was permitted, that it would not contravene a condition prohibiting the use of premises for any trade or business which might be hurtful, nauseous or noxious to houses and inhabitants in the neighbourhood and that such use would not contravene the obligation was abandoned at the hearing on the ground that the tribunal could not grant such a declarator.[16]

In an application where two flats had been altered, contrary to a land obligation, apparently with the verbal consent of the superior, the tribunal said that it did not have jurisdiction to determine a question of alleged acquiescence by a superior rendering land obligations unenforceable.[17] In another case the tribunal did consider whether or not alterations to a number of houses without the consent of neighbours in a street, where the burdens required the consent of neighbours, had resulted in the obligation having fallen into disuse.[18]

Where a land obligation appears, on the face of the title, to be constituted validly the tribunal is not concerned "with whether it appeared in the title in error or had never been agreed".[19]

If an applicant intends to challenge the title and interest of the intended respondent to enforce the land obligation, that has to be done in another forum.[20]

In England, the Lands Tribunal has been discouraged from adjudicating on title, given that there is a statutory jurisdiction for application by any person interested to the High Court.[21]

[13] *Trustees of the Hindu Mandir & Cultural Society v. Thomson*, February 27, 1989; LTS/LO/1988/42 and 43.

[14] *Edinburgh Southern Harriers v. Sellar*, August 9, 1989; LTS/LO/1988/10.

[15] *Lee v. Inverness District Council*, October 10, 1994; LTS/LO/1994/9, where held that an obligation to build a shop to a design and of materials approved by the superior did not prevent an extension being added subsequently by the proprietor.

[16] *Ramsay v. Holmes*, 1992 S.L.T. (Lands Tr.) 53 at 54C.

[17] *Harris v. Douglass*, 1993 S.L.T. (Lands Tr.) 56 at 58C; *Bankier v. Barloch Properties Ltd*, December 23, 1992; LTS/LO/1992/21: "the question of alleged acquiescence by a superior rendering a land obligation unenforceable is not within the jurisdiction of the Tribunal".

[18] *Stoddart v. Glendinning*, 1993 S.L.T. (Lands Tr.) 12 at 15B–C.

[19] *MacDonald v. Abbotshall Evanton Ltd*, February 16, 1989; LTS/LO/1988/89.

[20] *Bachoo v. George Wimpey & Co. Ltd*, 1977 S.L.T. (Lands Tr.) 2 at 4.

[21] *Re Purkiss's Application* [1992] 1 W.L.R. 902; [1962] 2 All E.R. 690 at 693H.

"(a) to declare whether or not in any particular case any freehold land is, or would in any given event be, affected by a restriction imposed by any instrument; or

(b) to declare what, upon the true construction of any instrument purporting to impose a restriction, is the nature and extent of the restriction thereby imposed and whether the same is, or would in any given event be, enforceable and if so by whom"[22]

although it was recognised that in certain circumstances:

"it might be that the tribunal would have to come to a conclusion whether the land in question was affected by any restriction in order to found its own jurisdiction to proceed".[23]

These comments in *Re Purkiss's Application* have been subject to comment in *Shepherd Homes Ltd v. Sandham (No. 2)* where Megarry J. said[24]:

"*Re Purkiss's Application* is a case which has been the subject of some comment and, perhaps, some misunderstanding. Even if what is said about difficult points of law is not of the ratio, the dicta are no mere passing remarks but statements by members of a powerful Court of Appeal after what, from the names of counsel engaged in the case, I imagine to have been powerful arguments. If the Lands Tribunal is confronted by some difficult point of law on which its jurisdiction depends, such as whether an ancient building scheme exists which entitles objectors to the benefit of the covenant, it seems to me clear from the judgments of Upjohn and Diplock LJ that the Lands Tribunal should proceed to hear and determine the application on its merits after either assuming or deciding that the objectors are entitled to the benefit of the covenant. Such an assumption or decision, being on a matter for the court under S 84 (1), will not be binding on those concerned, and may subsequently be questioned in the courts. Like any other tribunal of limited jurisdiction, the Lands Tribunal must have power to determine whether or not the case falls within the limits of its jurisdiction: but as with other inferior tribunals, that power does not enable it to expand or contract the jurisdiction that Parliament has conferred on it, and so no party who is minded to challenge that decision on jurisdiction

---

[22] 1925 Act, s. 84(2).
[23] *Re Purkiss's Application* [1982] 1 W.L.R. 906 at 908.
[24] [1971] 1 W.L.R. 1062 at 1071.

will be bound by it in the courts. As a matter of convenience and prudence, the Lands Tribunal will no doubt decide the matter in most cases where the legal complexities are not overburdensome, and assume the point where they are. Indeed, in *Spruit v. John Smith's Tadcaster Brewery Ltd*, the Court of Appeal remitted the case to the Lands Tribunal for a further hearing in which the title of certain objectors to the benefit of the restriction could be investigated. The dicta in *Re Purkiss's Application* give a valuable warning as to the extent to which decisions of the Lands Tribunal are binding on the parties, and offer a counsel of prudence to the Lands Tribunal: but I do not think that the case is authority for any general rule that the Lands Tribunal is bound to abstain from resolving points of law merely because they are said to be difficult."

Where the Lands Tribunal has doubts about the jurisdictional competency of an application service may be ordered on the Lord Advocate in the public interest.[25]

The tribunal does have an explicatory jurisdiction, where there is an undoubted land obligation, to determine who are benefited proprietors and to distinguish between who may be benefited proprietors, perhaps having a *jus quaesitum tertio*, and who are just affected proprietors.[26]

---

[25] *Macdonald, Applicant*, 1973 S.L.T. (Lands Tr.) 26.
[26] *Smith v. Taylor*, 1972 S.L.T. (Lands Tr.) 34; *McCarthy & Stone (Developments) Ltd v. Smith*, 1995 S.L.T. (Lands Tr.) 26. The situation would appear to be the same in England; *Re Purkiss's Application* [1992] 1 W.L.R. 902 at 912 citing *Spruit v. John Smith's Tadcaster Brewery* (1957) P. & C.R. 24.

CHAPTER 4

THE APPLICATION AND PROCEDURE

General

An application to the Lands Tribunal for a variation or discharge **4–01** of a land obligation requires to be made by a burdened proprietor in terms of rules 3–5 of the Lands Tribunal for Scotland Rules 1971,[1] in Form 1.[2] The tribunal procedure is considered in detail in Chapter 2.[3]

The Applicant

An application to the Lands Tribunal for discharge or variation **4–02** of a land obligation may be made only by "a burdened proprietor".[4] The application may relate only to some obligation to which the burdened proprietor's land is subject and not to land belonging to another person.[5]

In *Murrayfield Ice Rink Ltd v. SRU*[6] the Lord Justice-Clerk said:

"Under s. 1 of that Act (and that is the section with which we are concerned here) it is only the burdened proprietor who may apply to the Tribunal for the variation or discharge of obligations. Furthermore, he may apply only to have varied or discharged some obligation to which his land is subject. The Tribunal, if the appropriate circumstances are established, may vary or discharge the obligation(s) of which the burdened proprietor complains. So far as I am aware, however, there is no provision in the Act—and we were referred to none— which empowers the Tribunal, even when they are relieving the burdened proprietor's land of some obligation, to impose

---

[1] S.I. 1971 No. 218.
[2] 1971 Rules, Sched. 1, Form 1. See App. 8.
[3] See above, para. 2–01.
[4] 1970 Act, s. 1(3) and 1971 Rules, r. 3.
[5] *Mrs Young, Applicant*, 1978 S.L.T. (Lands Tr.) 28, following *Murrayfield Ice Rink Ltd v. Scottish Rugby Union*, 1973 S.C. 21, *per* Lord Justice-Clerk at 31.
[6] 1973 S.C. 21, *per* Lord Justice-Clerk at 31.

an extended obligation on some other land in which the 'burdened proprietor' (or indeed anybody else) has an interest."

A "burdened proprietor" in relation to a land obligation "means a proprietor of an interest in land upon whom, by virtue of his being such proprietor, the obligation is binding". It includes: (1) where land is held by two or more persons jointly or in common, all those persons or any of them; and (2) where the interest in land is subject to an *ex facie* absolute conveyance or assignation in security, the person who, if the debt were discharged, would be entitled to be vested in that interest.[7]

Where there are a number of *pro indiviso* burdened proprietors with mutual obligations in their titles, although they do not all have to join in the application, the application will not be granted in the face of opposition by any of the other burdened proprietors.[8]

The definition by reference to the enforcement being "by virtue of his being such proprietor" emphasises that the Act is dealing with obligations relating to land and not personal obligations.

One effect of the provision is that where there are missives of sale conditional upon a discharge, only the seller will have the right to apply for the variation. If ownership changes during the course of the application, the purchaser may be sisted as a party to the application and the seller may withdraw.[9]

While it is competent for the seller under conditional missives to make an application, if the application is made, not for the benefit of the subjects in question, but for the benefit of neighbouring or other proprietors, it will be incompetent.[10]

The English provision which allows an application to be made by "any persons interested in any freehold land affected by any restriction arising under covenant or otherwise"[11] is a wider category of applicant than "burdened proprietor". The restrictive covenant does not have to be enforceable by a person with an interest in land.[12]

The proprietor of a dominant tenement of a servitude is not a benefited proprietor.[13] A person in right of a restricted right of

---

[7] 1970 Act, s. 2(6).

[8] *Mrs Young, Applicant*, above, where some of the proprietors objected to an application which sought to increase their contribution to the costs of maintaining a common garden.

[9] 1971 Rules, r. 26 and 27.

[10] *Henderson v. Mansell*, November 9, 1993; LTS/LO/1992/41.

[11] 1925 Act, s. 84(1). See Scammell, p. 320 ("Who may apply").

[12] See above, para. 3–10 re English jurisdiction to vary planning conditions or conservation conditions agreed with the National Trust.

[13] *McCarthy & Stone (Developments) Ltd v. Smith*, 1995 S.L.T. (Lands Tr.) 19 at 23I–J.

access is not a burdened proprietor for the purposes of applying to have the restriction on the right of access removed.[14] A proprietor with a *jus quaesitum tertio* is not a burdened proprietor, nor is a person with a qualified right of *jus quaesitum tertio* subject to the superior's veto in respect of that veto. The veto is the qualification of the right and not a separate land obligation in its own right.[15]

Existing land obligation

There has to be in existence an enforceable land obligation at **4–03** the time that the application is made. An ineffective conveyance or land obligation, granted by a person with no right in the lands, can be validated retrospectively by acquisition of the property and recording of the disposition during the course of the application. The "doctrine of accretion also serves to validate the original application" in circumstances where a land obligation was created by feu charter, before the superior had acquired the lands in question and accordingly, there had been no enforceable obligation at the time of making the application.[16]

Benefited proprietors

An application requires to be served on the benefited proprietor, **4–04** who has title and interest to oppose the application.[17] Section 2(2) of the 1970 Act provides that a burdened or benefited proprietor "shall be entitled, within such time as may be prescribed, to oppose or make representation in relation to the application".

In cases of dispute, for the purposes of the application, the Lands Tribunal may determine who is a benefited proprietor, entitled to enforce undisputed land obligations. This jurisdiction arises from the terms of section 2(1) of the 1970 Act which requires that the tribunal give notice of an application to "persons who . . . appear to them to be either benefited or burdened proprietors".[18] There is a similar jurisdiction in England for the Lands Tribunal to investigate the title of individual objectors.[19] In *Stoddart v. Glendinning*[20] the tribunal had to determine who were the "neighbours", as benefited proprietors whose permission for alterations to a dwelling-house had to be obtained, and held:

---

[14] *Mackay v. Burton*, 1994 S.L.T. (Lands Tr.) 35. See above, para. 3–17.
[15] *Reid v. Stafford*, 1979 S.L.T. (Lands Tr.) 16; see above, para. 3–16.
[16] *Murrayfield Ice Rink Ltd v. SRU*, 1972 S.L.T. (Lands Tr.) 20 at 21.
[17] 1970 Act, s. 2(2) and 1971 Rules, r. 4(1)(a).
[18] *Smith v. Taylor*, 1972 S.L.T. (Lands Tr.) 34; *McCarthy & Stone (Developments) Ltd v. Smith*, 1995 S.L.T. (Lands Tr.) 19.
[19] *Re Purkiss's Application* [1962] 1 W.L.R. 902, *per* Upjohn L.J. at 912.
[20] 1993 S.L.T. (Lands Tr.) 12 at 15.

"The word 'neighbours' must accordingly be given its ordinary meaning of persons who live close or near to one another."

A benefited proprietor "means a proprietor of an interest in land who is entitled, by virtue of his being such proprietor, to enforce the obligation" and includes, where the interest in land is held by two or more persons jointly or in common, all those persons or any of them.[21]

In appropriate circumstances both a superior and a mid-superior might be benefited proprietors, and the mid-superior may enforce the obligation even if the superior consents.[22]

A heritable creditor is not a benefited proprietor, although he might be an affected person.[23]

Where there is no longer a subsisting land obligation, as occurs where there is a consolidation of the feu and superiority, or where an obligation is spent,[24] there is no burdened proprietor or benefited proprietor entitled to enforce the obligation.[25]

The phrase "benefited proprietor" includes not only those proprietors who are benefited specifically in terms of their title deeds or the title deeds of the burdened property,[26] but also those proprietors who in law can be held to have a *jus quaesitum tertio* to enforce the land obligation.[27]

A benefited proprietor is entitled to act on behalf of his feuars or the local community to oppose an application.[28] Where the application is made under section 1(3)(b) the benefited proprietor cannot act in the public interest because, under ground (b) the tribunal is comparing the burden to the burdened proprietor with the benefit to the benefited proprietor alone.[29]

A local authority which is the benefited proprietor is not entitled to be treated any differently from any other benefited proprietor.[30]

---

[21] 1970 Act, s. 2(6). The definition includes the person, where there is a conveyance in security, who would be entitled to a vested interest in property if the debt were discharged.

[22] *Smith v. Taylor*, above; *Ramsay v. Holmes*, 1992 S.L.T. (Lands Tr.) 53 at 56H (superior not objecting but mid-superior the objector).

[23] *Smith v. Taylor*, above.

[24] *e.g.* a spent pre-emption clause: *Geddes v. Cluny Trs*, January 25, 1993; LTS/LO/1992/23.

[25] *McCarthy & Stone (Developments) Ltd v. Smith*, 1995 S.L.T. (Lands Tr.) 19.

[26] *Ness v. Shannon*, 1978 S.L.T. (Lands Tr.) 13.

[27] *Leny v. Craig*, 1982 S.L.T. (Lands Tr.) 9 at 10; *McCarthy & Stone (Developments) Ltd v. Smith*, above.

[28] *MacDonald v. Stornoway Trust*, 1987 S.L.T. 240 at 242K; *Lothian Regional Council v. George Wimpey & Co.*, 1985 S.L.T. (Lands Tr.) 2.

[29] *MacDonald v. Stornoway Trust*, above; *Noble v. Viscount Reidhaven*, June 17, 1991; LTS/LO/1989/98.

[30] *MacDonald v. Stornoway Trust*, above, at 242K.

The superior

A superior's interest to enforce a feuing condition is presumed. **4–05**
The tribunal has commented that:

"A superior's continuing interest to enforce a feuing condition
of this nature is always presumed and is not departed from
because they are prepared to grant a minute of waiver for a
financial consideration; see *Howard De Walden Estates
Limited v. Bowmaker Limited*, 1965 S.C. 163, 1965 S.L.T. 254.
In the present case, moreover, the superiors' interest is
conceded by virtue of the application to the Tribunal under s.
1 (3). But the superiors appear to be confusing their interest
to enforce the feuing conditions at common law with the
somewhat different interests which are involved and which the
Tribunal has to take into account when applying the Conveyancing and Feudal Reform (Scotland) Act 1970."[31]

A superior can act on behalf of his feuars or the general public
in the area, except in relation to an application under ground (b).
In *Noble v. Viscount Reidhaven*,[32] where there was strong local
opposition to a proposal on the ground of its effect on the amenity,
the tribunal said:

"A superior has every right to try to protect that amenity, and
to control a particular environment in the public interest, by
maintaining private land obligations."

The tribunal has allowed a developer superior to maintain feuing
conditions over the estate it has developed because there was:

"no disagreement between the parties that it is desirable to
have a mechanism to protect an estate such as Prospect Hill as
a whole from unacceptable development and to protect proprietors within the estate from each other"[33]

although each application has to be considered on its own merits.
Where the developers argued that as well-known builders they
had an interest to make it known that they would protect the
interest of persons to whom they had sold a house on their estate,
the tribunal has said that:

"superiors, as builders and estate developers, have a legitimate
interest to protect the overall amenity of the estate seeking to

[31] W*est Lothian Co-operative Society Ltd v. Ashdale Land and Property Co. Ltd*,
1972 S.L.T. (Lands Tr.) 30 at 32; see *Bachoo v. George Wimpey & Co. Ltd*, 1977
S.L.T. (Lands Tr.) 2 at 4.
[32] June 17, 1991; LTS/LO/1989/98.
[33] *Graham v. Wimpey Homes Housing Ltd*, July 11, 1990; LTS/LO/1989/92.

enforce such obligations, and that it might be of considerable benefit to their business to do so".[34]

The tribunal is prepared to have regard to the superior's wider interest, particularly where there are a number of family connected superiors, with a general interest to maintain the amenity of a particular area. In *Noble v. Viscount Reidhaven*[35] the tribunal had regard to the fact that:

> "The Seafield and Strathspey estates, which include Viscount Reidhaven's estate and are owned by various members of the Seafield family and are administered together"

had an interest to maintain the amenity of the Boat of Garten area. The tribunal will, in appropriate cases, pierce the corporate veil where a land-holding company has title to the land for the benefit of a subsidiary or related company using the land.[36]

Where a superior has not taken any interest for a long period of time or cannot be found, the tribunal will assume that he has no real continuing interest to enforce an obligation and so will more readily grant an application for discharge or variation.[37]

The Crown, through the Queen's and Lord Treasurer's Remembrancer, might be the superior if the ownership of the subjects has fallen to the crown as *bona vacantia* either on the death of a person without heirs or on the dissolution of a company.[38]

Affected persons

4–06   The Lands Tribunal "may allow any other person who appears to them to be affected by the obligation or by its proposed variation or discharge, to be heard in relation to the application".[39] Such a person is known as "an affected person". The power:

> "conferred on the Tribunal to canvass, in appropriate cases, the views of affected persons is a real one and not mere

---

[34] *Anderson v. Murray & Burrell Ltd*, May 4, 1990; LTS/LO/1989/56; see also *Mitchell v. MacTaggart & Mickel Ltd*, May 21, 1980; LTS/LO/1979/26, where it was said: "The superiors still have a continuing interest in ensuring that the estates they have developed do not deteriorate—they continue to build houses and intending purchasers may be influenced by their insistence on keeping control of the estate."
[35] June 17, 1991; LTS/LO/1989/98.
[36] *Currie v. Alliance Property Co. Ltd*, February 26, 1995; LTS/LO/1992/19 and 20. Alliance were the property-holding company for Safeway plc.
[37] *Penmax v. Murphy*, July 11, 1990; LTS/LO/1989/6.
[38] e.g. *Trs of Lady Coats Memorial Church v. QLTR*, June 24, 1985; LTS/LO/1984/31.
[39] 1970 Act, s. 2(2); 1971 Rules, r. 26.

window-dressing and that the Tribunal have a discretion to take into account the views of such persons in cases falling under s. 1 (3) (a) and (c). It may not, however, be appropriate to canvass the views of affected persons in cases falling exclusively under s. (1) (3) (b)".[40]

In determining who is an affected person:

"[T]he concept of 'affected person' must involve the concept of neighbourhood or that of proximity to the land affected and must exclude the wider public interest as represented by the planning authority".[41]

This is similar to the test applied under section 16(1) (a) of the Licensing (Scotland) Act 1976 in determining who is "any person owning or occupying property situated in the neighbourhood of the premises". The test is "the likelihood or otherwise of the amenity of the objector's property being adversely affected by the grant of any licence".[42]

This is a discretionary power and the Lands Tribunal may refuse a party a right to be heard as an affected person if the affected person's position can be protected adequately by the benefited proprietor who is a party to the action.[43]

One of the anomalies of section 2(2) is that an affected person has a right to be heard before the tribunal only if there is a current application. If the benefited proprietor grants a waiver or otherwise loses the right to enforce a land obligation (*e.g.* by acquiescence, etc.), an affected proprietor has no right to be heard. Where a benefited proprietor cannot be found or does not enter the process to oppose an application, the affected proprietor acquires a right to be heard. The anomaly sometimes allows affected proprietors, in effect, to appeal a planning decision.[44]

The right to be heard is not extended to an affected person in applications under section 1(3)(b), because a person is unlikely to be affected by an application which relates to the burdensomeness of the obligation as between benefited and burdened proprietors.[45]

---

[40] *McArthur v. Mahoney*, 1975 S.L.T. (Lands Tr.) 2 at 6.

[41] *Eadie v. Nenadic*, May 28, 1996; LTS/LO/1995/11.

[42] Greens Annotated Acts, *The Licensing (Scotland) Act 1976* (4th ed.), note to s. 16(1)(a), approved in *Khan v. City of Glasgow District Licensing Board*, 1995 S.L.T. 332.

[43] *Manz v. Butter's Trs*, 1973 S.L.T. (Lands Tr.) 2 at 4.

[44] *e.g. T & I Consultants Ltd v. Cullion*, 1998 Hous. L.R. 9.

[45] *Manz v. Butter's Trs*, above; *Tully v. Armstrong*, 1990 S.L.T. (Lands Tr.) 42 at 45B.

The views of an affected proprietor or a third party are irrelevant in considering an application under ground (b).[46]

A heritable creditor may be an affected person entitled to be heard.[47]

An affected person is "allowed . . . to be heard" by the Lands Tribunal. While the affected person should put in written representation at the procedural stage, the tribunal cannot have regard to written representations if the affected person does not appear to speak to their representations at the hearing, because:

> "The tribunal are thus forced to the conclusion that the use of the words 'to be heard in relation to the application' can only mean to be heard by the tribunal at a hearing. Hence we are unable to take cognisance of the written objections submitted on behalf of the two neighbours who did not attend the hearing in person to state their views."[48]

The tribunal "are also entitled to take into account the views of the local community as affected persons, where such are not unreasonable and where a benefited proprietor does not wish to offend them",[49] but the tribunal usually will not allow representatives of a residents' association or the views of a councillor to be taken into consideration, as they are not "affected persons".[50]

In appropriate circumstances the tribunal might treat a superior also as an affected proprietor of neighbouring property and consider his separate interests as such in reaching a determination of the application:

> "[T]he tribunal in [*MacArthur v. Mahoney*, 1975 S.L.T. (Lands Tr.) 2] said in effect that the objectors were both superiors and had an interest to enforce the relevant land obligation as affected proprietors, because of the damage which the new

---

[46] *McArthur v. Mahoney*, 1975 S.L.T. (Lands Tr.) 2 at 6; a claim to a "benefit" by the affected person is irrelevant—see below, para. 6.15.

[47] *Smith v. Taylor*, 1972 S.L.T. (Lands Tr.) 34 at 36.

[48] *Scott v. Wilson*, 1993 S.L.T. (Lands Tr.) 51. Unless all parties have agreed under r. 31 to a disposal without a hearing. See *Strathclyde Regional Council v. Mactaggart & Mickel*, 1984 S.L.T. (Lands Tr.) 33 at 34, where such written representations were taken into account.

[49] *MacDonald v. Stornoway Trust*, 1987 S.L.T. 240 at 242K; see also *Bolton v. Aberdeen Corporation*, 1972 S.L.T. (Lands Tr.) 26; *Lothian Regional Council v. George Wimpey & Co.*, 1985 S.L.T. (Lands Tr.) 2.

[50] *Eadie v. Nenadic*, May 28, 1996; LTS/LO/1995/11; but see *Scott v. Wilson*, May 19, 1992; LTS/LO/1991/7 (Reported on another point at 1993 S.L.T. (Lands Tr.) 51) where Mr Wilson, a benefited proprietor as trustee, was also allowed to speak as Chairman of the Killearn Trust for himself and on behalf of the other local persons as affected persons.

building proposed by the applicants would do to the objectors' view of the River Clyde".[51]

The application

An application is made to the tribunal on Form 1,[52] which can be **4–07** obtained from the tribunal. The application form has to be lodged with the current application fee, unless that has been waived.[53] On lodging, the application is given a reference number which, in the case of section 1(3) of the 1970 Act, is usually in the form "LTS/LO/199*/**".

With Form 1, the applicant requires to lodge his own title deeds, any burdened proprietors' title deeds, a location plan showing details of surrounding properties and the names and addresses of their proprietors and, where any planning permission has been granted, the permission and any associated plans.[54]

Where a superior is a benefited proprietor, the applicant should, if possible, provide the name and address of the current superior. If the applicant is unable to obtain this information, the application may have to be advertised at his expense.

The tribunal will require the applicant to provide as much information as is possible from which it may be able to identify the superior or other benefited or burdened proprietor and any persons who might be affected by the application.

Intimation, answers and representations

In terms of rule 4, on receipt of the application the Lands **4–08** Tribunal shall:

"(a) give notice thereof in writing to the persons who appear to it to be either benefited or burdened proprietors having an interest in the subject of the application;
Provided that if the Tribunal is satisfied that any such proprietor cannot by reasonably inquiry be identified or found notice may be given by advertisement or by such other method as the Tribunal thinks fit; and
(b) give notice in writing or by advertisement or by such other method as the Tribunal thinks fit to any other persons whom it considers should receive notice."

An application has to be intimated by the Lands Tribunal to "the persons who appear to it to be either benefited or burdened

---

[51] *Henderson v. Mansell*, November 9, 1993; LTS/LO/1992/41.
[52] 1971 Rules, r. 3, Form 1; App. 7.
[53] See below, paras 4–11 and 4–12.
[54] 1971 Rules, Form 1, n. 1.

proprietors having an interest in the subject of the application".[55] This is usually done by recorded delivery letter.

Where the tribunal is satisfied that any such proprietor cannot by reasonable inquiry be identified or found, notice may be given by advertisement or such other method as the tribunal thinks fit.[56] This is usually done by the tribunal placing a notice in appropriate national or local papers.

The tribunal is required to "give notice in writing or by advertisement or by such other method as the tribunal thinks fit to any other person whom it considers should receive notice".[57] Rule 4(1)(b) is directed towards giving intimation to affected proprietors who, in terms of section 2(2), may be allowed by the tribunal to be heard in relation to the application.

The notice requires the benefited or burdened proprietors, who wish to oppose the application or to make representations in respect of it, to send intimation thereof in writing to the tribunal and the applicant within the period specified in the notice. The tribunal usually allows 21 days in which written answers or representations to an application must be intimated.[58]

The written answers or representations "shall contain a concise statement of the facts and contentions on which it is intended to rely".[59]

The notice also requires to intimate that, subject to the tribunal's discretion, any affected person to whom notice has been given may be heard in relation to the application.[60]

The importance of the intimation to a benefited proprietor is that a benefited proprietor may claim compensation under section 1(4) of the 1970 Act.

Application procedure

4–09   Details of tribunal procedure are given in Chapter 2.[61]

After a section 1 application has been lodged and intimated, and if answers are lodged, a period of 21 days' adjustment is usually given to the applicant to respond to any written answers or representation. This may be followed by such further period of adjustment as the tribunal might consider necessary.

[55] 1971 Rules, r. 4(1)(a).
[56] *ibid.* proviso.
[57] *ibid.* r. 4(1)(b).
[58] *ibid.* r. 4(2). The rule requires not less than 14 days.
[59] *ibid.* r. 4(2).
[60] *ibid.* r. 4(3).
[61] See above, para. 2–01.

A debate on any legal question may then be fixed, although the tribunal is slow to dismiss an application without a hearing and a site visit. In *Walton's Exrs v. Farquharson of Invercauld*[62] the tribunal said:

"[T]he tribunal should be slow to dismiss as irrelevant a section 1 application without hearing evidence and should do so only in extreme cases in which neither the application nor any subsequent pleadings reveal any circumstances which would possibly reveal any circumstances of section 1(3) and where a proof and an inspection of the subjects would be merely a waste of time and expenses".

The tribunal may determine that the pleadings in the application are irrelevant and dismiss the application.[63]

The tribunal will fix a hearing and site visit upon 21 days' notice. The proof in opposed cases usually takes the following sequence:

"(1) The person conducting the case for the applicant may make a brief statement outlining his case. This is helpful where complicated questions of title are involved. An opening statement is not however essential.

(2) The applicant's evidence is then led. Evidence is given under oath or affirmation and witnesses will be open to cross-examination and re-examination if required. If the objectors are claiming compensation, any objection to such compensation may be put forward as part of the applicant's case with supporting evidence where appropriate; or alternatively, proof on compensation may be led in reply at the conclusion of the objector's case.

(3) The objectors (or their representatives) will then be invited to put forward their case in the same manner as the applicant's case was presented including any claim for compensation. Persons who are not benefited proprietors with a legal title to enforce the land obligation—but who may be affected by the proposed discharge or variation—may be allowed to be heard at the Tribunal's discretion but it is only in exceptional cases that the Tribunal will allow them to lead evidence or cross-examine witnesses. Affected persons however, are not strictly parties to the action entitled to enter the process.

(4) At the close of the evidence the parties will be invited to address the Tribunal in the order in which they presented

---

[62] January 26, 1978; LTS/LO/1977/7.
[63] *James Miller & Partners Ltd v. Hunt*, 1974 S.L.T. (Lands Tr.) 9 at 10.

their case, Any statement allowed to be made by an affected person will, however, precede the closing statement for the applicant."[64]

At the conclusion of the hearing, or at some future date, the tribunal will visit and inspect any relevant locations.[65] The parties involved will be at liberty to attend this inspection and to draw the tribunal's attention to any matter which may bear on the proposals or the objections. No new evidence will be heard at this stage of the proceedings.[66]

The decision will be intimated after the hearing. It usually takes about eight weeks for the decision to be produced. There is a right of appeal to the Court of Session on any question of law within 42 days of the decision.[67]

Unopposed applications

4–10   The tribunal has no power to grant an unopposed application without inquiry because the statutory provisions require the tribunal to be "satisfied in all the circumstances"[68] that the application has been made out. Where there is no opposition, the tribunal usually proceeds by way of written submissions without an oral hearing in terms of rule 31, and such applications usually succeed.[69]

Fees

4–11   Schedule 2 to the 1971 Rules specifies the fees payable to the tribunal in respect of various steps in the procedure, for example lodging and hearing fees. The hearing fees, unless the tribunal directs otherwise, are payable by the party who instituted the proceedings.[70]

The tribunal has a discretion to waive the fees in whole or in part "where it considers that the financial circumstances of the party are such that undue hardship would be caused by payment of the said fees".[71]

---

[64] Standard letter intimating hearing.
[65] The importance of a site visit is emphasised by *Mitchell v. MacTaggart & Mickel Ltd*, May 21, 1980; LTS/LO/1977/26 where the tribunal said that its first reaction was that the condition should be upheld but that it was only later, after the accompanied inspection, that "we became convinced the case had been made out".
[66] *Guidance Notes for Prospective Applicants*.
[67] See above, para. 2–22.
[68] 1970 Act, s. 1(3).
[69] Discussion Paper No. 106, p. 140, para. 6.13.
[70] 1971 Rules, r. 34(2).
[71] *ibid*. r. 34(1).

A list of the current fees is available by application to the Clerk to the Lands Tribunal and is printed in the *Parliament House Book.*[72]

Expenses

The tribunal has the power to make appropriate orders for **4–12** expenses.[73]

---

[72] 1971 Rules, Sched. 2 (S.I. 1971 No. 218); *Parliament House Book*, Section A, p. 101.

[73] See below, paras 8–11 to 8–14.

CHAPTER 5

GROUNDS FOR APPLICATIONS

General

5–01   Section 1(3) of the 1970 Act, gives the Lands Tribunal a general discretion to vary or discharge land obligations in whole or in part, provided that one or more of three particular grounds are made out to its satisfaction. The subsection provides:

> "(3) Subject to the provisions of this section and of section 2 of this Act, the Lands Tribunal, on the application of any person who, in relation to a land obligation, is a burdened proprietor, may from time to time by order vary or discharge the obligation wholly or partially in relation to the interest in land in respect of which the application is made and on being satisfied that in all the circumstances:
> (a) by reason of changes in the character of the land affected by the obligation or of the neighbourhood thereof or other circumstances which the Tribunal may deem material, the obligation is or has become unreasonable or inappropriate; or
> (b) the obligation is unduly burdensome compared with any benefit resulting or which would result from its performance; or
> (c) the existence of the obligation impedes some reasonable use of the land."

It can be seen that the three grounds deal with the past, the present and the future. Ground (a) refers to a land obligation which by reason of the passage of time has become unreasonable, in the content where feudal obligations would otherwise continue in perpetuity. Ground (b) deals with the present in regard to the balance of burdensomeness as between benefited and burdened proprietor. Ground (c) looks to the future and whether or not the land obligation will impede some future reasonable use of the land.

The tribunal has said:

> "In the exercise of their jurisdiction however under the Conveyancing and Feudal Reform (Scotland) Act 1970, the

68

tribunal is not intended to act like some kind of local authority
or substitute its own subjective views; but to consider whether
the maintenance of a particular title condition continues to be
reasonable; and whether a burdened proprietor seeking to
be relieved has discharged the onus upon him of satisfying the
tribunal that one or more of the conditions enacted by
Parliament in s. 1 (3) (a), (b) or (c) have been fulfilled."[1]
The tribunal is therefore not concerned with what might be
described as the wider social or planning considerations which
might influence a public body in granting planning permission or
some other approval for any particular activity.

Onus on applicant

The onus is on the applicant to establish the grounds upon which   **5–02**
the land obligation should be varied or discharged. The Lands
Tribunal, in holding that "the onus is therefore firmly upon the
applicants"[2] and that the applicant "must discharge the onus of
showing that its continued enforcement has become unreasonable
in terms of one or more of the subs(ections)"[3] followed the dictum
of Evershed M.R. in *Re Ghey and Galton's Application*[4] who said:

> "What has to be done if an applicant is to succeed, is
> something far more than to show that, to an impartial planner,
> the applicant's proposal might be called, as such, a good and
> reasonable thing: he must affirmatively prove that one or
> other of the grounds for the jurisdiction has been established;
> and, unless that is so, the person who has a proprietory right
> as covenantee of controlling the development of the property
> as he desires and protecting his own proprietory interest, is
> entitled to continue to enjoy that proprietory right."

Thus the onus lies firmly on an applicant to establish that one or
more of the grounds for a variation have been established. Even if
a ground is established, the tribunal retains a general discretion on
whether or not to vary or discharge the land obligation. A local
authority, which might be the planning authority, will be treated no
differently from an ordinary superior who is trying to enforce
"what may loosely be described as private planning control".[5]

---

[1] *Lothian Regional Council v. George Wimpey & Co. Ltd*, 1985 S.L.T. (Lands Tr.)
2 at 2.
[2] *Murrayfield Ice Rink Ltd v. SRU*, 1972 S.L.T. (Lands Tr.) 20 at 21; see *Bolton v.
Aberdeen Corporation*, 1972 S.L.T. (Lands Tr.) 26 at 28.
[3] *MacDonald v. Stornoway Trust*, 1987 S.L.T. 240 at 241B.
[4] [1957] 2 Q.B. 650 at 659.
[5] *Campbell v. Edinburgh Corporation*, 1972 S.L.T. (Lands Tr.) 38 at 39; *Bolton v.
Aberdeen Corporation*, 1972 S.L.T. (Lands Tr.) 26; *Grampian Regional Council v.
Viscount Cowdray*, 1985 S.L.T. (Lands Tr.) 6.

Premature applications

5–03   The tribunal will not entertain an application in the abstract, but
requires that there is an identified proposed use which is prevented
by the land obligation before it will consider whether or not to vary
or discharge the obligation. This is particularly so under ground (c)
where it has to be established that the obligation impedes some
reasonable use.[6]

In *Murrayfield Ice Rink Ltd v. Scottish Rugby Union*[7] the tribunal
commented that:

> "In our view the proper course when applying under
> s. 1 (3) (c) is to seek a full order which removes all the
> proprietory impediments **and which is based upon a specific
> proposal**. Otherwise compensation cannot be properly
> assessed nor can it be judged whether a reasonable use is
> being impeded in the particular circumstances of the case."
> (emphasis added)

This approach was upheld on appeal where it was "conceded that
the proposed new use must be an 'identifiable proposed use' "
(*Taylor v. Smith*, Court of Session, July 27, 1972, unreported).[8]

It has been recognised that prematurity relates to the application
and not to the perception of the benefited proprietor.[9]

In *Jackson v. Bell*[10] the applicant sought the discharge of an
obligation to use the land as agricultural land under all three
grounds, in order that it could be used as a motorway service area
(MSA) on a possible extension of the M77. Bell owned the
superiority of Jackson's land and owned the land on the opposite
side of the proposed motorway. At the time of the application
there were competing planning application for MSAs, neither of
which had been decided, nor had the route or timing of the
proposed motorway extension been confirmed. It was argued that
the application was premature because it could not be said that
planning permission would be granted or that the MSA would in
fact be sited at that location, if indeed the extension of the
motorway was to go ahead. The applicant's argument was that
prematurity could only apply to an application under ground (c).

[6] *United Auctions (Scotland) Ltd v. British Railways Board*, 1991 S.L.T. (Lands
Tr.) 71 at 76H, where the tribunal recognised that prematurity might not be
relevant to a ground (a) or (b) application.
[7] 1972 S.L.T. (Lands Tr.) 20 at 25.
[8] *Murrayfield Ice Rink Ltd v. Scottish Rugby Union*, 1973 S.C. 21 at 30.
[9] *United Auctions (Scotland) Ltd v. British Railways Board*, above at 76G.
[10] June 5, 1997; LTS/LO/1996/12 and 13.

The tribunal decided that the question of prematurity under any of the grounds could not be decided without evidence. Having allowed a proof, the application was dismissed later that year as premature, when the government announced that proposed extension was suspended pending a review of road building in Scotland.

Discretion of the Lands Tribunal

The Lands Tribunal has held that the provisions of section 1(3)   **5–04** give it an underlying general discretion to look at the whole situation in reaching a decision on whether or not to pronounce an order varying or discharging a land obligation.[11]

The opening part of subsection (1) provides that the Lands Tribunal "may . . . vary or discharge the obligation" and requires the tribunal to be "satisfied in all the circumstances" that the particular ground has been made out.

The question of exercising this discretion arises only where an applicant has established one of the statutory grounds (a), (b) or (c) "in all the circumstances". Once a statutory ground has been established, the tribunal has this underlying general discretion to decide whether or not to grant the application. As the tribunal said in *North East Fife District Council v. Lees*[12]:

"While the powers of the tribunal under s. 1 (3) are introduced by the word 'may', so indicating an element of discretion, the tribunal have nevertheless to be satisfied before granting a variation or discharge order, that one or more of the particular conditions contained in s. 1 (3) have been fulfilled. If so satisfied, there would have to be very special circumstances to justify the withholding of a variation or discharge order."

If one or more of the grounds is not made out, the application must be dismissed; the tribunal does not retain a general discretion to vary or discharge a land obligation in circumstances where a ground has not been made out.[13]

In the exercise of its general discretion under section 1(3), the tribunal has said "that it would be inequitable to grant discharge or variation orders due to self-created burdens or changes brought about by applicants".[14]

---

[11] *Keith v. Texaco Ltd*, 1977 S.L.T. (Lands Tr.) 16 at 19.
[12] 1989 S.L.T. (Lands Tr.) 30 at 33H.
[13] *Re Ghey and Galton's Application* [1957] 2 Q.B. 650.
[14] *Nicolson v. Campbell's Trs*, 1981 S.L.T. (Lands Tr.) 10 at 12; *Solway Cedar Ltd v. Hendry*, 1972 S.L.T. (Lands Tr.) 42 at 44; *North East Fife District Council v. Lees*, 1989 S.L.T. (Lands Tr.) 30 at 33.

The tribunal has a further discretion, where it has determined that it is minded to grant the application, either to require additional or substitutional provisions to be agreed[15] or to award compensation or, where ground (c) is invoked, to refuse the application if in exceptional circumstances money is not adequate compensation.[16]

This discretion requires to be exercised judicially and will be subject to review only if improperly exercised or if not exercised at all.[17]

"in all the circumstances"

5–05   Although section 1(3) provides for the three particular grounds that have to be made out, and on which the tribunal has to be "satisfied", before an order can be pronounced varying or discharging a land obligation, the preamble to the subsection nevertheless requires the tribunal to be "satisfied that in all the circumstances" the order should be granted.

Although this extends the discretion of the tribunal, it also provides that it can have regard to the whole surrounding facts and circumstances, even if they do not strictly fall within one of the three particular grounds. In *McArthur v. Mahoney*[18] the tribunal said:

> "[I]t emerges clearly from these English cases that the somewhat similar jurisdiction conferred on the Lands Tribunal there is discretionary and we have reached the conclusion that our jurisdiction under s. 1 of the Act is also discretionary, seeing that we are enjoined to consider what is reasonable or appropriate in all the circumstances—a direction which seems to lay stress on the discretionary nature of our jurisdiction. In taking this view we are not overlooking the existence of the proviso at the end of s. 1 (4) but we do not consider that this is one of those statutory enactments where such proviso is intended to make the exercise of the power conferred by the statute imperative in all cases. To say that in any set of circumstances we have no discretion appears to us to negate an essential feature of the Act—for the wording of the statute clearly indicates that the legislature has contemplated that there may be special circumstances in which the application of a rigid code would produce an unsatisfactory or unjust result".

[15] 1970 Act, s. 1(5).
[16] *ibid*. s. 1(4).
[17] See above, para. 2–20.
[18] 1975 S.L.T. (Lands Tr.) 2 at 5.

In *Main v. Lord Doune*[19] the tribunal went on to say:

"[A] Tribunal may judicially determine whether a contractual right to maintain a particular environment should be upheld or modified. Unlike the amended s. 84 (1) (aa) of the Law of Property Act 1925, which has appended under subs. (1A) its own specific guidelines, we are merely directed by the opening words of s. 1 (3) to have regard to 'all the circumstances'. This appears to be a looser style of legislation requiring us to give consideration to such circumstances as the Tribunal consider relevant".

There is thus a general overriding discretion vested in the tribunal which it exercises upon judicial lines and which is subject to review by the Court of Session upon familiar principles.

Even if one or more of the grounds for variation or discharge is **5–06** made out on the ground that the land obligation is obsolete, the tribunal can nevertheless refuse the application if the obligation still serves a practical purpose in another way.[20]

In *Driscoll v. Church Commissioners for England* the covenant was to use very large houses for a single family. The Church Commissioners had been given permission to divide the houses into flats or use them as guest houses but wished to retain the covenant so that they could keep the area residential. The applicant applied for a discharge of the covenant. Lord Denning said[21]:

"In one sense, therefore, the covenant is obsolete, because it can be said no longer to serve the purposes originally contemplated; but . . . the covenant still serves a useful purpose in another way; it enable the landlords . . . to keep control over the use to which these houses are put. It enables the landlords . . . to keep the area as a residential area, instead of it being used, as it might have been, for commercial purposes. It seems to me that, so long as the landlord uses this covenant reasonably for a useful purpose, then, even though the purposes goes beyond what was contemplated ninety years ago, the covenant is not obsolete; whereas if the covenant is shown no longer to serve any useful purpose, then, of course it is obsolete. And in considering whether it still serves a useful

---

[19] 1972 S.L.T. (Lands Tr.) 14 at 18.
[20] *McArthur v. Mahoney*, 1975 S.L.T. (Lands Tr.) 2; *Merchant Company Education Board v. Bailey*, October 12, 1995; LTS/LO/1994/51; *Driscoll v. Church Commissioners for England* [1957] 1 Q.B. 330; *Re Ghey and Galton's Application* [1957] 2 Q.B. 650.
[21] *Driscoll v. Church Commissioners for England*, above at 341.

purpose, I think it is important to see how the landlord, or whoever is entitled to the benefit of the covenant, has used it in the past and seeks to use it in the present. If he uses it reasonably, not in his own selfish interests but in the interests of the people of the neighbourhood generally, as for instance, when he gives his consent for any sensible change of user, then it serves a useful purpose. I should have thought that if he uses it unreasonably, for instance, to exact a premium as a condition of his consent; or if he refuses consent altogether when he ought to give it . . . it would no longer serve a useful purpose."

A similar approach was taken, in considering a similar Jamaican provision, in *Stannard v. Issa*[22] where Lord Oliver said:

"The question is not 'what was the original intention of the restriction and is it still being achieved?' but 'does the restriction achieve some practical benefit and if so is it a benefit of sufficient weight to justify the continuance of the restrictions without modification?' "

In *Merchant Company Education Board v. Bailey*[23] the tribunal confirmed this approach in Scotland, saying:

"The overall effect of the statutory provisions (including the provision directing the tribunal to take into account the representations of affected proprietors) is, as it was put by the Lord-Justice Clerk in *Murrayfield Ice Rink Ltd v. Scottish Rugby Union*, 1973 SLT 99, to require the tribunal to look at the whole picture. And if, having done so, it is clear either that the same purpose which led to the creation of any obligation can still usefully he served or (according to [*McArthur v. Mahoney*, 1975 S.L.T. (Lands Tr.) 2]) even that some different yet useful purpose can be served, then, in our discretion, we may properly refuse to discharge it."

5–07   An important point to come out of that dictum is that in considering whether or not to allow a discharge of a land obligation, the tribunal should have regard to the motives and actions of the benefited proprietor in seeking to maintain a burden.

Motive can be a particularly relevant consideration.[24] Where the motive shows that the applicant is in fact seeking a personal

---

[22] [1987] 1 A.C. 175, *per* Lord Oliver at 188E.

[23] October 12, 1995; LTS/LO/1994/51.

[24] *Currie v. Alliance Property Co. Ltd*, February 26, 1995; LTS/LO/1992/19 and 20; *East Fife District Council v. Lees*, 1989 S.L.T. (Lands Tr.) 30; *Spafford v. Brydon*, 1991 S.L.T. (Lands Tr.) 49; *Henderson v. Mansell*, November 9, 1993; LTS/LO/1992/41.

licence, the application will be refused.[25] In a retrospective application, if an applicant has operated deliberately in breach of the obligation, that is a factor the tribunal may take into consideration.[26]

In deciding whether or not to discharge a land obligation the tribunal will have regard to the original purpose for which the obligation was imposed and see if it still fulfils a purpose.[27] The fact that there may have been some breaches of the land obligation does not mean that the land obligation cannot still fulfil a useful role.[28]

Public policy and public interest could well be factors that the tribunal should take into account as part of "in all the circumstances". In England section 84(1A)(b) of the 1925 Act authorises the discharge or modification of a restriction if it "is contrary to the public interest". The tribunal has had regard to the fact that an applicant is a public body seeking to carry out its statutory functions.[29] The tribunal may have regard to the fact that something is government policy.[30]

The fact that the obligation was imposed in a gift as one of the conditions of gift may be a relevant consideration.[31]

As part of the general discretion relating to a consideration of "all the circumstances" the tribunal will sometimes leave out of consideration matters such as planning, police, fire, tree preservation, etc., where it considers that these are best left to statutory authorities. It has said:

> "This implies, in our view, that we must consider each application submitted to us on its own individual merits

---

[25] See below, para. 5–08.

[26] See above, para. 3–04.

[27] *Tully v. Armstrong*, 1990 S.L.T. (Lands Tr.) 42 at 45E–F.

[28] *Hunt v. Molnar* (1956) 7 P. & C.R. 224, where some houses had been converted into flats in breach of the restrictive covenant, but the restriction was held useful to prevent bungalows being built in the garden ground.

[29] *Banff and Buchan District Council v. Earl of Seafield's Estate*, 1988 S.L.T. (Lands Tr.) 21 (discharge of pre-emption clause interfering with tenant's right to buy); *Independent Television Authority's Application* (1961) 13 P. & C.R. 222, where the tribunal had regard "that the applicant is a public body and requires the modification to enable it to perform its statutory duty".

[30] *Re Lloyds and Lloyd's Application* (1993) 66 P. & C.R. 112 (application granted on ground of government policy regarding community care for the mentally ill); *Lothian Regional Council v. George Wimpey & Co. Ltd*, 1985 S.L.T. 2 (regard had to such a policy, but policy did not prevail).

[31] *Westminster City Council v. Duke of Westminster* [1991] 4 All E.R. 136, *per* Harman L.J. at 146h. But see s. 84(7) of the 1925 Act which disapplies the section to restrictions "imposed on the occasion of a disposition made gratuitously or for a nominal consideration for public purposes".

according to the special facts and circumstances. This would entitle us, we think, to decline in some cases to import into our decisions consideration of matters normally regulated by the town planning, fire, police or cleansing departments of the local authority but does not preclude us from taking a fresh look at the reasonableness or otherwise of discharging or modifying a land obligation. This Tribunal have already issued decisions based on the understanding that possible adverse effects of discharging or varying land obligations can be dealt with as part of the functions of town planning, police, fire brigade and cleansing and have kept this aspect well to the forefront of their thinking."[32]

Personal licence

5–08   The tribunal is concerned with varying or discharging land obligations which affect the land. The power cannot be used to grant a variation or discharge to confer a personal benefit or licence on the then owner of the interest in land.[33]

In purporting to follow *Re Ghey and Galton's Application*,[34] in considering an application to remove a restriction on use as shop premises so that it could be used as a licensed betting office because the shop could be more profitably used as a licensed betting office, the tribunal commented:

> "The applicant's existing business difficulties may therefore be purely personal or purely temporary. Any discharge, however, which the Tribunal grants will operate in favour of the applicant's land for all time and we cannot grant an order in the form of a personal licence."[35]

The tribunal would appear to have misunderstood *Re Ghey and Galton's Application*. The case concerns the form of the order that may be granted, rather than that it is the current individual who seeks a removal of the restriction so that he may benefit personally. The fact that the permanent discharge of a land obligation may be of personal benefit, or a personal licence, should not be a reason for refusing the discharge if that discharge or variation could also be of benefit to subsequent proprietors.

The tribunal has recognised that in deciding whether or not to vary or discharge a land obligation it must be judged by its

---

[32] *McArthur v. Mahoney*, 1975 S.L.T. (Lands Tr.) 2 at 5–6.
[33] *Re Ghey and Galton's Application* [1957] 2 Q.B. 650, *per* Evershed M.R. at 660. See below, para. 8–03.
[34] *Re Ghey and Galton's Application*, above.
[35] *Bolton v. Aberdeen Corporation*, 1972 S.L.T. (Lands Tr.) 26 at 29.

consequences for any proprietor who might be burdened by it, rather than by its consequences for one particular proprietor.[36] Similar considerations should apply in relation to the benefited proprietor.

The "thin end of the wedge" argument

The question of whether or not the "thin edge of the wedge" or **5–09** "floodgates" argument should be a relevant consideration is subject to contrary decisions by the tribunal. The issue is now usually taken into consideration as a relevant factor, particularly where the application relates to a possible first variation or discharge.

In *Bolton v. Aberdeen Corporation*[37] the tribunal took into account evidence that if it discharged an obligation not to use a shop for a purpose not approved of by the superiors in a shopping precinct they had provided, because "A discharge by the Tribunal would therefore be likely to constitute 'the thin edge of the wedge'", whereas in *Ness v. Shannon*[38] the tribunal rejected a "thin edge of the wedge" argument, saying:

"It does not seem to the tribunal that the possibility of such further application or applications in the future should deter them from considering the present case on its own merits."

In *Anderson v. Trotter*[39] the tribunal, in considering a submission that if it allowed the application it would be the thin edge of a wedge, allowing a change from residential use in the area, said:

"The Tribunal should be slow in a case such as this to exercise its unique power to vary what is in effect, a mutual contract, binding on a number of different proprietors, when that would involve a first departure from that contract."

In some cases the tribunal will consider the "thin end of the wedge" argument and then make clear in its decision that the decision is special to the facts of the application and should not be regarded as a first departure which can be founded upon as the thin end of the wedge.[40]

---

[36] *Davie v. G. S. Brown Construction Ltd*, June 20, 1997; LTS/LO/1996/41.
[37] 1972 S.L.T. (Lands Tr.) 26 at 29.
[38] 1978 S.L.T. (Lands Tr.) 13 at 16.
[39] August 12, 1997; LTS/LO/1996/46.
[40] *e.g. Alexandra Workwear Ltd v. Lothian Regional Council*, October 21, 1992; LTS/LO/1991/62. See *Love's and Love's Application* (1994) 67 P. & C.R. 101 at 108–109 (argument rejected "on the special facts of this case" because "Each case will still turn on its own particular facts").

It is clear that this argument may be a relevant consideration, but much will depend on the facts of the particular case and whether the application would be the first departure or, if a first departure, whether the application subjects are sufficiently special to take them out of the "first departure" concern.

5–10   The "thin end of the wedge" argument is considered a relevant consideration in England, although the relevance or strength of the issue depends on the whole facts and circumstances of each case.[41] The weight to be given to the "thin end of the wedge" argument in England is different because an application under section 84(1)(c) requires the tribunal to be satisfied that the discharge or modification "will not injure the persons entitled to the benefit of the restriction". The tribunal therefore has to consider whether the discharge or modification makes future applications more likely and if that is the case this might be an "injury" in terms of the subsection.[42]

Recently created obligations

5–11   The tribunal has no power to consider an application made within two years of the creation of the obligation which is the subject of the application.[43] In view of this time-limit it is clear that the tribunal has jurisdiction to vary or discharge a land obligation after two years. The tribunal does take into account the fact that an obligation has been recently created, or that it is an application by the original parties to the application, as considerations relevant to a determination of whether or not to discharge the obligation.

There is no equivalent English provision preventing an application being made immediately after a covenant was entered into.

Although an application is competent after the two years, the tribunal is reluctant to discharge a recently created land obligation, particularly where the applicant is one of the original contracting parties:

> "The Tribunal would in any event be slow to interfere between original contracting parties where the conditions regulating the use of the land had been so recently formulated and had

---

[41] *Land Covenants*, p. 353 and cases there cited.
[42] *Re Teagle's and Sparks' Application* (1962) 14 P. & C.R. 68 at 73; *Re Beech's Application* (1990) 59 P. & C.R. 502.
[43] 1970 Act, s. 2(5); *Watters v. Motherwell District Council*, 1991 S.L.T. (Lands Tr.) 2.

been accepted by the party which now wishes to have one of them set aside."[44]

In the first case where this argument was considered by the tribunal, in an application by the original feuar made ten years after an obligation was created, to be allowed to subdivide his house contrary to an obligation to use the house as a single dwelling, the tribunal said:

"We cannot construe reasonableness without reference to what was recently accepted by both parties as reasonable unless there appears to be some compelling argument for doing so."[45]

In *Crombie's Exr v. Burns*[46] the tribunal allowed another application to vary an obligation varied in 1972 allowing two houses to be built, primarily on the ground that the original applicants had died and in any event the tribunal had not considered a variation to three houses in 1972.

In England the matter was originally put more strongly.[47] The applicants had bought an extension to their garden ground under a covenant not to build on the land and to use it as a private garden. Two years after the purchase, without there having been any change of circumstances in respect of the land, the applicants applied to the Lands Tribunal for a modification so that they could build a house on the land for which they had received planning permission. The tribunal, in the exercise of its discretion, refused the application even though it appeared to qualify under section 84(1)(c). On appeal Harman L.J. said[48]:

"The idea that a covenant, voluntarily entered into, can be modified within a year or so, without any change in circumstances of the property at all, is to me shocking. It is not beyond the jurisdiction of the court to modify a covenant the day after it is made if it saw fit to do so; but the powers of the court, or the tribunal indeed before whom the matter first

5–12

---

[44] *Wallace v. Yeaman*, December 19, 1995; LTS/LO/95/30 (application to discharge obligation not to park caravan on a feu in new housing scheme refused). This is consistent with *Ridley v. Taylor* [1965] 1 W.L.R. 611, *per* Harman L.J. at 618B: "the court should be slow to relieve an applicant of covenants which he has himself entered into" and *Re Rudkin's Application* (1963) 15 P. & C.R. 85 at 88 where it was said that "The Tribunal is I think justified in requiring from an original convenator a somewhat higher proof of justification for the modification sought".

[45] *Logie v. Eagle Star Insurance Co. Ltd*, July 30, 1980; LTS/LO/1980/6.

[46] May 16, 1977; LTS/APP/1/157.

[47] *Cresswell v. Proctor* [1968] 1 W.L.R. 906.

[48] *ibid.* at 913F.

comes, are discretionary powers, and I cannot imagine circumstances in which, within a few months, a covenant solemnly entered into would be released. . . . It seems to me to be a matter within the discretion of the court and one member of the tribunal who decided the case decided it in the exercise of his discretion, saying that he felt that what he called 'public policy' demanded that such an application should not be acceded to, even if the applicant could bring himself within the grounds of s. 84(1)(a), (b) or (c) of the Law of Property Act 1925."

Danckwerts L.J. considered that "The sanctity of contract must have some relevance".[49]

It must be noted that Winn L.J., while not dissenting on the ground that it could not be said that the tribunal had abused its discretion in that case, was not so firmly against the view that such a covenant might not be modifying in appropriate circumstances.

The approach in *Cresswell v. Proctor*[50] is not consistent with the approach in the earlier case of *Ridley v. Taylor*[51] where Harman L.J.[52] suggested that a tribunal should be slow to modify covenants entered into by the parties, but Russell L.J. said that[53]:

"I do not for myself think that the particular situation of the tenant, as having not very long since struck a bargain inconsistent with this particular outcome, is a factor in the exercise of discretion. I do not think that the personality of the tenant or his past behaviour is relevant to the exercise of the discretion. I refer again to the fact that tomorrow an assignee may make the same application."

These inconsistent approaches were brought together in *Jones v. Rhys-Jones*[54] where Stephenson L.J. said:

"Without the assistance of authority I would have thought that the shortness of time which has elapsed since the burden of a covenant was imposed on an original convenantor or was transferred to a subsequent purchase was a factor which could properly be put in the scale against modification or discharge whether application under section 84 be made by an original purchaser (when it would weigh more) or by a subsequent

---

[49] *Cresswell v. Proctor* [1968] 1 W.L.R. 906 at 914G.
[50] *ibid.*
[51] [1965] 1 W.L.R. 611.
[52] *ibid.* at 618.
[53] *ibid.* at 623.
[54] (1974) 30 P. & C.R. 451 at 459.

purchaser (when it would weigh less) . . . It is enough for our purposes that according to that judgement [*Re Wickin's Application* (1962) 183 E.G. 541] the shortness of time is not a decisive factor which forbids the grant of such an application."

The approach now taken in England is that the recency of the **5–13** covenant and whether or not the parties are originally covenanting parties, are factors to be taken into account in the exercise of the tribunal's discretion but that the discretion is not automatically to be exercised against the applicant.[55]

Where the covenant no longer serves the purpose for which it was imposed or any practical purpose[56] or if the covenant, from its inception,[57] has served no useful purpose, then it might be appropriate to discharge it in early course.

Right of access

A servitude right of access is a land obligation which the tribunal **5–14** may vary or discharge. In general the tribunal will only vary the right of access provided that a comparable alternative access can be provided.[58]

The tribunal has commented that it was "by no means certain how s. 1 (3) (b) should be applied in the case of servitudes"[59] and on this basis has said that "it was doubtful whether it could ever be appropriate for the tribunal to discharge a servitude right of access outright in terms of section 1(3) (b)".[60]

Accordingly, variations of access are usually approached on the basis of ground (c) and may be granted where the applicant is willing and able to provide a comparable alternative right of access.

"A right of access is usually such a fundamental right that it would be virtually unthinkable for the tribunal to consider discharging it without at the same time substituting some other right of access in its place."[61]

The tribunal has said that while it was important as a matter of fairness to ensure, so far as possible, that any substitute right of

---

[55] Scammell, p. 348.
[56] *Re Quaffers Ltd's Application* (1988) 56 P. & C.R. 142 (covenant imposed to preserve amenity, but new motorway system meant that amenity could not longer be protected).
[57] *Re Barclays Bank plc's Application* (1990) 60 P. & C.R. 354 (agricultural occupancy condition imposed on "farm" cottage, where farming on that property was never a viable prospect from its inception).
[58] *Buist v. Merson*, March 8, 1995; LTS/LO/1994/31.
[59] *Murrayfield Ice Rink Ltd v. SRU*, 1972 S.L.T. (Lands Tr.) 20 at 23.
[60] *Buist v. Merson*, above.
[61] *ibid*.

access should be equally convenient to the objector as that presently enjoyed, the 1970 Act did not require the tribunal to ensure that the substitute right of access should be in every way the same, or indeed in every way as convenient, as the previous right of access.[62]

The tribunal has refused to exercise its powers under section 1(3) to close a footpath right of access because the residents considered it to be dangerous and a matter of public safety, particularly as it was still used by some of the benefited proprietors.[63] The tribunal commented that as long as a significant number of benefited proprietors wished to continue to use it, it had to be regarded as serving a useful purpose and that it would be unreasonable to take away those rights.[64]

Where a right of access is general and the terms undefined, the tribunal will not "vary a servitude in order to set precise limits to the way in which the objectors may exercise their rights of access".[65] The tribunal will not grant a variation order "simply in order to clarify rather than to vary the original land obligations".[66]

The tribunal has no power to vary a servitude right of access so as to increase the right or burden, for example from a right of access for agricultural purposes to a general right of access.[67]

The tribunal will consider varying a designated line of access where a different route has been established on the ground to that of the designated route.[68] The route of a right of access has been varied or narrowed without affecting the extent of the right, to allow an extension to a house to be built.[69]

Trade restraint

5–15   While a land obligation the sole purpose of which is to operate in restraint of trade may be unenforceable as a matter of public policy,[70] if the sole purpose is not restraint of trade but for instance protection of the amenity or character of the area, the obligation is one that may be considered by the tribunal.[71]

---

[62] *Nisbet v. Meikle*, June 23, 1995; LTS/LO/1993/52 and 56.
[63] *Spafford v. Brydon*, 1991 S.L.T. (Lands Tr.) 49.
[64] *ibid.* at 53D.
[65] *Buist v. Merson*, above.
[66] *Crichton Brain Ltd v. Messrs Robertson*, December 3, 1984; LTS/LO/1983/8.
[67] *Mackay v. Burton*, 1994 S.L.T. (Lands Tr.) 35; see above, para. 3–16.
[68] *Stewart v. Kazim*, June 22, 1995; LTS/LO/1993/49.
[69] *Christine v. Miller*, February 23, 1990; LTS/LO/1988/91; *Christie v. Carson*, April 30, 1991; LTS/LO/1990/53.
[70] *Aberdeen Varieties Ltd v. James F. Donald (Aberdeen) Cinemas Ltd*, 1940 S.C. (H.L.) 52; *Phillips v. Lavery*, 1962 S.L.T. (Sh.Ct.) 57.
[71] *Co-operative Wholesale Society v. Ushers Brewery*, 1975 S.L.T. (Lands Tr.) 9.

In England the tribunal discharged a restriction which it found originally intended to protect an amenity allowing a hotel to be built. The tribunal refused to continue it on the ground that it should protect the trade of a neighbouring hotel.[72] While it was accepted that in England "there is no reason in law why a restrictive covenant should not be taken for the protection of trade", such a restriction could be continued only if that was the purpose for which it was imposed.[73]

---

[72] *Re Quaffer Ltd's Application* (1988) 56 P. & C.R. 142.
[73] *ibid.* at 152.

CHAPTER 6

THE SPECIFIC GROUNDS

General

6–01   Having dealt with the general considerations which the tribunal takes into account in determining whether or not to discharge a land obligation, the specific grounds are now considered. If an applicant fails to establish one or more of the specific grounds in section 1(3) of the 1970 Act then his application necessarily fails. Each ground is considered in turn.

GROUND (A)

Terms

6–02   Ground (a) is in the following terms:

"(a) by reason of changes in the character of the land affected by the obligation or of the neighbourhood thereof or other circumstances which the Tribunal may deem material, the obligation is or has become unreasonable or inappropriate".

The ground is directed towards past changes which have taken place since the land obligation was imposed, which now render the obligation unreasonable or inappropriate. There are three factors to which the Lands Tribunal is directed to have regard, namely changes in the character of the land or the neighbourhood or other material circumstances.

The tribunal has said:

"For the application to be relevant under subs. (3) (a)—which is the only subsection relied upon—facts must, therefore, be averred which, if proved, could constitute material changes arising since 1962 and involving a distinct change from the original contracting position of both parties."[1]

---

[1] *James Miller & Partners Ltd v. Hunt*, 1974 S.L.T. (Lands Tr.) 9 at 10.

In considering whether the obligation has become unreasonable or inappropriate, the tribunal must:

"consider only those changes which have occurred since the actual imposition. If material changes had occurred beforehand then the obligation need not have been accepted."[2]

In considering "the land affected" and "the neighbourhood thereof", the tribunal has said that the neighbourhood must be greater in area than the land affected by the obligation.[3]

English provision

The English provision is in the following terms: **6–03**

"(a) that by reason of changes in the character of the property or the neighbourhood or other circumstances of the case which the Lands Tribunal may deem material, the restriction ought to be deemed obsolete".

The significant distinction is that the "restriction ought to be deemed obsolete", whereas the 1970 Act provides that "the obligation is or has become unreasonable or inappropriate", which is a much less strict test. The Halliday Report recommended that the provision in Scotland should be "the condition or servitude has become obsolete or inappropriate or of little practical value to the person or persons entitled to enforce it."

In the English context "obsolete" has been explained in *Truman, Hanbury, Buxton & Co. Ltd's Application*[4] to mean that:

"if, as sometimes happens, the character of an estate as a whole or of a particular part of it gradually changes, a time may come when the purpose [of the convenants in question] can no longer be achieved, for what was intended at first to be a residential area has become either through express or tacit waiver of the covenants, substantially a commercial area. When that times does come, it may be said that the covenants have become obsolete because their original purpose can no longer be served, and in my opinion, it is in that sense that the word 'obsolete' is used in section 84(1) (a) of the 1925 Act".

The tribunal has explained the distinction between ground (a) and the English provision thus[5]:

[2] *Murrayfield Ice Rink Ltd v. Scottish Rugby Union*, 1972 S.L.T. (Lands Tr.) 20 at 22.
[3] *Thomson v. Birch*, May 31, 1994; LTS/LO/1993/42.
[4] [1956] 1 Q.B. 261, *per* Romer L.J. at 272.
[5] *Merchant Company Education Board v. Bailey*, October 12, 1995; LTS/LO/1994/51.

"The English cases cited to us[6] by the applicants were of course concerned with section 84 of the Law of Property Act 1925 and in particular with the interpretation of the word 'obsolete' therein. While the draftsman of section 1(3) (a) of the 1970 Act may well have drawn upon the terms of section 84 of the 1925 Act (as subsequently amended) it is striking that he eschewed the use of the word 'obsolete'. There can be no doubt but that that was deliberate and that an entirely different approach was intended. For the tribunal are enjoined first of all to ask themselves whether there have been changes in the character of the land affected by the obligation or of the neighbourhood thereof (or whether there are other circumstances which the tribunal may deem material). Having done so however the tribunal are not then directed to come to an opinion as to whether, by reason of such changes, the obligation has become 'obsolete'. Instead we are required to satisfy ourselves that 'in all the circumstances' and by reason of those changes 'the obligation is or has become unreasonable or inappropriate'. The intention of the 1970 Act is thus to permit the variation, or even discharge, of any obligation which, however reasonable or appropriate it may have been when it was created, has become less so or is now wholly inappropriate in the light of subsequent events. The overall effect of the statutory provisions (including the provision directing the tribunal to take into account the representations of affected proprietors) is, as it was put by Lord-Justice Clerk in *Murrayfield Ice Rink Ltd v. Scottish Rugby Union*, 1973 S.L.T. 99, to require the tribunal to look at the whole picture. And if, having done so, it is clear either that the same purpose which led to the creation of any obligation can still usefully be served or (according to [*McArthur v. Mahoney*, 1975 S.L.T. (Lands Tr.) 2]) even that some different yet useful purpose can be served, then, in our discretion, we may properly refuse to discharge it."

Changes brought about by the applicant

6–04   In general the tribunal will disregard changes in the character of the land or the neighbourhood deliberately brought about by the applicant[7] and in particular will discount works undertaken in breach of a land obligation prior to the application being made.[8]

---

[6] *Truman, Hanbury, Buxton & Co. Ltd's Application* [1956] 1 Q.B. 261; *The Luton Trade Unionists Club and Institute Ltd's Application* (1968) 20 P. & C.R. 1131.

[7] *North East Fife District Council v. Lees*, 1989 S.L.T. (Lands Tr.) 30 at 33G; *Solway Cedar Ltd v. Hendry*, 1972 S.L.T. (Lands Tr.) 42.

[8] See above, para. 3–04.

In *North East Fife District Council v. Lees*[9] an acre of land was subject to a condition that it would be used only for a swimming pool and ancillary offices. As a result of a decision to build a leisure complex including a swimming pool on neighbouring land, which could not be accommodated on the acre, the council applied for a discharge of the obligation *inter alia* on the ground that there had been a material change of circumstances because the leisure complex had now been built elsewhere. The tribunal did not consider that the relevant change had been due to any fault on the part of the council from which they sought to profit and so had regard to the change of circumstances.

Nevertheless where there has been a use in contravention of a land obligation, the tribunal will have regard to evidence of the actual effect of that use on amenity of the area (*e.g.* noise and traffic generation) in determining whether or not to grant a variation or discharge.[10]

Changes in character of land

The first change to be considered is "changes in the character of the land affected". In the English provision "property" is used in lieu of "land" and this has been construed to mean the property which is the subject of the application.[11]   **6–05**

The "land affected" clearly means land affected or burdened by the land obligation, so that changes outwith that land are not a relevant consideration under this head although such changes might be relevant under neighbourhood or "in all the circumstances".[12]

The emphasis is on "land" and not something personal to the applicant or the business associated with the premises or land. "Land" is defined by section 3 of the Interpretation Act 1889[13] to include "messuages, tenements, and hereditaments, houses, and buildings of any tenure", so the meaning of "land" is wider than the dictionary definition.

It is difficult to define what amounts to a change in the character of the land, but the tribunal appears to have approached the

---

[9] 1989 S.L.T. (Lands Tr.) 30 at 33F.

[10] *Anderson v. Trotter*, 1999 S.L.T. 442.

[11] 1925 Act, s. 84(1)(a). See Scammell, p. 377, citing *Re Solarfilms (Sales) Ltd's Application* (1993) 67 P. & C.R. 110, where proprietor made internal changes to the house to suit its use as a nursery. See also *Re Davies's Application* (1971) 25 P. & C.R. 115 where the tribunal was "not satisfied that the application site itself had changed".

[12] *Re Davies's Application* (1971) 25 P. & C.R. 115; *Re Wilson's Application* (1954) 164 E.G. 269.

[13] 52 & 53 Vict. c. 63.

question on the basis that it relates to changes in the use to which the land is being put or to which it can be put. If the use to which the land is restricted is no longer practical that amounts to a change in the character of the land.

Professor Halliday cites unreported cases where the tribunal has granted discharges on this ground where: (1) nine smallholdings, a use to which the land was restricted, were amalgamated into two and a surplus dwelling-house was permitted to be sold; (2) a prohibition of buildings other than a public hall was discharged where that facility was provided by a new community centre and the old public hall had been demolished; and (3) a restriction to use land as a garage was varied when the bus service for which it had originally been used had been discontinued and private car hiring had also ceased so that the basis for the original restriction had gone.[14]

These cases suggest that it is changes in the use to which the land is being put that is relevant in determining a "change in character". Further confirmation for this approach comes from *Macdonald, Applicant*[15] where the tribunal notes that the land "is clearly passing out of agricultural production into use as a small private housing estate". In *Solway Cedar Ltd v. Hendry*[16] the tribunal observed that "there have been no changes in the character of what is still . . . a low density housing scheme", thus having regard to the use of the land as the material factor.

6–06   In England, the tribunal has approached the question of change in the character of the property on the basis that the property is no longer used or likely to be used for the use which was permitted in the covenant.

In *Re Greaves' Application*[17] a restriction to use land only as allotments was discharged on the ground that, although theoretically it could still be so used, there was in fact no demand for allotments, *i.e.* the land was not being used as allotments. In *Re Forestmere Properties Ltd's Application*,[18] where a covenant in a lease restricted the use of a building as a cinema, the tribunal issued an interim decision indicating that because there was no

---

[14] Halliday, Vol. 2, para. 34–77 and Halliday, *Conveyancing and Feudal Reform (Scotland) Act 1970*, pp. 21–22 and unreported cases there cited.

[15] S.L.T. (Lands Tr.) 26 at 29. The application was refused on the ground that it was not competent to vary a pre-emption clause imposed by statute, but the tribunal indicated that but for this competency issue it would have granted the application on the ground that there had been a change in the character of the land.

[16] 1972 S.L.T. (Lands Tr.) 42 at 44.

[17] (1965) 17 P. & C.R. 57.

[18] (1980) 41 P. & C.R. 390.

prospect of the building being used as a cinema it was minded to grant the application, provided that the applicants agreed to new restrictions.

The fact that the land can now only be used less profitably is not **6–07** a change in the character of the land.[19] Nor is increased business competition. In *Bolton v. Aberdeen Corporation*[20] the applicant sought to have a feuing condition imposed on a licensed grocer's shop, that there would be no change of use without the superior's consent, varied to allow the premises to be used as a licensed betting shop, because increased competition in the area made the shop unprofitable. The tribunal said:

> "The Tribunal do not, however, consider that increased local competition leading to a decline in the applicant's business is a change in the character of his land. The building remains the same and it remains a grocer's shop."

In *Glasgow City Council v. Carson*[21] the tribunal accepted that a change in the perception of the suitability of ground conditions for building could be a relevant change within section 1(3)(a). In that application, a land obligation that an area should not be built upon, appeared from the evidence to have been incorporated because the parties considered that the ground conditions were unsuitable for building. At the time of the application it was practical to build on the land and so the condition was discharged under ground (a).

A mere change in the condition of the land, for example by being in a neglected state, is not a change in character under ground (a).[22]

Changes in character of neighbourhood

The second change is "changes in the character ... of the **6–08** neighbourhood". There is no statutory definition of "neighbourhood". What is the neighbourhood is a question of fact and degree in the whole circumstances for the Lands Tribunal and "may differ in different cases and in some cases may be difficult to determine".[23] "What is comprehended within that description is, in our view, a question of fact in each case."[24]

---

[19] *Murrayfield Ice Rink Ltd v. SRU*, 1972 S.L.T. (Lands Tr.) 20.
[20] *Bolton v. Aberdeen Corporation*, 1972 S.L.T. (Lands Tr.) 26 at 28.
[21] February 7, 1997; LTS/LO/1996/6.
[22] *Re Davies's Application* (1971) 25 P. & C.R. 115 at 133.
[23] *Bolton v. Aberdeen Corporation*, above, at 28.
[24] *Anderson v. Trotter*, 1999 S.L.T. 442.

As the ground is concerned with changes in the character of the neighbourhood, it is submitted that the relevant neighbourhood must be considered and determined by reference to the time of the imposition of the land obligation, so that changes from that status can then be considered.

This was recognised as a matter of fact in *Bolton v. Aberdeen Corporation*[25] where the tribunal held that the "neighbourhood has certainly changed since 1948" when the obligation was imposed. In other cases the tribunal is not so clear that it has to determine what was the neighbourhood at the time of the imposition of the obligation.

In *Main v. Lord Doune*[26] the tribunal determined "neighbourhood" by reference to the situation at the time of the application, rather than what was the "neighbourhood" at the time of the imposition of the condition. The applicant relied "upon changes having occurred in Ainslie Place viewed as a whole (which was certainly how Gillespie Graham originally designed it)", but went on to define "neighbourhood" for the purposes of the application by reference to the fact the north side had retained a residential characteristic, which the south side had not. It is submitted that this approach was wrong.

If the extent of the neighbourhood, generally the area which might be affected by a variation or discharge of the land obligation,[27] at the time of the application is different from the neighbourhood as it would have been perceived at the date of imposition of the obligation, that may amount to a change in the character of the neighbourhood. It is changes in the "character" and not changes in the extent of the neighbourhood that are relevant.

6–09 In some English cases the tribunal has had regard to an enlarged neighbourhood, where there had been development around the original *locus*, as the neighbourhood for the purposes of the application.[28] Scammell[29] suggests that the neighbourhood can be enlarged only if the surrounding development is of the same or a similar kind

6–10 The extent of the neighbourhood may be determined from the scope of a particular feuing condition. In *Anderson v. Trotter*[30] the

---

[25] 1972 S.L.T. (Lands Tr.) 26 at 28.

[26] 1972 S.L.T. (Lands Tr.) 14 at 17.

[27] See below, para. 6–10.

[28] *Re Herbert Ferryman Ltd's Application* (1952) 7 P. & C.R. 69: "Southampton has altered its character"; *Re F & H Joyce Ltd's Application* (1956) 7 P. & C.R. 245: "not bound to have regard only to the area which belonged to the Trustees in 1925, but might consider a 'much wider area'".

[29] p. 382.

[30] August 12, 1997; LTS/LO/1996/46; upheld on appeal: *Anderson v. Trotter*, 1999 S.L.T. 442.

tribunal referred to the land obligation as defining the neighbourhood, saying:

> "The clear object and intent of the land obligation with which we are here concerned is to impose a particular character upon the one acre of ground described in the feu charter. *Prima facie* therefore the one acre comprises the neighbourhood for the purposes of section 1(3)(a). The obligation envisages a community of dwellinghouses of a superior sort being erected on that one acre and prohibits any other buildings. Clearly therefore the character of the neighbourhood is conceived as strictly residential."

A neighbourhood may be defined by reference to whether "the land affected forms part of a coherent development based on mutuality of feuing conditions".[31]

The boundaries of the original feuing estate may be the relevant neighbourhood, although, in the absence of evidence as to those boundaries, the tribunal will have to make an assessment of the appropriate relevant neighbourhood.[32]

Where the neighbourhood is not "defined" by the deed imposing the obligation or the boundaries of the estate, there is no satisfactory definition of "neighbourhood". Professor Halliday suggested that:

> "it is thought that the test for the purposes of the Act is that it will include all the properties of proprietors benefited by the land obligation of which variation or discharge is sought and also by the properties of persons who may appear to the Tribunal to be affected by the obligation or by its proposed variation".[33]

While it has been suggested that Professor Halliday's definition is too widely stated[34] neither approach is satisfactory. It is suggested that what is the neighbourhood will depend on a whole range of circumstances. The subsection refers to "changes in the character . . . of the neighbourhood", which suggests that regard must be had to the coherence of an area by reference to its character. This is consistent with the approach that in determining neighbourhood the tribunal is not concerned with the rights of individuals, which are protected by the requirement for service on all benefited

[31] *Anderson v. Trotter*, 1999 S.L.T. 442.
[32] *Leney v. Craig*, 1982 S.L.T. (Lands Tr.) 9 at 11.
[33] Halliday, 1st ed., para. 19–76.
[34] Halliday, 2nd ed., Vol. 2, para. 34–78.

proprietors and for service on affected proprietors, but with the wider public interest of protecting the coherence of the character of a neighbourhood.

"Neighbourhood" has been described as the "area of protection"[35] and this is consistent with the construction of "neighbourhood" in the Licensing (Scotland) Act 1976.[36]

In *McNeil v. Gordon*[37] the tribunal said that what was:

"to be regarded as the neighbourhood of any subjects for the purposes of section 1(3)(a) is very much a matter of circumstances, and depends on the extent of the area within which changes can reasonably be regarded as having an effect on those subjects or as being of real significance to their use".

In *Main v. Lord Doune*[38] the tribunal held that part of Ainslie Place, Edinburgh, which had retained its residential character could be considered to be the neighbourhood. It was argued that Ainslie Place was the neighbourhood and, as part had been changed to office use, there had been a change in the character of the neighbourhood. The tribunal rejected this argument and held that the part which had retained its residential character was to be taken as the neighbourhood. This suggests that the tribunal was not having regard to which properties might or might not be affected by any variation, but was looking to the "character of the neighbourhood" in determining what was the neighbourhood. The tribunal commented that "separate sides of a street might be regarded as having separate characters."[39]

In *Owen v. Mackenzie*,[40] without considering the question of neighbourhood, the tribunal appears to have treated Gairloch village and its surrounding area as the neighbourhood.

In *Cameron v. Stirling*[41] the tribunal held that the neighbourhood was the homogeneous area of single building plots of about one-third acre subject to a 1962 restriction on use for no more than one dwelling-house.

---

[35] Gordon, para. 25–19.

[36] *Khan v. City of Glasgow Licensing Board*, 1995 S.L.T. 332 where it was held that the appropriate test for the application of s.16(1)(a) ("person owning or occupying property in the neighbourhood of the premises") was the likelihood or otherwise of the amenity of the objector's property being adversely affected by the grant of any licence.

[37] October 2, 1992; LTS/LO/1992/1.

[38] 1972 S.L.T. (Lands Tr.) 14 at 17.

[39] *ibid*. at 16.

[40] 1974 S.L.T. (Lands Tr.) 11. See *Re Herbert Ferrymans Ltd's Application* (1952) 7 P. & C.R. 69, where Southampton was treated as the neighbourhood.

[41] 1988 S.L.T. (Lands Tr.) 18 at 20H.

In other circumstances it might be appropriate to take those properties affected by the burden or its discharge if there is otherwise no coherence to an area of property. In *Anderson v. Trotter*[42] the Second Division rejected an argument that in defining "neighbourhood" the affected property should be treated as lying at the centre of the neighbourhood, which on that definition would then include shops and garages. Clearly, the location of the application subjects by reference to the position in the neighbourhood will be a relevant consideration for the tribunal. Thus properties on the border of a neighbourhood might fall to be treated differently from properties at its centre.[43]

In considering changes to the neighbourhood, the tribunal has had regard to growth in population, growth in industry and a growth in tourism as factors amounting to change.[44] It has taken into account changes in the character of the neighbourhood by the infilling of garden ground of large houses.[45]

Changes such as the removal of redundant chimneys, the installation of double glazing and even the building of garages have been held not to change the character of a residential neighbourhood, at least not in a way that was relevant to an application under ground (a).[46]

Where the original "neighbourhood" as defined by the tribunal has become affected by external factors, such as noise from the construction of nearby council housing, a school and a motorway, the tribunal has held that the neighbourhood was no longer a quiet residential area with a distinctive character of its own.[47]

Other material circumstances

The third factor is "other circumstances which the Tribunal may deem material". The Lands Tribunal has held[48] that: **6–11**

"the general words 'other circumstances' fall to be read *ejusdem generis* and as comprehending only things of the same

---

[42] 1998 G.W.D. 28–1438.
[43] See *Re Beech's Application* (1990) 59 P. & C.R. 502, where an application to modify a residential restriction was refused. The house in question was on the boundary between residential houses and houses that had been converted to shops and offices and the tribunal held that no case had been made out to move the boundary.
[44] *Co-operative Wholesale Society v. Ushers' Brewery*, 1975 S.L.T. (Lands Tr.) 9 at 13, although on the facts in that case the application was refused under ground (a).
[45] *Gardener v. Pickard*, April 24, 1992; LTS/LO/1991/56.
[46] *Stoddart v. Glendinning*, 1993 S.L.T. (Lands Tr.) 12 at 16B.
[47] *Leney v. Craig*, 1982 S.L.T. (Lands Tr.) 9 at 11.
[48] Gordon, in *Scottish Land Law* para. 25–20, says "questionably".

kind as are designated by the preceding words—Maxwell on the *Interpretation of Statutes*, 12th edition, p. 297 and *Eton R.D.C. v. River Thames Conservators* [1950] Ch. 540. So interpreting the words 'other circumstances' we consider that they embrace material changes akin to changes in the character of the land or the neighbourhood which have rendered unreasonable or inappropriate the original obligation".

"(S)ignificant changes in social habits" can be considered as one of the other circumstances which the tribunal is entitled to take into account.[49]

In *Main v. Lord Doune*[50] and in *Anderson v. Trotter*[51] the tribunal regarded the fact that nurseries for children were now in demand as a relevant factor, although the tribunal reaches different conclusion in each case, having regard to all the circumstances.[52]

In *Manz v. Butter's Trs*[53] the tribunal decided that changes in drinking habits was a major change in social habits which justified a discharge of a land obligation that a hotel was to be maintained as a temperance hotel. The tribunal found that in 1924 there was a strong temperance movement, which made a temperance hotel attractive, but that by the 1970s drinking habits had become more civilised and there were more tourists looking for a drink with their meal and so a temperance hotel was a deterrent to most visitors.

In *Owen v. Mackenzie*,[54] when relaxing a restriction against the sale of alcohol, the tribunal took into account the changes in social habits and the presence of local caravanners, campers and other tourists who were not hotel residents and who desired to purchase alcohol along with other provisions in a local tourist store.

In *United Auctions (Scotland) Ltd v. British Railways Board*[55] the tribunal found that a burden that a site next to the railway station was to be used as an auction mart was unreasonable and inappropriate under ground (a), because livestock no longer travelled by rail and this was a major change going to the root of the need to impose the restriction.

---

[49] *Murrayfield Ice Rink Ltd v. SRU*, 1972 S.L.T. (Lands Tr.) 20 at 21.
[50] 1972 (Lands Tr.) 14 (application granted).
[51] August 12, 1997; LTS/LO/1996/46 (application refused).
[52] See also *Re Solarfilms (Sales) Ltd's Application* (1993) 67 P. & C.R. 110, where the tribunal in England had regard to the need for nurseries, but still refused the application.
[53] 1973 S.L.T. (Lands Tr.) 2.
[54] 1974 S.L.T. (Lands Tr.) 11.
[55] 1991 S.L.T. (Lands Tr.) 72.

In *Strathclyde Regional Council v. Barcaldine School Board*[56] the tribunal had regard to changes of legislation, being the introduction of the tenant's right to buy, as being "a change in circumstances which are material to the obligation" in rendering the obligation unreasonable and inappropriate, because the obligation restricted the use of a dwelling-house to be used by the resident teacher.

In *Biggerstaff v. SSPCA*[57] the applicant sought the variation or discharge of a land obligation to allow him to build an additional dwelling-house in the garden ground. It was argued under ground (a), that the increase in the value of the land as a building site made it unreasonable and inappropriate to require such a large plot to have only one house. The tribunal rejected the argument, holding that a rise in the value of building land did not constitute a change of circumstances such as to render a land obligation unreasonable or inappropriate under ground (a).

In *Avonside Homes Ltd v. Fyvie*[58] the tribunal rejected an argument that an obligation restricting the number of houses was no longer reasonable because of changes in demand for housing caused by high interest rates meant that the applicants were paying higher bridging finance than anticipated. The tribunal commented:

> "[N]or should title conditions be regarded as obsolete under section 1(3)(a) due to transitory changes in demand when the conditions are still conceded to be reasonable in their application over the rest of the site".

Such an argument could also have been rejected as one personal to the applications, rather than running with the land.

GROUND (B)

Terms

Ground (b) is in the following terms: **6–12**

> "(b) the obligation is unduly burdensome compared with any benefit resulting or which would result from its performance".

This ground is directed towards the present situation and compares how burdensome the land obligation is on the property compared to the benefit accruing to the benefited proprietor.

---

[56] September 23, 1992; LTS/LO/1991/27; see also *Banff and Buchan District Council v. Earl of Seafield's Estate* 1988 S.L.T. (Lands Tr.) 21 where pre-emption clause discharged having regard to a tenant's statutory right to buy.
[57] October 25, 1990; LTS/LO/1990/17.
[58] November 9, 1978; LTS/LO/1977/22.

The tribunal has said that "unduly" falls to be construed by reference to the primary definition in the *Shorter Oxford English Dictionary* ("without due cause or justification; unrightfully, undeservedly") and not by reference to the secondary definition ("to excess; beyond the due decree").[59]

No English provision

6–13   There is no corresponding English provision, which has been explained by the tribunal on the ground that:

> "Under the common law of England it is generally impossible to enforce covenants relating to freehold land except against the original covenantor. The only exceptions are restrictive covenants which create an equity binding on the land and which are enforceable against the holder for the time being— see Preston and Newsom on Restrictive Covenants, 5th edition, p. 55. Hence in England no power was needed for the Lands Tribunal to vary positive covenants which are usually of a transient nature. In Scotland on the other hand there is no significant distinction between land obligations to perform and land obligations to abstain—indeed the enforceability against successors (of both types of obligation) has been vital to the development of the Scots law of the tenement with ownership above ground level. One is enforceable by decree *ad factum praestandum* and the other by interdict."[60]

Scope of the ground

6–14   Ground (b) applies both to restrictive obligations and to those requiring specific performance.[61] In the early cases an attempt was made to argue that the ground applied only to "positive obligations that were capable of being performed and not obligations . . . which were merely restrictive" because of the provision in the subsection referring to "benefit resulting or which would result from its performance". In *Bolton v. Aberdeen Corporation*:

> "it was contended that this subsection only applies to positive obligations which require to be specifically performed. This was said to be the ordinary meaning of the word 'performance' and was reinforced by the preceding words 'resulting or which would result' which could not so readily be applied to a purely

[59] *Buist v. Merson*, March 8, 1995; LTS/LO/1994/31.
[60] *Murrayfield Ice Rink Ltd v. SRU*, 1972 S.L.T. (Lands Tr.) 20 at 23.
[61] *ibid.* at 22; 1973 S.C. 21.

restrictive obligation. The Tribunal, however, is not prepared to hold as a matter of law that s. 1 (3) (b) can only be applied to obligations requiring specific performance. Our jurisdiction applies to servitudes as well as obligations in registrable leases and there may be cases where a restrictive obligation has become unduly burdensome; but the facts of the case do not permit a discharge under s. 1 (3) (a) or 1 (3) (c) . The word 'performance' can be applied to the carrying out of a duty of abstention; see Shorter Oxford English Dictionary, vol. II, p. 1472, Stair's Institutes, I.17.20, and *Harman v. Ainslie* [1904] 1 K.B. 698".[62]

In rejecting this argument the tribunal commented on problems which might arise in seeking to invoke ground (b), where the land obligation was restrictive in nature, saying:

> "We are by no means certain how s. 1 (3) (b) should be applied in the case of servitudes and there may be other restrictive obligations which have become unduly burdensome which fall neither under s. 1 (3) (a) nor 1 (3) (c).[63] Having so said, however, we must add that as matter of practice in most cases where a restrictive obligation has become unduly burdensome it will be because it is impeding some reasonable use and it may be more appropriate to proceed under s. 1 (3) (c). Under s. 1 (3) (b) it will in many cases be difficult to discharge the onus of proving that a restrictive obligation is unduly burdensome compared with any corresponding benefit— because one is endeavouring to weigh imponderables. In the case of an obligation requiring specific performance, however, the cost of actual performance can usually be obtained and placed before the Tribunal. Certainly s. 1 (3) (b) is, therefore, more apt in practice for application to obligations requiring specific performance."[64]

The opinion of the tribunal that ground (b) applied to positive as well as negative obligations was upheld by the Court of Session, where the Lord Justice-Clerk said:

> "The first is whether 'obligation' in head (b) includes a negative as well as a positive obligation. *Prima facie* 'performance' is a word more apt to describe the 'doing' of something than 'refraining from doing'. However, looking back to

---

[62] *Bolton v. Aberdeen Corporation*, 1972 S.L.T. (Lands Tr.) 26 at 28.

[63] See *McQuiban v. Eagle Star Insurance Co*, 1972 S.L.T. (Lands Tr.) 39 for an example of an application relating to a restrictive obligation, where grounds (a) and (c) could not be invoked.

[64] *Murrayfield Ice Rink Ltd v. SRU*, 1972 S.L.T. (Lands Tr.) 20 at 23.

the passage from Stair (I.xvii.20) referred to by the Tribunal and having regard to their reasoned consideration of this issue, I am satisfied that their conclusion was right."[65]

The right to extract a waiver fee from a vassal is not a "benefit" within the meaning of the subsection. In *West Lothian Co-operative Society Ltd v. Ashdale Land and Property Co Ltd* the Lands Tribunal rejected a contention by the superior that:

> "they are being deprived of a substantial 'benefit' in terms of the subsection, as they will be losing the financial considera-tion which they are presently able to claim on granting a waiver. In the Tribunal's view this is the very situation which s. 1 of the 1970 Act was designed to prevent, namely a superior who has now become primarily an investor in feuduties and with no genuine desire to maintain the land obligations, merely using their existence to extract money. The subsection requires the Tribunal to compare the burdensome-ness of the obligation with any benefit which would result to the superior from its performance—not any financial benefit which, apart from the Act, might derive from its waiver".[66]

If the proposed use is impractical or cannot be carried out for reasons outwith the burden, such as no right of access, then the land obligation cannot be said to be unduly burdensome.[67]

Benefit, etc., to affected and other persons

6–15   Under ground (b) any benefit that might accrue to an affected person is not a relevant consideration. In *Manz v. Butter's Trs*[68] a temperance hotel sought a variation on the restriction against the sale of alcoholic liquor contained in its feu charter. The application was opposed by the superior and by another hotel holding under a feu charter from the superior, which contained an obligation on the superior not to consent to the conversion of any building into a licensed hotel or licensed house. The tribunal recognised that there would probably be financial disadvantage to the hotel if the application was granted but went on to hold:

> "that under s. 1 (3) (b) it is irrelevant to consider the question of possible benefits to a third party who is not a benefited proprietor in relation to the land obligation of which discharge

---

[65] *Murrayfield Ice Rink Ltd v. SRU*, 1973 S.C. 20 at 29.
[66] 1972 S.L.T. (Lands Tr.) 30 at 33. See below, para. 8–08.
[67] *Murrayfield Ice Rink Ltd v. SRU*, above, *per* the Lord Justice-Clerk at 32.
[68] 1973 S.L.T. (Lands Tr.) 2.

is sought. The subsection does not expressly state that the Tribunal must compare the burden with the benefit only to a benefited proprietor. If ss. 1 and 2 however are read as a whole it seems clear that this must have been Parliament's intention. Reference is made to the definitions contained in s. 1 (2) and 2 (6) and also to the compensation provisions which can only be operated in favour of benefited proprietors".[69]

That said, the tribunal may have regard to the interests of the persons in whose favour the superior originally imposed the benefit, where that interest is put forward by the superior. In *Grampian Regional Council v. Viscount Cowdray*[70] the tribunal had regard to a submission for the superior that the restriction on a house that it was to be used for educational purposes as the house for the local school teacher "was imposed for the benefit of the estate and estate workers on whose behalf the estate owner made the land available as a schoolhouse in return for a nominal sum".

How an affected proprietor or other person might be affected may be a relevant consideration under "all the circumstances", but it is not a consideration under ground (b).

The tribunal may be willing to "lift the veil" in corporate affairs so as to take into account the burden or benefit to a subsidiary company which is actually carrying on the business of the parent applicant/benefited company. In *Currie v. Alliance Property Co. Ltd*,[71] where a discharge of an obligation preventing an area of land from being used as a supermarket was sought, the tribunal was prepared to treat Safeway Stores plc, who operated a neighbouring supermarket and for whose protection the restriction had been imposed when they moved out of the premises to neighbouring premises, as the benefited proprietor even though the land title was held in the group property company *Alliance's* name.

The burden compared with the benefit

In determining whether or not to discharge or vary a land **6–16** obligation under ground (b), the tribunal has to be satisfied that "the obligation is unduly burdensome compared with any benefit". This is always a balancing exercise, with the onus on the applicant "of proving undue burden to herself compared with corresponding benefit to the objecting superior",[72] where considerations of burden or benefit to affected proprietors or others are not considered.[73]

---

[69] See also *Owen v. Mackenzie*, 1974 S.L.T. (Lands Tr.) 11.
[70] 1985 S.L.T. (Lands Tr.) 6 at 9.
[71] February 26, 1995; LTS/LO/1992/19 and 20.
[72] *Nicolson v. Campbell's Trs*, 1981 S.L.T. (Lands Tr.) 10 at 12.
[73] See above, para. 6–15.

The tribunal has recognised that "for a case to succeed . . . under s. 1(3)(b), the relevant land obligation, must in practice, have become a relatively pointless one giving no real benefit".[74] Thus it is that applications under ground (b) very seldom succeed. In the balancing exercise the tribunal "cannot be influenced by the applicant's purely personal circumstances in deciding whether an obligation attaching to land should be discharged for all time".[75] The tribunal has refused an application to extend a house where the reason was given as the applicant's health and the extension would outlast the applicant's occupation of the house[76]; an application to allow two blocks of flats to be built on vacant land, where developers could not realise the full potential of the land and therefore they personally required that the obligation required to be discharged.[77]

The fact that a developer has bought land for a price that did not take account of the land obligation could not be relied upon as making the restriction unduly burdensome because of what was agreed to be paid for the site.[78] Similarly, an inability to gain money from an unimpeded sale is an irrelevant consideration.[79]

The tribunal will not grant what is in effect a temporary suspensive condition, which has become necessary because of the applicant's personal failure to act timeously. An application was refused where an applicant sought the variation or discharge, by extension of the time-limit, of an obligation to rebuild a cottage that had been burned down, because, by her inactivity, the applicant had failed to rebuild within the stipulated time and was threatened with an irritancy.[80]

As a general rule, the Lands Tribunal will not hold a land obligation to be unduly burdensome if it merely restricts the full potential of the land being realised, particularly if the land can still be operated at a profit or if it prevents one use where the land can still be used for another purpose.[81] If the obligation, for example to

---

[74] *Lothian Regional Council v. George Wimpey & Co. Ltd*, 1985 S.L.T. (Lands Tr.) 2 at 3
[75] *Main v. Lord Doune*, 1972 S.L.T. (Lands Tr.) 14 at 17. See also *Bolton v. Aberdeen Corporation*, 1972 S.L.T. (Lands Tr.) 26 at 29.
[76] *Stoddart v. Glendinning*, 1993 S.L.T. (Lands Tr.) 12 at 16H.
[77] *Miller Group Ltd v. Gardner's Exrs*, 1992 S.L.T. (Lands Tr.) 62 at 67H.
[78] *ibid.* at 67L.
[79] *Mcneil v. Gordon*, October 2, 1992; LTS/LO/1992/1.
[80] *Nicolson v. Campbell's Trs*, 1981 S.L.T. (Lands Tr.) 10 at 13,
[81] *Smith v. Taylor*, 1972 S.L.T. (Lands Tr.) 34 at 36; *Bolton v. Aberdeen Corporation*, 1972 S.L.T. (Lands Tr.) 26; *Sinclair v. Gillon*, 1974 S.L.T. (Lands Tr.) 18 at 20; *MacDonald v. Stornoway Trust*, 1987 S.L.T. 240 at 242D.

maintain a derelict building, has become "expensive and pointless" then a variation or discharge might be appropriate.[82]

The tribunal may have regard to the financial viability of the project in considering what benefit there might be to an applicant, particularly if the applicant's estimates are different from the findings of the tribunal.[83]

Loss of amenity is a relevant benefit which the tribunal should take into consideration under ground (b) because:

"So far as head (b) is concerned, one can think of many cases where, comparing the benefit to the objectors in whose favour the burden was created and to whom amenity was the essence and origin of the burden, that amenity benefit so far outweighed the burden on the 'burdened proprietor' as to preclude the latter from establishing that 'the obligation in question is unduly burdensome compared with any benefit resulting or which would result from its performance'. Where it is alleged that loss of amenity would result from the granting of an application under head (b), this is a matter which must, in my opinion, be considered by the Tribunal when deciding whether the conditions laid down by head (b) have been established."[84]

In *Stannard v. Issa*[85] the Privy Council said of a Jamaican provision similar to section 84 of the 1925 Act that:

"It hardly needs stating, that, for anyone desirous of preserving the peaceful character of a neighbourhood, the ability to restrict the number of dwellings permitted to be built is a clear benefit, just as, for instance was the ability in *Gilbert v Stoor* [1983] Ch 27 to preserve a view by restricting building."

A pre-emption right is not *per se* necessarily an undue burden, because as recently as 1974[86] Parliament confirmed that pre-emption clauses could competently be included in dispositions or feu contracts and so must be taken to have held that they are not unduly burdensome. The tribunal has said that it might be difficult to justify the discharge of a pre-emption right on any of the section 1(3) grounds.[87] In *Banff & Buchan District Council v. Earl of Seafield*[88] the

---

[82] *West Lothian Co-operative Society Ltd v. Ashdale Land and Property Co. Ltd*, 1972 S.L.T. (Lands Tr.) 30 at 33.

[83] *MacDonald v. Stornoway Trust*, above, at 242B–D.

[84] *Murrayfield Ice Rink Ltd v. SRU*, 1973 S.C. 20 at 29.

[85] [1987] 1 A.C. 175, *per* Lord Oliver at 188F.

[86] See s. 9 of the Conveyancing Amendment (Scotland) Act 1938, amended by s. 13 of the Land Tenure Reform (Scotland) Act 1974.

[87] *Macdonald, Applicant*, 1973 S.L.T. (Lands Tr.) 26 at 29.

[88] 1988 S.L.T. (Lands Tr.) 21.

tribunal discharged a pre-emption clause because of its potential conflict with the statutory right of a local authority tenant to buy his house.[89]

Where it is not possible to trace the benefited proprietor, the need to obtain his consent is in itself "unduly burdensome" and the fact that he cannot be traced is an indication of the fact that the land obligation is likely to be little benefit to him in enforcing the burden.[90]

An obligation to build to a specific design requirement of the superior may be held unduly burdensome, because it would add to the cost of the building and would affect all potential proprietors. This would be so particularly where the superior had no continuing benefit in maintaining the design requirement.[91]

Personal considerations

6–17   Where a party purchased development subjects for a higher price than their value warranted, when subject to the restriction in a land obligation, without making the purchase conditional on the restriction being discharged or varied, the fact of the higher price being paid did not make the obligation burdensome. The "burden" imposed by paying the higher price was personal and self-imposed and so did not fall to be taken into consideration.[92]

Similarly, where a party lives in a house subject to a restrictive land obligation the tribunal has held that the obligation is not unduly burdensome because:

> "The restriction is one from which any owner can readily relieve himself by simply selling the house and buying another in a more suitable location which is not so restricted. This was what the tribunal held in *Bachoo v. George Wimpey & Co. Ltd.*, 1977 S.L.T. (Lands Tr.) 2, in a case involving a similar deed of conditions relating to another Wimpey housing estate and where one proprietor wished to build a major extension to the detriment of his neighbours after obtaining planning permission to do so"[93]

[89] Now under s. 61 of the Housing (Scotland) Act 1987; see *Ross and Cromarty District Council v. Patience*, 1997 S.C. (H.L.) 46, where the House of Lords held that the pre-emption clause did not affect statutory sales under the 1987 Act.

[90] *Porter v. Rhodes*, January 11, 1996; LTS/LO/1995/43.

[91] *Hopcroft v. Smith*, March 23, 1992; LTS/LO/1991/43. See *Noble v. Lord Reidhaven*, June 17, 1991; LTS/LO/1989/98, where the superior had a continuing interest in maintaining the amenity of an area for his pecuniary interest.

[92] *County Properties and Development Ltd v. Cumbernauld Development Corporation*, April 5, 1995; LTS/LO/94/20.

[93] *Lothian Regional Council v. George Wimpey & Co. Ltd*, 1985 S.L.T. (Lands Tr.) 2 at 3.

and so the burden is in fact personal. Extraneous financial benefits to third parties are not a relevant consideration for the tribunal. Thus the tribunal refused to consider the benefit a restriction against the sale of alcohol gave to a hotel proprietor who was an affected proprietor.[94]

GROUND (C)

Terms

Ground (c) is in the following terms: **6–18**

"(c) the existence of the obligation impedes some reasonable use of the land."

This ground "looks principally to the proposed new use and we have to gauge whether this is a reasonable use in all the circumstances, which is being impeded".[95] Ground (c) looks to the proposed future use of the subjects and the tribunal has to determine whether or not such a reasonable use is being impeded. It is essential that there is a current proposed use before this ground can be invoked. This is the ground that succeeds most often.

Unlike grounds (a) and (b), the subsection does not look to the land obligation itself, but to the reasonableness, in all the circumstances, of the proposed new development.[96]

English provision

The equivalent English provision in section 84(1)(aa) of the 1925 **6–19** Act is:

"(aa) that (in a case falling within subsection (1A) below) the continued existence thereof would impede some reasonable user of the land for public or private purposes or, as the case may be, would unless modified so impede such user; . . .
(1A) Subsection (1)(aa) above authorises the discharge or modification of a restriction by reference to its impeding some reasonable user of land in any case in which the Lands Tribunal is satisfied that the restriction, in impeding that user, either—

---

[94] *Manz v. Butter's Trs*, 1973 S.L.T. (Lands Tr.) 2.
[95] *Smith v. Taylor*, 1972 S.L.T. (Lands Tr.) 34 at 36.
[96] *MacDonald v. Stornoway Trust*, 1987 S.L.T. 240 at 242F.

(a) does not secure to persons entitled to the benefit of it any practical benefits of substantial value or advantage to them; or
(b) is contrary to the public interest;
and that money will be an adequate compensation for the loss or disadvantage (if any) which any such person will suffer from the discharge or modification."

It will be noted that while the English provision is also related to "impede some reasonable user of the land for public or private purposes" the grounds upon which the restriction can be varied or discharged are more restrictive. The Lands Tribunal has to be satisfied the restriction does not secure to the person entitled to the benefit any practical benefits of substantial value or advantage or that it is contrary to the public interest and that money will be an adequate compensation for the loss or disadvantage. This later requirement is the equivalent of the proviso to section 1(4) of the 1970 Act, but under that proviso the Lands Tribunal of Scotland has a discretion which it is to exercise only in exceptional circumstances.

Reasonable use

6–20   In dealing with applications under ground (c), the tribunal has to be satisfied that there is a proposed use and that the use is reasonable in all the circumstances.

The proposed use has to be a new use. If the proposed use is the current use, then ground (c) cannot be invoked. Where it was intended to sell a schoolhouse to the present occupant (who was a school teacher) to live in, no new use in contravention of the restrictive land obligation was intended and accordingly it could not be said to impede some proposed new use of the land in terms of section 1(3)(c).[97]

The division of a house into two houses is a new use.[98] In *Leach & Son v. Croabh Haven 2000 Ltd*[99] the tribunal had to consider whether the current use of land for a diving centre with a wooden accommodation shed was the same use as that diving centre with a dwelling-house, three chalets and offices and held that the "new use was qualitatively different from the Diving Centre as it has hitherto been run".

The proposed new use must be a use by the applicant. In *Henderson v. Mansell*[1] the tribunal held an application to be

---

[97] *Grampian Regional Council v. Viscount Cowdray*, 1985 S.L.T. (Lands Tr.) 6.
[98] *Syer v. Mitchell*, July 5, 1985; LTS/LO/1984/44.
[99] August 31, 1993; LTS/LO/1992/52.
[1] November 9, 1993; LTS/LO/1992/41.

incompetent where the burdened proprietor sought the discharge of an obligation to maintain a tree, a wall and metal fence in order that a developer of nearby ground could remove the tree and realign the road to form a clear line of site in accordance with their planning permission. The tribunal held that this was not a proposed use by the proprietor and said:

> "it is clear to us that in the context of the 1970 Act use 'by the applicant' is predicated. The whole scheme of the Act is, in relation to section 1 applications, that there must be an applicant who is a burdened proprietor and that, in our opinion, connotes that any intended new use must mean use by the burdened proprietor".

The tribunal went on to hold that the removal of the tree, the realignment of the wall and metal railing to form a line of sight was in itself not a "use" of the ground by the burdened proprietor, because:

> "It is also pertinent to note that not even those who are sponsoring Mr Henderson in his application (namely the Walker Group) would be taking advantage of that new use. The Walker Group simply propose to use the garden ground . . . temporarily—long enough to provide a sight line for the benefit of the general public. Thereafter, the new 'use' will be use by members of the public—that is by road users surveying the junction."

In an application to vary or discharge a right of pre-emption on grounds which included ground (c), the tribunal left unanswered the question:

> "whether a sale of land is 'use' in the sense of 1(3)(c) where such a sale is to leave unchanged the actual functional use of the land"[2]

In considering whether a proposed use is reasonable or not it is: **6–21**

> "essential to look at the whole picture and not at 'reasonableness' in the abstract. For example, if A conveys a part of his extensive garden to B (who is a market gardener) under the burden that the land conveyed shall not be built upon, the time may come when, from the point of view of a singular successor of B it is 'reasonable' that he should build a house, or a hotel, or some business premises on that land—and if the

---

[2] *Macdonald v. Begg*, August 24, 1979; LTS/LO/1978.29.

restriction still holds, B's singular successor will be the loser of the potential profit which he has done nothing to earn. In deciding, however, whether the particular proposed use is 'reasonable' it is, in my opinion, essential to take into account the effect on the amenity of the land still held by A (or his successor)".[3]

The tribunal is not concerned with whether or not a proposed use is reasonable or desirable in itself, but whether the proposed use of the particular subjects is reasonable in all the relevant circumstances of the case.

In *Lothian Regional Council v. George Wimpey & Co. Ltd*[4] the council sought a variation of an obligation to use a house as a single dwelling-house for one family to allow a house in a housing scheme as supported accommodation for children in care aged about 16 to 18 years with some outside supervision. The tribunal said:

> "The tribunal have experienced greater difficulty in deciding the second and stronger branch of the applicants' case under s. 1 (3) (c), namely, that the land obligation, unless varied, impedes some reasonable use of the land. This is particularly so when the aims of providing supported accommodation appear to be reasonable in themselves and underprivileged children need all the care and support they can get at a formative stage in their lives. But the tribunal cannot decide this branch of the case simply on the ground that supported accommodation is in itself good or desirable: *see Murrayfield Ice Rink v. Scottish Rugby Union* 1973 S.L.T. 99. We have to decide whether the proposed new use of a particular house at no. 12 Clerwood Terrace as supported accommodation is reasonable in all the relevant circumstances of the case which include the character of the neighbourhood; the still experimental nature of supported (but loosely supervised) accommodation; and the attitude of the local community which could prove harmful to the children and the experiment as a whole."[5]

Where the proposed use is reasonable "it is immaterial who are the persons for the time being making use thereof" and therefore

---

[3] *Murrayfield Ice Rink Ltd v. SRU*, 1973 S.C. 21 at 29.
[4] 1985 S.L.T. (Lands Tr.) 2 at 3.
[5] See *Re Lloyd's and Lloyd's Application* (1993) 66 P. & C.R. 112, where the tribunal modified a restriction to allow a house to be used for community care of the mentally ill, because it was accepted that the user was reasonable, but that the restriction was contrary to the public interest as government policy required the provision of care homes in the community.

the tribunal is not concerned with whether it is the burdened proprietor, who intends to use the land himself or proposes that another, for example, a lessee, make the proposed use of the land.[6]

As an almost invariable rule, the tribunal will only grant a variation of the land obligation to permit the particular use proposed and will not just discharge the obligation.[7]

Where a superior no longer has any legitimate interest to enforce an obligation or where there is no continuing usefulness to the superior, particularly where he might have been seeking to enforce it mala fide, the tribunal may discharge the obligation rather than varying it.[8]

"Impedes"

Before ground (c) can be invoked it has to be shown that the **6–22** obligation impedes some reasonable use. Before such a use can be impeded there has to be a specific proposal before the tribunal. In rare circumstances, where there are a number of possible proposals before the tribunal, it has issued a draft decision indicating that it is minded to allow the application provided that a specific proposal is put to it for consideration.[9]

What is meant by "existence of the obligation impedes some reasonable use" has given rise to difficulties. In *Murrayfield Ice Rink Ltd v. Scottish Rugby Union*[10] the tribunal rejected a narrow construction of "impedes",[11] that the word meant "a situation where the use of the land was so impeded by the restrictive obligation that it could not be put to reasonable use at all", inclining:

---

[6] *Ross and Cromarty District Council v. Ullapool Property Company Ltd*, 1983 S.L.T. (Lands Tr.) 9 at 13.

[7] *T & I Consultants Ltd v. Cullion*, 1998 Hous. L.R. 9; *Ramsay v. Holmes*, 1992 S.L.T. (Lands Tr.) 53 at 59L; but see *Harris v. Douglass*, 1993 S.L.T. (Lands Tr.) 56 at 59C, where a restriction on making any alteration to a flat was discharged.

[8] *Murray v. Farquharson*, July 28, 1995; LTS/LO/94/47.

[9] *East Kilbride Development Corporation v. The Norwich Union Life Insurance Society*, March 29, 1995; LTS/LO/1993/34, where a number of possible development proposals, none of which had planning permission, were put forward during the course of the hearing. The tribunal issued a draft decision indicating that the application would be refused for want of a specific proposal, but inviting the applicants to put forward a particular proposal, subject to conditions acceptable to the objectors. When this was done the application was granted.

[10] 1972 S.L.T. (Lands Tr.) 20 at 24.

[11] Based on *Re Leeds Road, Wakefield* (1953) 103 L.J. 188 and *Re M Howard (Mitcham) Ltd's Application* (1955) 7 P. & C.R. 219, which construed s. 84(1)(a) of the 1925 Act ("would impede . . . the reasonable user") narrowly, prior to its amendment in 1965 to "some reasonable user".

"towards a wider interpretation which will allow the subsection to operate under circumstances where there have been no material changes to satisfy s. 1 (3) (a), but where, nevertheless, 'some reasonable use' is being impeded. The existence of restrictive obligations appropriate to the conditions operating when they were made may nowadays impose unacceptable restraints upon development. This is particularly so in the case of the feuing system with its imposition of obligations in perpetuity. ... Nevertheless a wider interpretation must clearly have some limits and no judicial tribunal could be called upon to decide whether a particular use is reasonable in the abstract".

In *Ramsay v. Holmes*[12] consideration was given to the meaning of "impedes"[13] in contrast with the word "prevent", where the tribunal suggested that impede meant something less than prevent,[14] which is consistent with the wider approach taken in *Main v. Lord Doune*.[15]

Before it can be said that the obligation impedes a reasonable use, there has to be a specific proposal before the tribunal. In *Murrayfield Ice Rink Ltd v. Scottish Rugby Union*[16] the tribunal commented that:

"In our view the proper course when applying under s. 1 (3) (c) is to seek a full order which removes all the proprietory impediments **and which is based upon a specific proposal**. Otherwise compensation cannot be properly assessed nor can it be judged whether a reasonable use is being impeded in the particular circumstances of the case." (emphasis added)

This approach was upheld on appeal where it was "conceded that the proposed new use must be an 'identifiable proposed use' " (*Taylor v. Smith*, July 27, Court of Session, 1972, unreported).[17] It is not enough that it is one of the factors preventing the proposed use. As was said by the Lord Justice-Clerk[18]:

"In essence, if the proposed use is impracticable as, in my opinion, it is, the obligation cannot be said to be 'unduly

---

[12] 1992 S.L.T. (Lands Tr.) 53 at 56I and 58E.
[13] *Shorter Oxford English Dictionary*: "to impede" meant "to obstruct progress or action, to hinder, or to stand in the way of".
[14] *Ramsay v. Holmes*, 1992 S.L.T. (Lands Tr.) 53 at 58G.
[15] 1972 S.L.T. (Lands Tr.) 14 at 17–18.
[16] 1972 S.L.T. (Lands Tr.) 20 at 25.
[17] *Murrayfield Ice Rink Ltd v. SRU*, 1973 S.C. 21 at 30.
[18] *ibid.* at 32.

burdensome': nor can the existence of the obligation be said to impede 'some reasonable use of the land' when the removal of the alleged impediment would leave the appellants still in statu quo ante and in a situation where they had failed to establish that, even if the application were granted, the subjects could be used for the purpose proposed."

In *Murrayfield Ice Rink Ltd v. Scottish Rugby Union*[19] the tribunal found that there was inadequate parking for the proposed use as a supermarket, there were difficulties regarding access and a further obligation not to alter the buildings, which the applicants were not seeking to discharge and considered that therefore the land obligation was not the only impediment to the proposed use.

In *Cameron v. Stirling*[20] the use of land and a house was restricted to one house. The applicant sought a discharge of the obligation under ground (c) to allow another house to be built. The tribunal observed that the refusal of planning permission was probably conclusive evidence that the relevant land obligation did not of itself impede the proposed new use of the land. In *Scott v. Fulton*[21] the tribunal said:

"[H]ere the neighbours have been consulted and planning permission has not been granted but, after full consideration, has been refused. It would be difficult for an applicant to satisfy the conditions of s. 1 (3) (c) where he had been refused planning permission for a proposed development. For it cannot then be said that the relevant land obligation is impeding some reasonable use of the land: see Murrayfield Ice Rink Ltd. v. Scottish Rugby Union, 1972 S.L.T. (Lands Tr.) 20, 1973 S.L.T. 99".

The absence of a grant of planning permission, as opposed to a refusal, need not be fatal to the application in all circumstances if such planning permission is reasonably likely to be granted.[22]

In an earlier decision the tribunal had said that an obligation to obtain a superior's consent to a permitted development was not an obligation that impeded a reasonable use, because:

"It is difficult therefore to understand how the existence of these particular obligations can be said to impede some reasonable use of the land. Their existence does not in itself

---

[19] 1972 S.L.T. (Lands Tr.) 20 at 25.
[20] 1988 S.L.T. (Lands Tr.) 18 at 20J.
[21] 1982 S.L.T. (Lands Tr.) 18 at 20.
[22] *United Auctions (Scotland) Ltd v. British Railways Board*, 1991 S.L.T. (Lands Tr.) 71 at 76D.

provide any impediment. It is only the way in which the district council might exercise their rights which could impede a use of the land. It is no more than a hypothetical possibility that in this case the district council might act unreasonably in the exercise of their rights under these obligations."[23]

In *Ramsay v. Holmes*[24] it was held, not following *British Bakeries (Scotland) Ltd v. City of Edinburgh District Council,*[25] that the obligation contained in the land obligation to obtain consent from a superior for any development could itself impede a reasonable use. The tribunal said:

"In [counsel's] submission, however, a proposed use of land could always be said to be impeded by the mere existence of a need to obtain a consent to the use. If that view is sound, it follows that such an obligation may always be varied or discharged under subs. (3) (c) simply on it being shown that the proposed use is reasonable and that the necessary consent to it has not been obtained. Obviously, if consent had actually been given, the existence of the obligation to obtain it could hardly be said still to impede the use.

In our opinion, that approach is correct, although it may make little difference in practice. One would not normally expect an application under subs. (3) (c) to be made to the tribunal unless either the necessary consent had been sought and refused or there was some difficulty in obtaining it, perhaps because a superior could not be traced. In that latter case it would indeed be the existence of the obligation to obtain a consent which was impeding the proposed use of the land. In a sense that must always be the case. Where an obligation is to obtain a consent, then if that has not been obtained, for whatever reason, even if it is because it has not been sought, the use of the land is impeded by the need to obtain it. Some significance must be attached to the use of the word 'impede' rather than 'prevent', for while an actual refusal of consent would always prevent a proposed use of land, that use could be regarded as impeded by something less, such as by the need to obtain consent."

In *Orsi v. McCallum*[26] the tribunal refused an application to vary a servitude right of access over which an ashbin shelter had been

---

[23] *British Bakeries (Scotland) Ltd v. City of Edinburgh District Council*, 1990 S.L.T. (Lands Tr.) 33 at 37B. See *Re Reynold's Application* (1987) 54 P. & C.R. 121 for the discharge in England of an obligation to obtain prior approval for plans.

[24] 1992 S.L.T. (Lands Tr.) 53 at 56I and 58E.

[25] 1990 S.L.T. (Lands Tr.) 33.

[26] 1980 S.L.T. (Lands Tr.) 2.

built, on the basis that the evidence that it could have been built elsewhere without obstructing the access was not disproved and so it could not be said that the obligation impeded the erection of the ashbin.

In *Irving v. John Dickie & Sons Ltd*[27] it emerged during the course of the hearing that the applicant might not have a right of access to the development subjects. In respect that this lack of access impeded the proposed reasonable use and so the application might have to be refused, the tribunal continued the application giving the applicant an opportunity to obtain a grant of access and to lodge a draft of the agreed deed with the tribunal prior to the application being determined.

In *MacDonald v. Stornoway Trust*[28] the tribunal considered that the fact that the proposed conversion of a croft house into a public house was unviable meant that it was the unviability which would prevent the conversion rather than the land obligation.

In contrast, in *Smith v. Strathkelvin District Council*[29] the tribunal, upheld on appeal, took a practical approach to a restriction in title. It held that a declaration in the feu contract which was enforceable by the superior, but not by a benefited proprietor with a *jus quaesitum tertio*, which might have impeded the development, did not in fact impede it, because the superior was also the council. The First Division said:

"That is plainly a restriction which is conceived in the interests of the superior alone and which could never be enforced, say, by Mrs Smith. But, as we have mentioned already, the council acquired the superiority in 1974. Therefore at present— whatever might be the position if the council were no longer the superiors—as a practical matter the declaration is not an impediment of the kind which faced the owners of the ice rink in the *Murrayfield* case. As we understand the position, the council are anxious to sell the land to developers who wish to build seven houses in terms of the planning application which Strathkelvin District Council granted to them. Since this is what the council want to happen, they will obviously not invoke the declaration to prevent it."

The court recognised that the existence of the declaration might cause difficulties for the council in granting title to a purchaser, but as that issue was not before the court, no opinion was expressed on the point.

[27] August 31, 1995; LTS/LO/94/17.
[28] 1987 S.L.T. 240 at 242F.
[29] 1997 S.C. 98 at 102B–E.

Significant factors

6–23   While the tribunal has to have regard to all the relevant circumstances, there has been a trend to show that certain factors are of particular significance for the tribunal in reaching a decision on whether or not to allow a discharge or variation on ground (c).

Purpose of the obligation

6–24   The tribunal will consider the reasons for which the restrictions were imposed in the first place and then the relevance of the restriction to the particular area of land at the present time.[30]

In *Tully v. Armstrong*[31] an obligation to build only one house on a building site was imposed to protect the disponer's veterinary and kennel business from complaints of noise by too many neighbouring houses. There had been a number of complaints. The applicant sought a variation to allow another house to be built on his garden ground. While the tribunal considered this to be reasonable in itself, it took into account the original aim of the obligation and held that it was not a reasonable use of land to allow another house to be built and therefore possibly another complainer about the kennel business.

Changed social circumstances

6–25   The tribunal will have regard to changes in social circumstances. One of the most common applications relates either to the division of a large house into a number of flats or the building of an additional house or houses in a large garden.

> "Changed social circumstances, due to lack of domestic staff and increased costs of upkeep have caused many large houses, like the present one, to be subdivided. For the same reason many gardens nowadays have become too large for convenient upkeep and are sometimes reasonably able to accommodate another dwelling-house without significant harm to local amenity and still leaving the original house with a more manageable garden."[32]

The tribunal has noted that a common thread running through many of its decisions is that in principle the erection of a dwelling-house is a reasonable use of land, but each case has to be decided in the circumstances of the particular facts.[33]

---

[30] *Biggerstaff v. SSPCA*, October 25, 1990; LTS/LO/1990/17.
[31] 1990 S.L.T. (Lands Tr.) 42.
[32] *Scott v. Fulton*, 1982 S.L.T. (Lands Tr.) 18 at 19.
[33] *Thomson v. Birch*, May 31, 1994; LTS/LO/1993/42.

Social need for the proposed use

The tribunal will have regard to the social need for the proposed **6–26** use and may take into account any changes from the "social conditions operating, when they were created".[34] However good or desirable the social need is, it has to be considered in the context of the whole circumstances of the particular application site.[35]

In *Main v. Lord Doune*[36] the tribunal granted an application under ground (c) because it held it proved "that a new nursery school situated within the Moray Feu would help to fulfil a social need". Changes in social drinking habits, whereby tourists now expected to be able to buy a drink at hotels or off-sales, have led to the discharge of restrictions against selling alcohol.[37] In *Sinclair v. Gillon*,[38] the fact that a proposed variation to allow a coffee house which "would also doubtless fulfil the needs of local office staff who are now the main users of houses in the street" weighed with the tribunal in granting an application. In *Smith v. Taylor*[39] the tribunal had regard to "a continuing demand for modern hotel accommodation" and the fact that "People using hotels nowadays, expect licensed facilities" in granting a variation permitting an unlicensed boarding house to be upgraded to a licensed hotel. In *Church of Scotland General Trustees v. Fraser*[40] the linking of three charges because of changes in church attendance was considered as a change in social circumstances warranting the discharge of an obligation that a manse and church were to be used for church purposes only.

Planning permission, licences, etc.

The tribunal can have regard to whether or not planning **6–27** permission has been granted, the local plan and local planning policies[41] as part of "all the circumstances" in section 1(3).

---

[34] *Main v. Lord Doune*, 1972 S.L.T. (Lands Tr.) 14 at 18; *Manz v. Butter's Trs*, 1973 S.L.T. (Lands Tr.) 2 at 3.
[35] *Lothian Regional Council v. George Wimpey & Co. Ltd*, 1985 S.L.T. (Lands Tr.) 2 at 3.
[36] above at 18.
[37] *Manz v. Butter's Trs*, above; *Owen v. Mackenzie*, 1974 S.L.T. (Lands Tr.) 11.
[38] 1974 S.L.T. (Lands Tr.) 18.
[39] 1972 S.L.T. (Lands Tr.) 34 at 36.
[40] January 8, 1985; LTS/LO/1984/24.
[41] *Scott v. Wilson*, May 19, 1992; LTS/LO/1991/7 (reported 1993 S.L.T. (Lands Tr.) 51 on another point), where the tribunal had regard to the local authority's "window development envelope" concept, that infilling would be permitted within envelopes drawn round certain villages; *Merchant Company Education Board v. Bailey*, October 12, 1995; LTS/LO/94/51, where regard had to local planning policy.

Although section 84(1B) of the 1925 Act made specific provision for the English tribunal to "take into account the development plan and any declared or ascertainable pattern for the grant or refusal of planning permissions in the relevant area" and the 1970 Act does not make similar provision, the tribunal does take such issues into consideration, but considers that its discretion "is not precisely a function of town planning".[42]

The tribunal will not entertain a challenge to the validity of a planning permission. In *Rae v. Anderson*[43] where the validity of the permission was challenged on the grounds of failure to serve on neighbours and therefore that the tribunal should not take it into account, the tribunal said:

> "[I]t is not . . . for the Tribunal to decide whether a grant of planning permission has been lawfully made or otherwise".[44]

Although not determinative, the fact that planning permission has been granted for the proposal is usually taken as an indicator that the proposed use is reasonable, although the tribunal does take into account the fact that planners do not have regard to the contractual and other private arrangements between the parties.[45] Similarly, in England, the grant of planning permission is not decisive of whether a covenant restricting development should be lifted and does not prevent the Lands Tribunal from exercising its discretion to refuse to lift a restriction.[46]

In considering what weight to give to a planning permission, the tribunal will have regard to the circumstances in which it was granted. It has said:

> "[I]t is still open to the Tribunal to consider the circumstances in which it was granted, in order to assess what weight should be attached to it when deciding whether the proposed use of the land is reasonable in the context of private land obligations"[47]

In *Cunninghame District Council v. Fforde*[48] the tribunal took into account that the application for planning permission had not

---

[42] *McArthur v. Mahoney*, 1975 S.L.T. (Lands Tr.) 2 at 7.

[43] August 14, 1992; LTS/LO/1991/57.

[44] See ss. 237 and 238 of the Town and Country Planning (Scotland) Act 1997, which impose a six-week time-limit in which challenges to any planning permission, etc., have to be made: see *Pollock v. Secretary of State for Scotland*, 1993 S.L.T. 1173.

[45] *Solway Cedar Ltd v. Hendry*, 1972 S.L.T. (Lands Tr.) 42 at 45.

[46] *Gilbert v. Spoor* [1983] Ch. 27.

[47] *Noble v. Viscount Reidhaven*, June 17, 1991; LTS/LO/1989/98, where the tribunal took into account that the voting was two to two and the permission granted on the chairman's casting vote against the planning officer's advice and where there was a lot of local opposition.

[48] December 24, 1992; LTS/LO/1992/8.

been advertised so that the planners could not have known the weight of local opposition and the fact that the committee vote for the grant was divided eight to seven. In *Thomson v. Birch*[49] the tribunal noted and gave weight to the fact that the planning authority had carefully looked at the whole proposal in the full knowledge of the conservation area, the listed status of the street and that the objectors' views had been made clear to it. In *Walker v. Wilson*[50] the tribunal considered it relevant that the planning application had been granted on appeal contrary to the wishes of the planning authority and thus the permission "was less persuasive than normal".

The tribunal has recognised that its function is to have regard to the private rights and wishes of neighbouring proprietors because planning control is unconcerned with such rights and in general such proprietors have no *locus* in a planning application.[51]

It is of concern to the tribunal that public planning controls might not involve architectural planning at all, and might in practice lead neither to the creation nor conservation of fine townscapes.[52]

In *Bolton v. Aberdeen Corporation*[53] where the corporation was both superior and planning authority, the tribunal recognised that:

"In practice it might indeed have been more difficult for the Corporation to 'speak with two voices' and to try and maintain before the Tribunal that use as a betting shop was unreasonable, if their own planning committee had already granted planning permission for the desired change of use. We have to add, however, that it would still be technically open to them as proprietors to maintain the restriction—even if planning permission had been granted by the Secretary of State himself. Small burghs in Scotland are not local planning authorities and it may be their only means of control. As proprietors, just like any other private proprietor, they would be exercising private rights, which may involve benefits not in practice taken into account under public planning, and moreover be able to control 'permitted development' which does not fall under statutory control at all. Parliament has not yet indicated that control of a particular environment may not continue to be exercised (in supplement of public control) by private obligation. It has only provided that if it is so exercised such exercise must now be reasonable."

---

[49] May 31, 1994; LTS/LO/1993/42.
[50] May 4, 1990; LTS/LO/1989/57.
[51] *Crombie v. Heriot's Trs*, 1972 S.L.T. (Lands Tr.) 40 at 42.
[52] *Main v. Lord Doune*, 1972 S.L.T. (Lands Tr.) 14 at 19.
[53] 1972 S.L.T. (Lands Tr.) 26 at 29.

The tribunal has outlined its approach in *Cameron v. Stirling*[54]:

"The district planning authority has of course only to be guided by local planning considerations; whereas the tribunal have to consider broadly whether local controls by private land obligation are being unreasonably exercised or should otherwise be changed by discharge or variation orders. But Parliament, when passing the 1970 Act, obviously did not intend public planning totally to oust local environmental control by land obligations which are not infrequently used even by local authorities themselves in their proprietary capacity: see *Bolton v. Aberdeen Corporation*, 1972 SLT (Lands Tr.) 26, for they are more easily controllable as indeed are agreements made under s. 50 of the Town and Country Planning (Scotland) Act 1972."

Where a land obligation was imposed by a local authority prior to the passing of the Planning Acts, but for planning purposes, then the grant of planning permission by the local authority makes it difficult to envisage circumstances in which it remains reasonable to enforce the condition.[55]

A similar presumption does not arise where planning permission is not required by reason of provision in the Planning Acts or that it is a permitted development, because:

"That . . . cannot be treated as evidence that a proposed use of land is reasonable. It cannot be assumed that the exemption from the need to apply for planning permission is because of a presumption that adding to a house by less than a prescribed percentage is always to be regarded as constituting a reasonable use of land. The exemption may well be because to require the full planning procedure to be followed in the case of minor additions would be costly and impractical. However that may be, the result in the case of a permitted development is that a planning authority has never had to come to a decision on its merits. If it had been required to come to such a decision, planning permission might not have been granted."[56]

The tribunal is concerned that its jurisdiction is to consider whether private rights should be discharged or varied and that the tribunal should not be treated as a forum for appeal against a planning decision. The tribunal has said:

[54] 1988 S.L.T. (Lands Tr.) 18 at 20K.
[55] *British Bakeries (Scotland) Ltd v. City of Edinburgh District Council*, 1990 S.L.T. (Lands Tr.) 33 at 34J.
[56] *Stoddart v. Glendinning*, 1993 S.L.T. (Lands Tr.) 12 at 17A.

"[I]t cannot have been the intention of Parliament that the procedures of the 1970 Act should be used in such a way as to enable members of the public to, in effect, appeal to the tribunal against any decision of the planning authority, with which they, in the public interest, disagree".[57]

The distinction usually arises where affected, rather than benefited, proprietors seek to involve the tribunal in reviewing a grant of planning permission, where a land obligation remains enforceable and the benefited proprietor does not enter process. The tribunal will be careful to exclude evidence or submissions which relate to the public interest, rather than to the private rights of benefited or affected proprietors.

In some circumstances, particularly where the development is small, the tribunal, in granting a discharge of a land obligation, will give the benefited proprietor some continuing "planning" control over the development. The tribunal has recognised, in accordance with the approach outlined in *Bolton v. Aberdeen Corporation*, that:

"The problem is, therefore, one of preserving a measure of private control over a fine residential neighbourhood under circumstances which have altered since the original feuing obligations were imposed—namely a situation in which it is difficult to maintain such large gardens. Statutory planning control, however, cannot be solely relied upon for it is unconcerned with the rights and wishes of the neighbouring proprietors who have no locus in any planning application."[58]

In *Robinson v. Hamilton*[59] the tribunal granted a discharge of the restriction against further building without consent, by allowing a single dwelling-house to be constructed "subject to its plans and elevations, before construction, being agreed in writing by the" benefited proprietor. The tribunal made it clear that if agreement still cannot be reached the applicant may make a further application to the tribunal for variation of the varied order.[60]

Similarly, in applications to discharge or vary a land obligation against the use of premises for the sale of alcoholic liquor, the fact that a licence has been granted[61] is taken as a pointer that the proposed use is reasonable.[62] In *Inehaze Ltd*[63] the tribunal found

[57] *T & I Consultants Ltd v. Cullion*, 1998 Hous. L.R. 9.
[58] *Crombie v. George Heriot's Trust*, 1972 S.L.T. (Lands Tr.) 40 at 42.
[59] 1974 S.L.T. (Lands Tr.) 2.
[60] *Crombie v. George Heriot's Trust*, 1972 S.L.T. (Lands Tr.) 40 at 42.
[61] *e.g.* under the Licensing (Scotland) Act 1976 or the Civic Government (Scotland) Act 1982.
[62] *Owen v. Mackenzie*, 1974 S.L.T. (Lands Tr.) 11 at 12; *MacDonald v. Stornoway Trust*, 1987 S.L.T. 240 at 241H.
[63] October 6, 1995; LTS/LO/95/8.

that there were other licensed premises in the street and that
therefore it was reasonable to vary the prohibition against using
the premises for the sale of alcohol. The tribunal commented that
the fact that the licensing board might refuse an application on the
ground of overprovision[64] "need have no impact on the tribunal's
decision in this case".

In *Pickford v. Young*[65] in considering whether to discharge an
obligation preventing a hotel from selling alcohol, the tribunal
commented that a "licensing court is not . . . so concerned with
amenity questions and accordingly the question of control by
private land obligation . . . becomes a matter of particular importance". That observation must now be treated with caution as the
current Licensing Acts require a licensing board to have regard to
amenity.[66]

Objections

Amenity

6–28   Objections usually relate to harm to the amenity of the area, and
often include complaints about change in character of the neighbourhood, increased noise, traffic (including parking), smell, loss of
privacy and loss of a view. In England it has been held
that loss of view, not from the property itself, but from nearby, can
be part of the loss of amenity, particularly in regard to the amenity
of the estate of which the property is part.[67]

Many of the objections founded on amenity can be overcome or
alleviated by the imposition of additional or substitutional conditions under section 1(5).[68]

In considering amenity issues "It is legitimate . . . to take into
account personal tastes and predilections—provided they are
reasonable".[69]

---

[64] s. 17(1)(d) of the Licensing (Scotland) Act 1976.

[65] 1975 S.L.T. (Lands Tr.) 17.

[66] *e.g.* s. 17(1)(b) of the Licensing (Scotland) Act 1976; Betting, Gaming and
Lotteries Act 1963 (c. 2), Sched. 1, para. 19 (b)(i); Civic Government (Scotland)
Act 1982, Sched. 1, para. 5(3)(c)(i); and *Leisure Inns Ltd v. Perth & Kinross District
Licensing Board*, 1991 S.C. 224, where the court held that when considering
"location" under those provisions that amenity was a relevant consideration.

[67] *Gilbert v. Spoor* [1983] Ch. 27, albeit that the case turned on the interpretation
of s. 84(1A) and whether the view from near the land was "a practical benefit" said
to touch or concern the land.

[68] See below, paras 8–04 to 8–06.

[69] *Bolton v. Aberdeen Corporation*, 1972 S.L.T. (Lands Tr.) 26 at 30, following
Re Chandler's Application (1958) 9 P. & C.R. 512 and *Re Munday's Application*
[1953] 7 P. & C.R. 130.

The tribunal recognises that private planning control of the amenity remains a relevant consideration because:

"Parliament has not yet indicated that control of a particular environment may not continue to be exercised (in supplement of public control) by private obligation. It has only provided that if it is so exercised such control must now be reasonable."[70]

This aspect of private control is sometimes given effect to by allowing a discharge or variation to permit an additional house to be built on garden ground, subject to giving the benefited proprietors a right to see and approve the plans for new houses.[71]

Architectural harmony of an area may be an aspect of amenity. In *Stoddart v. Glendinning*[72] it was said of the objectors that:

"there is a concern shared by all of the objectors that the proposed development would cause injury to the visual amenity of St Ninian's Road. The objectors value what they consider to be the architectural harmony represented by the three blocks of symmetrical buildings. The tribunal accept that various aspects of amenity in the area may be important to a proprietor in St Ninian's Road. Although he may not be able to see the house at no 1 from inside his own house, the overall appearance of the road in which he lives may still be important to him, and the value of his interest in land may be affected by any damage to its appearance".

Where the proposed building of two houses on an area that had to be maintained as open space "would not be out of character with the existing housing any more than in any other local areas where modern houses have been built on gap sites and where existing gardens have become too large" the development was permitted.[73]

The residential character of an area, where the proposal involves a change to a non-residential use, is usually a major consideration in questions of amenity. Such considerations have influenced the decisions in applications to allow large houses to be used as

---

[70] *Bolton v. Aberdeen Corporation*, above, at 29.
[71] *Crombie v. George Heriot's Trust*, 1972 S.L.T. (Lands Tr.) 40; *Robinson v. Hamilton*, 1974 S.L.T. (Lands Tr.) 2.
[72] 1993 S.L.T. (Lands Tr.) 12 at 15F.
[73] *Gorrie and Banks Ltd v. Musselburgh Town Council*, 1974 S.L.T. (Lands Tr.) 5 at 8.

licensed hotels or guest houses.[74] Sometimes the tribunal will find that "the neighbourhood . . . is no longer a quiet residential area with a distinctive character of its own".[75]

Privacy can be an important aspect of amenity and the tribunal will take into account whether or not the proposals will lead to one property overlooking another.[76]

So will a good view or aspect, particularly as this is something that the planners do not have to take into account. In refusing to discharge an obligation to keep land as garden or ornamental ground or as a pleasure ground, whose principal purpose was to safeguard the outlook of a number of houses, the tribunal said:

> "The loss of a view enjoyed by residents on one side of a street as a result of housebuilding on the other side is not relevant to a planning judgment as to the acceptability of the proposal. But where a private land obligation affords a right to that view to those residents, then any assessment of the reasonableness of the proposed development in the context of s. 1(3)(c) of the Act must take account of the loss of view, even if planning permission has already been granted."[77]

[74] *Smith v. Taylor*, 1972 S.L.T. (Lands Tr.) 34 (potential noise, smell, cars parking gave compensation, but as character of neighbourhood already lost the application granted); *Morris v. Feuars of Waverley Park*, 1973 S.L.T. (Lands Tr.) 6 (application granted as the proposed use as guest house would not detract from residential character of neighbourhood); *Leney v. Craig*, 1982 S.L.T. (Lands Tr.) 9 at 11 (extra traffic, noise at night, floodlighting, noxious fumes—application granted subject to conditions to protect against loss of amenity); *Anderson v. Trotter*, August 12, 1997; LTS/LO/1996/46 (noise from children in proposed nursery, traffic caused by drop-off and collection—application refused).

[75] *Leney v. Craig*, above, at 11.

[76] *Ramsay v. Holmes*, 1992 S.L.T. (Lands Tr.) 53 at 55L; *Stoddart v. Glendinning*, 1993 S.L.T. (Lands Tr.) 12 at 15H and 17F.

[77] *Miller Group Ltd v. Gardner's Exrs*, 1992 S.L.T. (Lands Tr.) 62 at 68C.

CHAPTER 7

COMPENSATION

General

Section 1(4) of the 1970 Act provides that compensation to be **7-01** paid to a benefited proprietor on the variation or discharge of any land obligation. It provides:

> "(4) An order varying or discharging a land obligation under this section may direct the applicant to pay, to any person who in relation to that obligation is a benefited proprietor, such sum as the Lands Tribunal may think it just to award under one, but not both, of the following heads—
> (i) a sum to compensate for any substantial loss or disadvantage suffered by the proprietor as such benefited proprietor in consequence of the variation or discharge; or
> (ii) a sum to make up for any effect which the obligation produced, at the time when it was imposed, in reducing the consideration then paid or made payable for the interest in land affected by it;
> but the Tribunal may refuse to vary or discharge a land obligation on the ground specified in subsection (3) (c) of this section if they are of the opinion that, due to exceptional circumstances related to amenity or otherwise, money would not be an adequate compensation for any loss or disadvantage which a benefited proprietor would suffer from the variation or discharge."

The important points to note are that:

(1) the tribunal has a discretion as to whether or not a direction to pay compensation should be given;
(2) no guidance is given on the assessment of the sums, which has to be one that the tribunal "may think it just to award";
(3) the award may be made under one or other, but not **both**, of the relevant heads; and

(4) the tribunal has a discretion to refuse to vary or discharge a land obligation, but only under ground (c), if in exceptional circumstances it considers that money would not be an adequate compensation.

It is competent to make the claim in the alternative, under both section 1(4)(i) and 1(4)(ii).[1]

English provision

7–02   Section 84(1) of the 1925 Act provides:

"[A]n order discharging or modifying a restriction under this subsection may direct the applicant to pay to any person entitled to the benefit of the restriction such sum by way of consideration as the Tribunal may think it just to award under one, but not both, of the following heads, that is to say, either—
(i) a sum to make up for any loss or disadvantage suffered by that person in consequence of the discharge or modification; or
(ii) a sum to make up for any effect which the restriction had, at the time when it was imposed, in reducing the consideration then received for the land affected by it."

The provision is very similar to that found in section 1(4) of the 1970 Act, but it should be noted that the 1970 Act provides for compensation "to the proprietor as such benefited proprietor", which is a narrower class than those entitled to compensation in England. In England the class of person entitled to compensation is "any person entitled to the benefit of the restriction", thus allowing compensation to be paid for personal loss of amenity or other advantage even if not strictly related to the land itself.

Further, sub-head (i) in Scotland refers to "substantial" loss and disadvantage.

The compensation provisions in England have to be read against the provision in section 84(1A) that a modification or discharge under section 84(1)(aa) (impede some reasonable user, *e.g.* ground (c) equivalent) may be granted only if "money will be an adequate compensation for the loss or disadvantage (if any) ".

Right to claim compensation

7–03   The right to a payment of compensation is vested in "any person who in relation to that obligation is a benefited proprietor". It is therefore only the benefited proprietor who is entitled to compensation. In respect of any land obligation, there may be more than

---

[1] *Laing v. Cleghorn Housing Association Ltd*, April 26, 1991; LTS/LO/1987/15 & 52–60.

one benefited proprietor, including, for example, a superior and neighbouring proprietors with a *jus quaesitum tertio*.

An affected person may well suffer a disadvantage by reason of the discharge or variation of a land obligation but is not entitled to claim compensation. In *Manz v. Butter's Trs*[2] a hotel sought the removal of a land obligation providing that the hotel was to be used as a temperance hotel. While the tribunal noted that "there will probably be a financial disadvantage to" a neighbouring hotel without such a restriction, if the restriction was discharged, it commented that the neighbouring hotel "have no locus in the present proceedings to claim compensation".[3]

Tribunal's discretion

It is clear that the tribunal has a discretion in that it "may direct **7-04** the applicant to pay". In the exercise of this discretion, and the fact that the award is to be "just", the tribunal may take into account the whole circumstances surrounding the application and the claim for compensation.

In *Re Bradley Clare Estates Ltd's Application*[4] the Lands Tribunal held that where the benefited proprietor had contributed to the changes in the neighbourhood, which rendered a covenant obsolete, no compensation should be due. In that case there was a covenant restricting land use to dwelling-houses, but in 1937 there had been a permission to use one building as a doctors' surgery. The surgery opposed a further variation of the covenant and were refused compensation on the grounds that:

> "the relevant restrictions are obsolete, the objectors have caused or contributed to that state of affairs, and such injury is not of the kind which the restrictions are intended to prevent".

Quantification of any award

There are no statutory guidelines on how compensation should **7-05** be assessed, as is to be found, for example, in the six rules for statutory compensation for compulsory acquisition.[5] The tribunal is directed to order "such sum as the Lands Tribunal may think it just to award".

In considering the similar wording in section 84(1) of the 1925 Act, Lord Denning M.R. observed[6]:

---

[2] 1973 S.L.T. (Lands Tr.) 2.
[3] *ibid*. at 4.
[4] (1988) 55 P. & C.R. 126 at 132.
[5] s. 12 of the Land Compensation (Scotland) Act 1963 (as amended).
[6] *SJC Construction Co Ltd v. Sutton London Borough Council* (1975) 29 P. & C.R. 322 at 326.

"[W]hat is the basis or proper basis of compensation? It is simply to make up 'for [the] loss or disadvantage suffered' by the borough council. There is no method prescribed by the Act by which it is to be assessed; it is essentially a question of quantum. It is, however, to be assessed for loss of amenities, loss of view and so forth, which are things which it is hard to assess in terms of money. It is similar to compensation for pain and suffering, which cannot be translated into money terms; the courts have, therefore, to arrive at conventional sums which they award".

Similarly, Dillon L.J. said[7]:

"But there is no hard and fast formula which governs what sum should be awarded by way of compensation for loss or disadvantage occasioned by the modification of a restriction".

Scamell[8] has suggested that these cases lead to the conclusion that the tribunal should: (1) adopt a formal valuation (*e.g.* reduction of value) if there is one; or (2) if the compensation "does not lend itself to any precise method of valuation" a conventional sum should be awarded; or (3) where there is more than one method of valuation, the tribunal has a discretion to adopt the one it considers "just" in the circumstances.

The English approach has to be treated with caution because the right to compensation is not restricted to the proprietor "as such benefited proprietor". In England compensation is awarded for personal loss. As Lord Denning noted, compensation may be payable for loss of amenity, even if this does not relate to any loss of value, because "it is similar to compensation for pain and suffering".

Section 1(4)(i): substantial loss or damage

7–06   The first ground upon which compensation may be claimed is for "any substantial loss or disadvantage suffered by the proprietor as such benefited proprietor in consequence of the variation or discharge".

Any "substantial loss or disadvantage" does not include the right to extract a fee for waiver of any land obligation or to share in the released development value.[9]

---

[7] *Stockport Metropolitan Borough Council v. Alwiyah Developments* (1986) 52 P. & C.R. 278 at 285.

[8] Scammell, p. 446.

[9] See below, para. 7–18.

A claim under section 1(4)(i) may be made each time a land obligation is varied or discharged in part.[10] This is in contrast to a claim under section 1(4)(ii) where the claim may be made only once.

The words "in consequence" makes it clear that the loss must be **7–07** caused by the variation and discharge. It "is consequential harm to the proprietary interest caused by the discharge of the land obligation which requires to be compensated".[11] Where there is no causal link a claim for compensation will be rejected.[12]

In *Re Bennett's and Tamarlin Ltd's Application*[13] the President of the tribunal indicated that he might have accepted a claim for professional costs incurred in considering the request for approval of the applicant's proposals prior to the tribunal application being made. This has been criticised on the basis that such costs could not have been incurred "in consequence" of the variation or discharge.[14]

Unless a "substantial" loss or disadvantage can be proved, the **7–08** tribunal will not award compensation under this head.[15] The tribunal "are thus directed to disregard insubstantial harm to" a benefited proprietor's interests.[16] What is "substantial" will depend on relative values. In *Re Gaffney's Application*[17] the English tribunal said:

"A depreciation of £1,500 in the value of a property worth £5,000 is not to be compared in degree with the same amount payable in the case of a property worth £45,000. In one case the loss or disadvantage represents 30 per cent of the value of the whole; the value or advantage is clearly substantial. In the other case the proportion is 3.5 per cent; I do not consider that a value or advantage expressed in this way can be said to be substantial."

The claim relates to the loss to the owner of the land and not **7–09** any loss to the owner as an individual. The fact that compensation is restricted to the "proprietor as such benefited proprietor"

---

[10] *MacDonald v. Abbotshall Evanton Ltd*, February 16, 1989; LTS/LO/1988/89.
[11] *United Auctions (Scotland) Ltd v. British Railways Board*, 1991 S.L.T. (Lands Tr.) 71 at 78L.
[12] *Devlin v. Conn*, 1972 S.L.T. (Lands Tr.) 11 at 14.
[13] (1987) 54 P. & C.R. 378.
[14] Scammell, pp. 456–457.
[15] *Main v. Doune*, 1972 S.L.T. (Lands Tr.) 14 at 19; *Sinclair v. Gillon*, 1974 S.L.T. (Lands Tr.) 18 at 21.
[16] *Ness v. Shannon*, 1998 S.L.T. (Lands Tr.) 13 at 16.
[17] (1974) 35 P. & C.R. 440 at 442.

excludes the approach taken in England to compensate "any person entitled to the benefit",[18] where an individual can get compensation for the loss of his personal amenities, whether or not this affects the value of the property.[19]

7–10   In general, the tribunal will approach the value of this loss on the basis of the depreciation in the value of the subjects by reason of the discharge or variation of the land obligation.[20]

> "The practice has been to assess compensation under section 1(4)(i) on the basis of 'before and after' valuation of the benefited land and not by reference to any increment in the value of the burdened land."[21]

7–11   If a superior or benefited proprietor owns adjoining land, the value of which will be significantly reduced by the development permitted by the variation or discharge, the tribunal has said that might be a ground of claim.[22] In *McVey v. Glasgow Corporation*[23] the tribunal rejected an "extreme" argument by counsel for the applicants and affirmed this proposition, saying:

> "that s. 1 (4) (i) could only refer to loss to the benefited proprietor arising directly in connection with the subjects of the application. In this connection it has to be kept in view that s. 1 (4) (i) is not concerned only with feudal superiors but that compensation may be awarded to any benefited proprietor as defined in s. 1 (6) in respect of the discharge or variation of any land obligation however constituted, e.g., to the seller of land by an absolute disposition creating enforceable land obligations (or his successor); to a landlord under a

---

[18] 1925 Act, s. 84(1).

[19] *e.g.* Re Kershaw's Application (1975) 31 P. & C.R. 187: "consumer surplus" that is the loss peculiar to the occupier of the house, the mere alteration of the environment"; *Re Gaffney's Application* (1974) 35 P. & C.R. 440 (compensation included depreciation and disturbance); *Stockport Metropolitan Borough Council v. Alwiyah Developments* (1986) 52 P. & C.R. 278 (compensation awarded because value of borough's neighbouring property depreciated by the proposed development).

[20] *e.g. Smith v. Taylor*, 1972 S.L.T. (Lands Tr.) 34, where compensation was assessed on the basis of the depreciation in value of neighbouring residential houses, where the discharge allowed one of the houses to be used as a licensed hotel.

[21] *Gardner v. Pickard*, April 24, 1992; LTS/LO/1991/56, citing *Co-operative Wholesale Society v. Usher's Brewery*, 1975 S.L.T. (Lands Tr.) 9 and *Robertson v. Church of Scotland General Trustees*, 1976 S.L.T. (Lands Tr.) 11.

[22] *McVey v. Glasgow Corporation*, 1973 S.L.T. (Lands Tr.) 15 at 17; *Harris v. Douglass*, 1993 S.L.T. (Lands Tr.) 56 at 59L; *United Auctions (Scotland) Ltd v. British Railways Board*, 1991 S.L.T. (Lands Tr.) 71 at 78I. See *Stockport Metropolitan Borough Council v. Alwiyah Developments* (1986) 52 P. & C.R. 278.

[23] 1973 S.L.T. (Lands Tr.) 14 at 17.

long lease; or to the dominant proprietor in benefit of a right of servitude. It is accordingly clear that one kind of loss contemplated under s. 1 (4) (i) may be loss affecting the rights of proprietors, including superiors, qua proprietors of subjects other than the subject of the application in their capacities as benefited proprietors".

Any award of compensation is strictly related to loss or disadvantage suffered in terms of the Act, and any suggestion of solatium or a payment for waiver is rigidly excluded.[24] **7–12**

"The words 'as such benefited proprietor' appearing in the subsection appear to indicate that compensation is to be awarded in respect of loss caused to an objector as owner of the dominant tenement."[25]

In *Co-operative Wholesale Society v. Usher's Brewery*, where the tribunal had regard to the turnover of licensed premises in valuing them, it made it clear that:

"In estimating compensation in this case, however, we are not to be taken as endeavouring to compensate the objectors for loss of trade so much as for depreciation in the value of the dominant tenement."[26]

In *United Auctions (Scotland) Ltd v. British Railways Board*,[27] having discharged an obligation to use land only as an auction mart, the tribunal, in considering the valuation of the benefited proprietor's interest, said:

"We are therefore obliged to consider the value of the benefited proprietors' interest in their own land on a 'before' and 'after' basis, with and without the relevant restriction on use of the adjoining land to an auction mart."

In that case the tribunal concluded that there had been no consequential diminution in value.

The tribunal has rejected the proposition that evidence of the **7–13** diminution in value of subjects by reason of a variation or discharge of a land obligation can be cross-checked by reference to the *Stokes v. Cambridge*[28] ransom strip valuation method, saying

---

[24] *Ness v. Shannon*, 1998 S.L.T. (Lands Tr.) 13 at 16; *Henderson v. Mansell*, November 9, 1993; LTS/LO/1992/41. As noted above, the situation is different in England, where solatium-type or disturbance claims are allowed.
[25] *Co-operative Wholesale Society v. Ushers Brewery*, 1975 S.L.T. (Lands Tr.) 9 at 14.
[26] *ibid*. at 14.
[27] 1991 S.L.T. (Lands Tr.) 71 at 79B.
[28] *Stokes v. Cambridge Corporation* (1961) 13 P. & C.R. 77.

that the *Stokes* approach sought to maximise the value to be acquired from the ransom strip, whereas the "before and after" method of valuation sought to minimise the difference.[29]

7–14 Compensation has to be assessed by reference to the overall potential loss of amenity or other benefit by the proposed development, in comparison with any possible alternative developments which could take place without breaching the land obligation and for which there could have been no compensation.[30]

7–15 Where a section 1(5) additional or substitutional provision is imposed, this has to be taken into account. In *Leney v. Craig*[31] the tribunal agreed:

> "that the proper approach to this question was to consider the diminution in value to each of these houses if the licensed hotel were to be permitted and each house were now to be exposed for sale on the open market. We agree with this 'injurious affection' approach which involves a 'before' and 'after' valuation as at the present date. There must also, however, be taken into account the remedial conditions imposed under s. 1 (5) of the 1970 Act designed to lessen the resultant harm".

A similar approach has been adopted in compulsory purchase situations, where land subject to a restrictive covenant against building was compulsorily purchased and built upon. The court held that the proper measure of damages for breach of a restrictive covenant following compulsory purchase was the diminution in the value of the retained land and the compensation payable was limited to the diminution in value of the retained land and did not include the price that the owner of the retained land could have exacted for permitting the development.[32]

7–16 While it is generally advisable to lead expert evidence as to reduction in values, the tribunal has said:

> "It is not imperative for the objectors to lead the evidence of a professional witness to establish the fact of a reduction in value, where it is fully obvious from the other evidence and

---

[29] *Sillars' Exrs v. Farrimond*, May 8, 1991; LTS/LO/1989/25, where the tribunal awarded £2,000 to each of a number of houses valued at about £150,000 for diminution of value, where building was to be permitted on open ground behind the houses. The valuers considered that this open outlook had some value.

[30] *Elboramhor Ltd v. Brand*, October 4, 1990; LTS/LO/1989/97.

[31] 1982 S.L.T. (Lands Tr.) 9 at 13.

[32] *Wrotham Park Settled Estates v. Hertsmere Borough Council* (1993) 33 R.V.R. 56.

the inspection that substantial harm to the objectors' proprietory interests has been caused"[33]

particularly where levels of value are low and it would be difficult to distinguish a depreciation in market prices, even though there was a clear disadvantage.

The tribunal has left open for consideration whether a personal **7–17** loss or a disturbance claim unrelated to the heritage is competent under section 1(4)(i), although the tribunal would appear to doubt the competence of such claims.[34] A claim for inconvenience or disturbance over a limited period, for example while building works were undertaken, should qualify, because it is inconvenience that would be suffered by any proprietor of the land either as personal inconvenience or by a reduction in the sale or letting value during that year.

Similar claims have been allowed in England, although the analogous English provisions omit the words "as such benefited proprietor". In *Re Kershaw's Application*[35] the tribunal had regard to the fact that on the discharge of the restrictive covenant the occupier would suffer intense inconvenience for about a year, while building works were undertaken, but thereafter there would be a minor loss of amenity. The compensation appears to reflect this year's inconvenience.

Loss of a waiver payment

A problem which exercised the tribunal at an early stage was **7–18** whether the right to claim compensation "for any substantial loss or disadvantage" includes a right to claim compensation for the loss of the right to extract payment for a waiver or to claim for a share in the released development value.

The question first came before the tribunal in *McVey v. Glasgow Corporation*.[36] The facts of the case were that the applicants applied to the Lands Tribunal for discharge of certain land obligations under which the proprietor was required to use the two plots for a doctor's house and surgery only and was thus prevented from using any part thereof for a public house. The proposal was that the doctor's surgery be confined to a small part of both feus, leaving the remainder (the subject of the application) free for the

---

[33] *Ness v. Shannon*, 1978 S.L.T. (Lands Tr.) 13 at 16.
[34] *Co-operative Wholesale Society v. Ushers Brewery*, 1975 S.L.T. (Lands Tr.) 9 at 14.
[35] (1975) 31 P. & C.R. 187.
[36] 1973 S.L.T. (Lands Tr.) 15.

proposed development as a public house. The corporation, as local planning authority, granted planning permission for the proposed development and a public house licence had also been obtained. As superior, the corporation did not oppose the application on its merits but claimed compensation under section 1(4)(i) of the 1970 Act for substantial loss or disadvantage resulting from the discharge. It claimed that, as superior, it would be deprived of the right to obtain a substantial sum of money in return for granting a minute of waiver.

In considering this question the tribunal said:

"This brings us to the second main question . . . whether, in the event of a discharge or variation by the Tribunal under s. 1(3), compensation can be awarded under s. 1 (4) (i) in respect of the consequential loss of the power to obtain money. This is the sole remaining question in this case but it is a basic one. The contention of counsel for the Corporation is that it would be only just that the Tribunal should award such compensation in circumstances which are to some extent an innovation upon the position at common law, i.e., where there still subsisted an interest to enforce the particular land obligation. But the Tribunal is bound to follow the expressed intentions of Parliament as these are discernible from the wording of the Act. We have been unable to find any direction to us in the Act to award such compensation and are of opinion that compensation cannot be granted merely for deprivation of the power to obtain money."

The tribunal's reasoning was (1) that section 1(4)(i) related to all benefited proprietors and not just to superiors, so that the tribunal had to consider whether these other benefited proprietors might also be able to extract money; (2) that the compensation was for the loss or disadvantage "suffered by the proprietor *as such benefited proprietor*" and this indicated the necessity for there to be a direct relationship of damage to the removal of the restriction; (3) the reference to refusing a discharge under section 1(3)(c), where monetary compensation was inadequate for any loss or disadvantage, did not refer to the removal of a power to extract a monetary payment; (4) Parliament was unlikely to have intended that there should be a power to award compensation in relation to released development value; and (5) Parliament could not have intended the tribunal to speculate on what sum might have been extracted in any given circumstance.

7–19   Following the decision in the English case of *Re SJC Construction Company Ltd's Application*,[37] in which 50 per cent of the

[37] (1974) 28 P. & C.R. 200.

released development value was awarded as compensation by the Lands Tribunal after the modification of a restrictive covenant, the *McVey* decision was challenged in *Robertson v. Church of Scotland General Trustees*.[38]

The facts of *Re SJC Construction Company Ltd's Application* are different. In that case the council suffered loss and disadvantage by the discharge, because the amenity of neighbouring land owned by it was affected. The President of the tribunal valued this loss of amenity by reference to half of the development value. The Court of Appeal held that this method of valuing loss of amenity could not be challenged. It was not a case where the person in benefit of the restrictive covenant was paid a sum to represent the loss of bargaining power.

The proposition advanced by counsel for the trustees in *Robertson*:

"was that his clients, by virtue of the restrictive land obligation, had a right to control building on the strip of ground. Although they did not now wish in fact to prevent building, their right to impose a veto—if they so desired—was nevertheless a valuable asset which could be quantified in money terms. Prior to the Act, the resulting sum could have been obtained in exchange for a waiver of the obligation and he maintained that his clients' right to receive such payment had not been removed by the Act".

The tribunal distinguished the facts in *Re SJC Construction Company Ltd's Application* from those in *Robertson* and *McVey* and went on to uphold its decision. It said[39]:

"Their only interest (as in *McVey*) is in obtaining money in return for selling the superiority or granting a minute of waiver. It is unnecessary to repeat the detailed reasons already given by us in *McVey* for deciding that Parliament did not intend us to grant compensation for the removal of such a right. We would also add that *in West Lothian Co-operative Society Limited v. Ashdale Land & Property Company Ltd*, 1972 S.L.T. (Lands Tr.) 30, we decided that the 'benefit' to be taken into account under s. 1 (3) (b) of the 1970 Act did not include a right to extract money. The basic question is whether Parliament intended compensation to be awarded by the Tribunal for the removal of the right to extract money. We are clearly of the view that it did not."

[38] 1976 S.L.T. (Lands Tr.) 11.
[39] 1976 S.L.T. (Lands Tr.) 11 at 13.

The tribunal went on to reject a separate argument that the superiors owned a separate interest in the land and were entitled to share in the development value released, saying:

> "The Tribunal do not consider that any separate argument is open to superiors based on the feudal system and their ownership of the *dominium directum* as a separate estate in land. Such ownership never entitled superiors to share in any augmentation of value of the *dominium utile* unless the feu was terminated: Bell's Principles of the Law of Scotland, para. 737. The Tribunal cannot therefore agree with the objectors' averment already quoted, that they should be compensated for 'the loss of the development value of the feu vested in them by their control of building operations'. All that statement really means is that they were in a commanding position (just as would be any other benefited proprietor) to extract money in return for lifting their veto."

The tribunal found support for its approach from the judgment of Lord Denning M.R. in the *Re SJC Construction Company Ltd's Application* appeal[40] where, in commenting on *McVey*, the Master of the Rolls said:

> "The Lands Tribunal in Scotland held that a right or power to obtain money was not the subject of compensation under the statute, when no other loss or disadvantage had been involved. That seems to me entirely right. But I think the position would have been very different if there had been any loss or disadvantage, such as injury to the amenities or obstruction of view or increase in noise, or anything of that kind."

The Court of Appeal upheld the valuation of the compensation as 50 per cent of the released development value, but on the basis that this was a reasonable value of the "loss and disadvantage" to the council, being the loss of amenity to neighbouring properties.

7–20   Professor Halliday[41] criticised the decisions in *McVey* and *Robertson* because the right to require a waiver created a negotiating situation well recognised in practice. He said:

> "If Parliament had intended to expropriate superiors of a valuable right, based on contract and widely accepted in feudal theory and in daily practice, one would have expected that the legislation would have so provided in plain terms. It is at least

---

[40] *SJC Construction Co. Ltd v. London Borough of Sutton* (1975) 29 P. & C.R. 322 at 326.
[41] *The Conveyancing and Feudal Reform (Scotland) Act 1970* (2nd ed.), p. 41.

arguable that the object of the legislature was to ensure that the superior could not unfairly exploit the negotiating advantage".

McVey and *Robertson* were decided at a time when it was not competent to look at extrinsic material, such as *Hansard*, for guidance on the meaning of statutory provisions. Following *Pepper v. Hart*,[42] a court is entitled to have regard to Ministerial statements in *Hansard* as to the meaning of a particular statutory provision if there is ambiguity.

At a meeting of the Scottish Standing Committee on February 17, 1970 the Secretary of State for Scotland said[43]:

"The Clause . . . makes provision for the payment of compensation to superiors if the Tribunal considers this just. But—and underline this point—compensation will be payable only where the superior or his land suffers actual loss of disadvantage as a direct consequence of the variation or discharge as such, or where it is shown that the feuduty was originally fixed at a low level because of the restrictive condition imposed on the use of the land. It will not be paid simply because the superior has lost a potential source of profit arising from his exclusive right to relax a restrictive condition."

At a meeting of the Scottish Standing Committee on March 10, 1970 the Joint Under Secretary of State for Scotland, in discussing the meaning and effect of the proposed section 1(4)(i), said[44]:

"The superior's asset, the granting of the waiver, has been removed by the Tribunal, but this does not of itself lead to compensation . . . The Tribunal must look at it this way. . . . We are ensuring that the superior cannot base his estimate of loss on the sums that he has been able to obtain in the past in similar circumstances because on those occasions he has granted a minute of waiver. . . . It is not an asset to be compensated in that way. He will receive compensation only when he himself has suffered actual loss. . . . We are not intending to compensate superiors for the loss of the right which at present they hold to grant waivers, if they so choose."

Standing those Ministerial statements on the intention of section 1(4)(i), even if one were able to persuade the court that there was ambiguity in the subsection so as to allow it to look again at the

[42] [1993] A.C. 593.
[43] H.C. Standing Committees 1969–70 Vol. VI, Cols 6 and 7.
[44] *ibid.* Cols 74 and 75.

reasoning in *McVey* and *Robertson*, if it were to have regard to those Ministerial statements as the court is now entitled to do, it would undoubtedly uphold the decisions.

Having regard to these Ministerial statements, one may suspect that when the Lands Tribunal said in *McVey*[45]:

> "It seems unlikely that in this instance at least it can have been Parliament's intention that the Tribunal should be able to award compensation related to development value released"

and said in *Robertson*[46] that:

> "The basic question is whether Parliament intended compensation to be awarded by the Tribunal for the removal of the right to extract money. We are clearly of the view that it did not"

it may have been doing a little unofficial *Pepper v. Hart* consideration and perhaps took into account its knowledge of the debate that went on in 1970.

7-21   Subsequent English decisions, including the opinion of Lord Denning in *Re SJC Construction Company Ltd's Application*, have supported the Lands Tribunal for Scotland's approach that Parliament did not intend to provide for compensation for the loss of the right to extract money by way of waiver. It has now been held that the loss of the bargaining power to have a restrictive covenant released is not a "loss or disadvantage".[47]

Despite one or two attempts to challenge *McVey* and *Robertson*, the Lands Tribunal has consistently followed these earlier decisions.[48]

In *Keith v. Texaco Ltd*[49] the tribunal looked at the matter again and had regard to the Halliday Report, although it noted that "the tribunal would not be entitled to draw assistance from the report" except in so far as it identified the mischief which Parliament sought to remedy. Taking the mischief into account, the tribunal, in following *McVey* and *Roberston* said:

> "For the tribunal now to construe s. 1 (4) (i)—which forms part of other provisions all dealing with neighbourhood or

---

[45] 1993 S.L.T. (Lands Tr.) 15 at 20.

[46] 1976 S.L.T. (Lands Tr.) 11 at 13.

[47] *Stockport MBC v. Alwiyah Development* (1986) 52 P. & C.R. 278 (CA), *per* Everleigh L.J. at 281: "The benefit envisaged must be a practical one as opposed to a pecuniary one"; *Re Bennett's and Tamarlin Ltd's Application* (1987) 54 P. & C.R. 379 (LT); *Re Cornick's Application* (1994) 68 P. & C.R. 372.

[48] See, *e.g.*, *Harris v. Douglass*, 1993 S.L.T. (Lands Tr.) 56 at 59L; *United Auctions (Scotland) Ltd v. British Railways Board*, 1991 S.L.T. (Lands Tr.) 71 at 79D.

[49] 1977 S.L.T. (Lands Tr.) 16.

praedial rights—in such a way as to include within the ambit of the phrase 'loss or disadvantage' the loss of a mere power to extract money; or to apply it to the effect of apportioning to superiors in normal cases half the development value released by a discharge order, would be to perpetuate the very 'mischief' which Parliament sought to remedy."

Despite these strong judicial dicta both Professors Halliday[50] and Gordon are by no "means clear that the Act intended so radical a removal of the rights of feudal superiors as the Tribunal has assumed".[51] Even the tribunal "would certainly welcome higher judicial guidance on a disputed question so frequently raised under different guises—but which has not yet come to a heard appeal."[52]

Similarly, the tribunal will not give compensation under this heading for the deprivation of the right to irritate a feu. In *Highland Regional Council v. MacDonald-Buchanan*[53] the tribunal discharged a restriction requiring buildings to be used as a school and schoolhouse, which were subject to an irritancy clause, holding that "Parliament never intended a superior to be compensated for deprivation of his right to irritate the feu".[54] No compensation was awarded in a claim for the value of the buildings made on the basis that, but for the variation, they would have reverted to the estate.

The tribunal has rejected the argument that the right to extract payment for a waiver was a benefit under ground (b).[55]

Section 1(4)(ii): reduced consideration paid

A claim under the second head for "a sum to make up for any   **7–22** effect which the obligation produced, at the time when it was imposed, in reducing the consideration then paid or made payable for the interest in land affected by it" may also be made.

"an award under section 1(4)(ii) can only be made once in the case of each particular obligation. Accordingly, if a claim has been made for such an award and has been refused after due enquiry, that matter is *res judicata* and cannot be re-opened".[56]

---

[50] *The Conveyancing and Feudal Reform (Scotland) Act 1970*, (2nd ed.), p. 41.

[51] Gordon, *Scottish Land Law*, para. 25-34.

[52] *Keith v. Texaco*, 1977 S.L.T. (Lands Tr.) 16 at 22.

[53] 1977 S.L.T. (Lands Tr.) 41.

[54] *ibid*. Professor Gordon in *Scottish Land Law* at para. 25-34 considers that the Tribunal "misunderstood the nature of the superior's interest in the land".

[55] See above, para. 6–12; *West Lothian Co-operative Society Ltd v. Ashdale Land and Property Co. Ltd*, 1972 S.L.T. (Lands Tr.) 30 at 33

[56] *MacDonald v. Abbotshall Evanton Ltd*, February 16, 1989; LTS/LO/1988/89—in contrast to a claim under s. 1(4)(i) which can be made each time an obligation is varied or discharged in part; see above, para. 7–06.

In order to succeed under this head, the benefited proprietor will have to prove that a lower consideration was paid for the subjects at the time the land obligation was created. This is often a difficult, if not impossible, task, without such evidence the claim will be rejected, because the tribunal will not assume that a different feuing rate or consideration might have applied.[57]

7–23   In England, even though it is accepted that "the question whether a restriction had the effect in reducing the consideration" is a matter of proof,[58] the tribunal appears more willing to extrapolate a reasonable figure from the surrounding circumstances and "intelligent guesswork".[59]

7–24   The tribunal has expressed doubt as to whether or not a section 1(4)(ii) claim is restricted to the original seller. In a case:

> "where there is an intervening seller, the latter would be 'compensated' in respect of a 'loss' from which he has already derived the benefit from the original seller".[60]

Despite this dictum, claims by subsequent purchasers under this subsection have been considered and paid.[61]

7–25   Usually in the superior-vassal situation, the reduced consideration in question is a capitalisation of the feu duty differential that might have applied. In such situations the proper approach is[62]:

> "by capitalising, as at the present date (when the restriction is lifted and for the first time the superiors lose its benefit), what would have been the extra feuduty which would originally have been chargeable without the restriction".

The example upon which that dictum is given is found in *Manz v. Butter's Trs*[63] where the tribunal suggested that if the original feu duty with the restriction was, say, £10, but without restriction it would have been £50, the appropriate compensation would be a

---

[57] *Devlin v. Conn*, 1972 S.L.T. (Lands Tr.) 11; *West Lothian Co-operative Society Ltd v. Ashdale Land and Property Co. Ltd*, above; *Manz v. Butter's Trs*, 1973 S.L.T. (Lands Tr.) 2; *Ross & Cromarty District Council v. Ullapool Property Co. Ltd*, 1983 S.L.T. (Lands Tr.) 9; *Reid v. Trs of the Blythswood Friendly Society*, May 2, 1991; LTS/LO/1990/60 and 62.

[58] *Re Harper's Application* (1986) 52 P. & C.R. 104.

[59] *Re Cornick's Application* (1994) 68 P. & C.R. 372; *Re Bowden's Application* (1983) 47 P. & C.R. 455; *Re Watson's Application* (1966) 17 P. & C.R. 176.

[60] *Devlin v. Conn*, 1972 S.L.T. (Lands Tr.) 11 at 14; see also *West Lothian Co-operative Society Ltd v. Ashdale Land and Property Co. Ltd*, 1972 S.L.T. (Lands Tr.) 30 at 33.

[61] *Gorrie & Banks Ltd v. Musselburgh Town Council*, 1974 S.L.T. (Lands Tr.) 5.

[62] *ibid.* at 8.

[63] 1973 S.L.T. (Lands Tr.) 2 at 5.

capitalisation at the date of the variation of the difference, namely £40.

In *Gorrie* a 15-year purchase was applied, although it is now suggested that, following the redemption of feu duty provisions in sections 4 to 6 of the Land Tenure Reform (Scotland) Act 1974, the appropriate purchase value in terms of the 1974 Act is that applicable at the time of variation or discharge.

On either approach in a superior-vassal situation, even if a reduction in feu duty can be proved, the amount of compensation is usually insignificant.

In an ordinary sale and disposition, a particular problem is **7–26** whether the compensation to be awarded should be the difference in consideration paid at the time from what should have been paid or whether the tribunal should uprate that figure for inflation or in line with the Retail Prices Index.

In *Currie v. Alliance Property Co. Ltd*[64] the applicant sought to prove that the subjects had a value of £75,000 in 1984, but sold for £65,000 because of a restrictive condition. The applicant argued that the £10,000 should be uprated to take account of inflation between 1984 and 1995. Having held that the applicant had failed to prove that a lower consideration had been paid, the tribunal said that "the terms of section 1(4)(ii) are not such as clearly to exclude any updating of the amount of an award", but decided to reserve its opinion until the issues actually required to be decided.

An uplift would appear to be appropriate as the compensation has to be a sum which the tribunal "think it just to award" and which is "a sum to make up for any effect".[65] In *Re Harper's Application*[66] the tribunal rejected an argument that the objector should get one-third of the value of each building plot allowed by the discharge and allowed £250, being the sum calculated by the tribunal as the extra sum that would have been paid at the time the land was sold subject to the covenant. A similar approach was taken in *Re Bowden's Application*[67] where the tribunal calculated the extra sum that would have been paid for the land without the covenant. In neither case did the tribunal uprate the sum to take account of any loss in the value of money.

In contrast, in *Re Cornick's Application*[68] the tribunal had regard to the evidence of Mr Cornick that he had been advised that he

---

[64] February 26, 1995; LTS/LO/1992/19 and 20.
[65] In England no uplift is allowed: *Re Bowden's Application* (1983) 47 P. & C.R. 455.
[66] (1986) 52 P. & C.R. 104 (1981 covenant released in 1986).
[67] above.
[68] (1994) 68 P. & C.R. 372.

could share in the development value, when the restriction came to be lifted. The price therefore did not include an element of "hope" value for development. In reaching a figure of £5,000 for compensation the tribunal said:

> "I am bidden in that event to award 'a sum to make up for' that effect. I do not think that this sum is capable of precise calculation, having regard in particular to the lapse of time and the difficulty of attempting to surmise what might have been agreed had the restriction not been imposed. . . . Thus adapting the figures advanced . . . an award of £5,000 would be justified. Approaching the matter in another way, I think that amount is one which the parties would be likely to have reached themselves in friendly negotiation for a release of the covenant."

In *Cumbernauld Development Corporation v. County Properties and Developments Ltd*[69] the Court of Session upheld the tribunal's award of £206,000 under section 1(4)(ii), where a condition that subjects were to be used as an ice rink was varied to permit use as a bingo hall. The feu disposition provided that if the parties agreed a change from ice rink use to retail use an additional £650,000 would be paid. The tribunal held that as the change was to a bingo hall and not to retail use, £650,000 was not the correct valuation of the loss under section 1(4)(ii).

7–27   In considering the quantum of compensation under this head, if any prior payments had been made for waivers, to avoid double counting, account should be taken of the sums already paid for such waivers.[70]

Payment of compensation

7–28   Where a land obligation is varied or discharged subject to payment of compensation awarded by the tribunal:

> "[T]he order of the Tribunal shall not, so far as it affects such variation or discharge, take effect until the Tribunal has endorsed the order to the effect either that the compensation has been paid or that all person to whom any compensation has been awarded, but have not received payment of it have agreed to the order taking effect".[71]

The tribunal may direct that compensation shall be paid or satisfied within a specified time and that, unless it is so paid or

---

[69] 1996 S.L.T. 1106.
[70] *Taylor v. Nicholson*, March 20, 1996; LTS/LO/1995/39 and 40.
[71] Lands Tribunal for Scotland Rules 1971, r. 5(2).

satisfied, the variation or discharge order shall be void on the expiration of the time so specified.[72]

Refusal of discharge, etc., by reason of exceptional circumstances

Section 1(4) also provides that a discharge or variation on **7–29** ground (c) may be refused "due to exceptional circumstances related to amenity or otherwise" where money would not be adequate compensation for any loss or disadvantage suffered by a benefited proprietor.

The tribunal does not have a residual discretion to refuse a discharge or variation where it finds that ground (a) or (b) applies and has determined to exercise its discretion, even if compensation is not an adequate remedy.[73] It seems unlikely that the discretion can be exercised in respect of ground (c), if the tribunal has also determined to grant the application on ground (a) or (b) as well.[74] This is understandable because a finding under ground (a) is that the land obligation "has become unreasonable or inappropriate" and under ground (b) that it is "unduly burdensome". If either (a) or (b) applies, it would be inappropriate to continue the land obligation merely because money would not be adequate compensation.

Specific provision is made for such an additional discretion under ground (c), where money is not adequate compensation in exceptional circumstances. Any difficulty in assessing compensation is not an exceptional circumstance relating to amenity or otherwise in the proviso to section 1(4).[75]

There is no reported Scottish decision where this discretion has been exercised.[76] In *Anderson v. Trotter*,[77] a case where the application was refused on the merits, the tribunal commented that if it had been minded to grant the application under ground (c), it would have refused it under the proviso to section 1(4). In that

---

[72] Lands Tribunal for Scotland Rules 1971, r. 5(3); *e.g. Sillars' Exrs v. Farrimond*, May 8, 1991; LTS/LO/1989/25.

[73] See *United Auctions (Scotland) Ltd v. British Railways Board*, 1991 S.L.T. (Lands Tr.) 72 at 77H and 78E; *County Properties and Developments Ltd v. Cumbernauld Development Corporation*, April 5, 1995; LTS/LO/1994/20.

[74] *Cumbernauld Development Corporation v. County Properties and Developments Ltd*, 1996 S.L.T. 1106 at 1112 I.

[75] *United Auctions (Scotland) Ltd v. British Railways Board*, 1991 S.L.T. (Lands Tr.) 71 at 76J.

[76] *ibid.* (issue considered); *Cumbernauld Development Corporation v. County Properties and Developments Ltd*, 1996 S.L.T. 1106 at 1112 I (tribunal's refusal to exercise discretion upheld); *North East Fife District Council v. Lees*, 1989 S.L.T. (Lands Tr.) 30 at 36D (refusal to exercise discretion).

[77] August 12, 1997; LTS/LO/1996/46.

case the tribunal found that the objectors would be disadvantaged by noise from children at the proposed nursery and by the traffic generated, but that there was no diminution in the value of their property. Accordingly money would not be adequate compensation, effectively because there could be no compensation under section 1(4)(i).

In *Ross and Cromarty District Council v. Ullapool Property Company Ltd*[78] the tribunal said that:

"The proviso contemplates harm to amenity or like harm caused by a variation or discharge order and where, due to exceptional circumstances, money would not adequately compensate the benefited proprietor or mean anything to him."

Again, in *County Properties and Development Ltd v. Cumbernauld Development Corporation*[79] the tribunal commented that the proviso:

"is designed to apply mainly in those exceptional circumstances where the damage to the dominant tenement resulting from a variation or discharge is unquantifiable in money terms. The proviso has no application where it is accepted that money may be an adequate compensation, but the benefited proprietor is dissatisfied with the amount of money to which he is entitled as compensation and does not consider it to be adequate".

7–30   In England, the Lands Tribunal appears to have taken a similar approach to the equivalent provision. The English provision[80] requires that the tribunal finds that money will be an adequate compensation for the loss or disadvantage and does not give them a discretion in the matter or require that exceptional circumstances should apply. English cases therefore require to be treated with caution.

In *Re Quarterly's Application*[81] the tribunal refused the application because money would not be adequate compensation to the local authority which was seeking to enforce a section 52 condition that a house should be used for a person employed in agricultural. The removal of the condition would increase pressure on the council to permit the erection of a new house for an agricultural worker, contrary to planning policies.

---

[78] 1983 S.L.T. (Lands Tr.) 9 at 14.
[79] April 5, 1995; LTS/LO/1994/20.
[80] s. 84(1)(aa) and (1A) "and that money will be an adequate compensation for the loss or disadvantage".
[81] (1989) 58 P. & C.R. 518.

In *Re Beardsley's Application*[82] the tribunal considered that where a person's amenity would suffer (*e.g.* garden overlooked, increased noise and children playing in the street) even though that was personal and subjective, the person did not want to move, but the property would not decrease in value, that that was a circumstance, where money would not be adequate compensation.

[82] (1972) 25 P. & C.R. 233.

CHAPTER 8

ORDERS OF THE LANDS TRIBUNAL

General

8–01 The tribunal's orders include orders for variation or discharge, for additional or substitutional provisions, for compensation and for dates by which compensation falls to be paid and for expenses.

Variation or discharge

8–02 If the tribunal does not refuse an application, it has power to "vary or discharge the obligation wholly or partially".[1] The corresponding English provision relates to "any restriction arising under covenant or otherwise" and gives the Lands Tribunal the power "by order wholly or partly to discharge or modify such restriction".[2]

Where an application is made under ground (c), the tribunal will usually only grant a variation of the land obligation to permit the particular use proposed and in general will not just discharge the obligation.[3]

In granting a discharge or variation the tribunal does not have power to grant an applicant new or increased rights.[4]

The tribunal does not favour granting a variation by the deletion of words from an existing obligation, but prefers to issue an order that specifies the extent and effect of the use that is to be allowed. In *Forrest v. Gallacher*[5] the tribunal rejected a suggestion that a use as a licensed hotel contrary to restriction against use for any trade or business or as licensed premises could be achieved by the deletion of those words and granted a variation of the obligation to the "extent and effect of allowing the use of the subjects for the carrying on of a hotel with or without a restricted or full licence".

---

[1] 1970 Act, s. 1(3).
[2] 1925 Act, s. 84(1).
[3] *T & I Consultants Ltd v. Cullion*, 1998 Hous. L.R. 9; see para. 6–21 above.
[4] See above, para. 3–22; *George T. Fraser Ltd v. Aberdeen Harbour Board*, 1985 S.L.T. 384 (IH), *per* the Lord President at 386; *Mackay v. Burton*, 1994 S.L.T. (Lands Tr.) 35 at 38H.
[5] September 30, 1980; LTS/LO/1979/35.

Where an applicant is burdened by land obligations contained in a preceding deed of conditions executed and recorded in the Register of Sasines in terms of section 32 of the Conveyancing (Scotland) Act 1874 and incorporated into his conveyance by reference, the tribunal will only vary the condition as contained in the subsequent conveyance and will not vary the original deed of conditions.[6]

Personal licence

The tribunal has no power to grant what is in effect a personal **8–03** licence to the applicant.[7]

In *Re Ghey and Galton's Application*[8] the Court of Appeal disapproved an earlier order of the Lands Tribunal, which purported to modify a covenant so as "to permit the Metal Box Co. to use the said lands and premises as a convalescent home or rest home for their employees", saying:

> "Now it will be observed that that is no more than a licence to a particular company. The covenant is said to be modified so as to permit one individual . . . to use the lands as a convalescent home exclusively for their own employees. In the view that I take, it is unnecessary for me to express a final view on the matter; but when you start with a covenant binding the land, the benefit of which runs with the land, I doubt for my part whether it is competent for the tribunal, under cover of modifying the covenant, to give in effect no more than a personal license to one individual."

The tribunal will not vary a land obligation for a limited period. In *Nicolson v. Campbell's Trs*[9] the Lands Tribunal refused a submission asking the tribunal to vary a rebuilding obligation covered by an irritancy clause, to the effect that the obligation should not be applicable during a three-year period stating that the applicant would be better advised to apply to the sheriff in the irritancy action for an extension of time in which to purge the irritancy.

In England, in considering whether the power "partially to discharge"[10] included a power to lift a restriction for a limited

---

[6] *Bachoo v. George Wimpey & Co. Ltd*, 1977 S.L.T. (Lands Tr.) 2 at 3; *Mitchell v. Mactaggart & Mickel Ltd*, May 21, 1980; LTS/LO/1979/26.

[7] See *Bolton v. Aberdeen Corporation*, 1972 S.L.T. (Lands Tr.) 26 at 29.

[8] [1957] 2 Q.B. 650 at 660.

[9] 1981 S.L.T. (Lands Tr.) 10.

[10] s. 84(1) of Law of Property Act 1925.

period, the Lands Tribunal held that it had no such power, because "partially discharge" could not be partial in terms of time.[11]

Additional or substitutional provisions

8–04   In varying or discharging a land obligation, the tribunal may add or substitute any such provision as appears to it to be reasonable as a result of the variation or discharge, provided that this is accepted by the applicant. If such additional or substitutional provision is not acceptable to the applicant, the tribunal may refuse to vary or discharge the land obligation.[12] The tribunal has no power, under this provision, to make an award of money otherwise than by way of compensation under section 1(4).[13]

The test which the tribunal applies in determining whether or not to include an additional or substitute provision is:

> "that the tribunal's jurisdiction requires us to regard the present parties like any other proprietors and consider whether the successful burdened proprietors, released from the restrictive land obligation, should reasonably be subjected to onerous new provisions to protect the unsuccessful benefited proprietors in the light of the relaxation granted: see *Leney v. Craig and Others*, 1982 S.L.T. (Lands Tr.) 9, and *Bruce and Others v. Modern Homes Investment Co. Ltd.*, 1978 S.L.T. (Lands Tr.) 34, in which such suitable protective measures were imposed".

8–05   The new or substitute provision imposed must be directly related to the variation or discharge sought. They allow new conditions to be imposed which alleviate the consequences of the variation or discharge.[14] In considering the wording of section 1(5):

> "in the light of s. 1 viewed as a whole, the tribunal in any event reach the conclusion that the purposes of s. 1 (5) are of more modest scope than contended for by the objectors. Under s. 1 (4) monetary compensation can be directed to be awarded to a benefited proprietor by a successful burdened proprietor to make up for any loss or disadvantage caused by the discharge or variation order. Under s. 1 (5), the tribunal

---

[11] *Re Taroads Ltd's Application* (1951) 7 P. & C.R. 42 at 45.
[12] 1970 Act, s. 1(5); see *Strathclyde Regional Council v. Mactaggart & Mickel Ltd*, 1984 S.L.T. (Lands Tr.) 33 at 36.
[13] 1970 Act, s. 1(5).
[14] *Strathclyde Regional Council v. Mactaggart & Mickel Ltd*, 1984 S.L.T. (Lands Tr.) 33 at 36–37.

may also add or substitute any such provision as appears to them to be reasonable as the result of the variation or discharge of the obligation. We consider this to mean that any new or substitute provision imposed must be directly related to the variation or discharge order sought—in this case allowing the land to be used for residential rather than for school purposes. It allows new conditions to be imposed in order to alleviate the consequences. This is analogous to the limitations placed by the courts on conditions annexed to grants of planning permission which must directly relate to the grant and not to ultroneous matters. Provisions imposed under s. 1 (5) for the protection of benefited proprietors should likewise relate to the variation or discharge order".[15]

Where the tribunal allowed building on land restricted to a schoolhouse, it refused to include a pre-emption clause in substitution for the discharge, which was designed to allow the superiors to get the land back for developing themselves, on the ground that it was not directly related to the discharge sought.[16]

This is a power that has been used regularly, when a land obligation has been varied. Additional or substitutional provisions have included reserving a right to the benefited proprietor to agree plans,[17] discharging a condition to the extent of permitting the erection of additional buildings in accordance with approved plans,[18] by restrictions on the number and type of houses to be built on open ground[19] with provision for screening by trees,[20] restriction on height of buildings to be used in light industry near to residential property,[21] where a house was part built prior to the application a provision was made for an earth retaining wall to be built to the specification of a civil engineer to prevent land slip,[22] a provision requiring double glazing for sound insulation of all windows and all roof lights whether existing or in the future in a

---

[15] *Strathclyde Regional Council v. Mactaggart & Mickel Ltd*, 1984 S.L.T. (Lands Tr.) 33 at 36–37.

[16] *ibid.* at 37.

[17] *Robinson v. Hamilton*, 1974 S.L.T. (Lands Tr.) 2; *Crombie v. George Heriot's Trust*, 1972 S.L.T. (Lands Tr.) 40.

[18] *Smith v. Taylor*, 1972 S.L.T. (Lands Tr.) 34 at 37 (plans approved by the Dean of Guild).

[19] *Crombie v. George Heriot's Trust*, above; *Gorrie & Banks Ltd v. Musselburgh Town Council*, 1974 S.L.T. (Lands Tr.) 5.

[20] *Crombie v. George Heriot's Trust*, above; *Robinson v. Hamilton*, 1974 S.L.T. (Lands Tr.) 2; see *MacPhail v. Baksh*, November 10, 1995; LTS/LO/94/42 where a request for screening trees to be planted was refused.

[21] *Ashdale Land and Property Co. Ltd*, 1972 S.L.T. (Lands Tr.) 30 at 33.

[22] *Bruce v. Modern Homes Investment Co. Ltd*, 1978 S.L.T. (Lands Tr.) 34 at 37.

proposed functions suite of a dwelling-house to be converted into a hotel and provision for the extraction of kitchen fumes from the chimney head,[23] provision restricting the agreed new use to a particular purpose and number of occupants,[24] where land was burdened by a restriction to one house, which had a right to draw water from the benefited proprietor's land, the tribunal permitted another house to be built, subject to a condition that it could not draw water from the servient tenement,[25] that a variation to allow premises to be used as licensed premises subject to a restriction against the sale of alcohol except with meals and between the hours of 11 a.m. and 11 p.m., thus effectively preventing a regular or occasional extension of permitted hours,[26] and rights of access varied with provision to provide alternative access.[27]

Where a dwelling-house was to be converted to a hotel and noise was a threat to a neighbouring house, the tribunal considered it difficult to devise appropriate land obligations running with the land and controlling the use of sound amplifiers, which might be of different kinds and strengths. The tribunal ordered the installation of double glazing in lieu.[28]

8–06   The tribunal has no power to impose a condition or create obligations which affect subjects other than the applicant's subjects. This was recognised in *Murrayfield Ice Rink Ltd v. Scottish Rugby Union*[29] where the tribunal said that:

> "The Tribunal cannot, of course, vary the car parking rights which are a burden not on the applicants but on the superiors' land and are declared not to run with the land. Their transfer depends upon the superiors' consent."

Further, in *Irving v. John Dickie & Sons Ltd*[30] where the applicant sought a variation of a right of access, the other parties contended that the tribunal should impose a condition on all users regarding sharing the costs of maintenance. The tribunal held that this was not competent, as it was necessarily dealing with only the title to the applicant's subjects and could only impose conditions on that subject.

---

[23] *Leney v. Craig*, 1982 S.L.T. (Lands Tr.) 9 at 13.
[24] *Main v. Lord Doune*, 1972 S.L.T. (Lands Tr.) 14 at 19 (restriction to nursery school in basement of 15 pupils).
[25] *Courtesi v. Junker*, July 7, 1995; LTS/LO/95/4; *Jackson v. Graham*, June 16, 1981; LTS/LO/1980/1.
[26] *Nugent v. Downie*, March 27, 1981; LTS/LO/1980/29.
[27] See above, para. 5–14.
[28] *Leney v. Craig*, 1982 S.L.T. (Lands Tr.) 9 at 13.
[29] 1972 S.L.T. (Lands Tr.) 20 at 24.
[30] August 31, 1995; LTS/LO/94/17.

Proposed order

In certain circumstances the tribunal may issue a proposed order **8-07** and then allow parties to make further submissions in respect of the proposed order.

In an application to vary a prohibition on building on a particular area of land, the applicants put forward a number of development schemes none of which represented the applicants' firm proposals and none of which had planning permission. In respect that the tribunal considered that development was appropriate, they issued a proposed order, in which it was indicated that the application would be refused for want of an identified redevelopment proposal, but gave the parties time to agree a specific proposal and conditions. When these were agreed, the tribunal issued a final order granting the variation, subject to the agreed conditions.[31]

Where the tribunal proposed to grant a variation of an access route, it issued a proposed decision indicating that it was minded to grant the application but giving the objectors an opportunity to make representations that the variation should not be allowed for exceptional circumstances under the proviso to section 1(4) of the 1970 Act. As no representations were made, the application was granted.[32]

Where the tribunal was otherwise minded to allow a development, but during the course of the hearing it became apparent that the development might be impeded by a lack of access, the tribunal continued consideration of the application, giving a direction under rule 25(1)(d) that the applicant obtain and lodge a draft grant of access.[33]

Compensation

An order varying or discharging a land obligation may direct that **8-08** the applicant pay any compensation directed by the tribunal to be paid under section 1(4) to a benefited proprietor.[34]

The tribunal may direct that the compensation shall be paid or satisfied within a specified time and that, unless it is so paid or satisfied, the order shall be void on the expiration of the time so specified.[35]

---

[31] *East Kilbride Development Corporation v. The Norwich Union Life Insurance Society*, March 29, 1995; LTS/LO/93–34.
[32] *Stewart v. Kazim*, June 22, 1995; LTS/LO/93/49.
[33] *Irving v. John Dickie & Sons Ltd*, August 31, 1995; LTS/LO/94/17.
[34] 1970 Act, s. 1(4).
[35] r. 5(3); *Leney v. Craig*, 1982 S.L.T. (Lands Tr.) 9 at 13.

In addition an extract of an order of the tribunal may be recorded for execution in the Books of Council and Session and is enforceable accordingly.[36]

Effect of order

8–09   An order made under section 1 takes effect in accordance with the Lands Tribunal Rules.[37] Rule 5(1) provides:

> "Subject to the Provisions of paragraphs (2) and (3) of this rule, an order made by the Tribunal varying or discharging a land obligation shall take effect on the occurrence of whichever of the following events last occurs after the Tribunal has made the order, that is to say—
> (a) the expiry of a period of 21 days after the date when the order was made by the Tribunal;
> (b) the disposal by the Court of Session of a case stated by the Tribunal on appeal to that court or, if there is an appeal to the House of Lords, the disposal of the case by the House of Lords;
> (c) the abandonment or other termination of the proceedings on a case so stated without a decision having been given;
> (d) the abandonment or other termination of an appeal against the decision of the Court of Session in a case so stated or the expiry of the time for bringing any such appeal without it having been brought; or
> (e) the variation by the Tribunal of the order in compliance with any directions given by the Court of Session or the House of Lords in proceedings relating to such a case;
> Provided, that where the application is unopposed or all persons who have opposed or made representations in respect of the application have informed the Tribunal that they consent to the order taking effect immediately, and it is so certified in the order, such order shall take effect on the date on which it is made by the Tribunal".

Where a land obligation is varied or discharged subject to the payment of any compensation awarded by the tribunal, the order of the tribunal does not, so far as it affects the variation or discharge, take effect until the tribunal has endorsed the order to the effect either that the compensation has been paid or that all persons to

---

[36] 1949 Act, s. 3(12)(d).
[37] 1970 Act, s. 2(3).

whom any compensation has been awarded but who have not received payment of it have agreed to the order taking effect.[38] The tribunal may direct that the compensation shall be paid or satisfied within a specified time and that, unless it is so paid or satisfied, the order for variation or discharge shall be void on the expiration of the time so specified.[39]

An extract of an order made under section 1 may be recorded in the Register of Sasines or in the Land Register. Once duly recorded it is binding on all persons having an interest.[40]

These provisions are fortified by section 18(1) of the Land Registration (Scotland) Act 1979 which provides:

"The terms of any—
(a) deed recorded in the Register of Sasines whether before or after the commencement of this Act, where by a land obligation is varied or discharged;
(b) registered variation or discharge of a land obligation,
shall be binding on singular successors of the person entitled to enforce the land obligation, and of the person on whom the land obligation was binding".

The purpose of this section was to correct a possible lacuna in the 1970 Act whereby variations or discharges of land obligations, which might relate to the deed applicable to the application subjects, were binding on the proprietors of subjects whose deeds had not been varied or discharged.

In regard to the procedure for registration in the Land Register, the tribunal has said[41]:

"This is the first application for variation or discharge of a land obligation in which the burdened interest in land has been registered in the Land Register of Scotland under the provisions of the Land Registration (Scotland) Act 1979 . . . having given consideration to the relevant statutory provisions, the tribunal do not consider that they either can or should direct the Keeper to alter the burdens section of the certificate of title under s. 9. As presently advised in the tribunal's view it is simply a question of producing an order in a form suitable for registration under s. 2 (4) (c) of the Act.
It may be helpful, however, to observe that the 1979 Act did not amend or repeal any of the provisions of Pt. I of the

---

[38] 1971 Rules, r. 5(2).
[39] *ibid*. r. 5(3).
[40] 1970 Act, s. 2(4); see Land Tenure Reform (Scotland) Act 1974, s. 19.
[41] *Hughes v. Frame*, 1985 S.L.T. (Lands Tr.) 12.

Conveyancing and Feudal Reform (Scotland) Act 1970 dealing with the discharge or variation of land obligations. Section 2 (4) of the 1970 Act provides that 'Where an extract of an order made under section 1 of this Act which has taken effect is duly recorded, it shall be binding on all persons having interest.' In terms of the translation provisions contained in s. 29 (2) of the 1979 Act such a provision to record in the Sasine Register has to be construed, in relation to registered land, as registration in the Land Register. It would appear that this can now be achieved under s. 2 (4) (c) of the 1979 Act as an 'event' affecting title which the Keeper can be requested to register. The tribunal will, therefore, simply pronounce an order varying the land obligation."

The tribunal has no power to grant a retrospective variation or discharge of a land obligation,[42] which is of particular importance in relation to prior raised actions of irritancy.[43]

Irritant and resolutive clauses, etc.

8–10   Where the tribunal varies or discharges a land obligation which is fenced by any irritant or resolutive clause or other condition relating to the enforcement of the obligation, then after the date at which the order takes effect, the irritant, resolutive or other condition is effective (if at all) only in so far as it would have been effective if the obligation had been discharged or varied by the person entitled to enforce the obligation.[44] This provision was explained in *Strathclyde Regional Council v. Mactaggart & Mickel Ltd*[45]:

"We read the last lines of s. 1 (6), however, in their general context purely as enabling words designed to ensure that any existing irritancy clause should also apply to the new substitute provision; and not as directing that no new substitute provision can be inserted unless apt to be subject to the irritancy clause. In our opinion, a new provision must be a land obligation but not necessarily one capable of enforcement under an irritancy clause."

Any provision added or substituted under section 1(5) is enforceable in the same manner as the obligation to the variation or discharge of which it relates.[46]

---

[42] *Fraser v. Church of Scotland General Trustees*, 1986 S.L.T. 692 at 695C; *Ross and Cromarty District Council v. Ullapool Property Co. Ltd*, 1983 S.L.T. (Lands Tr.) 9 at 10.

[43] See above, para. 3–05.

[44] 1970 Act, s. 1(6).

[45] 1984 S.L.T. (Lands Tr.) 33 at 36.

[46] 1970 Act, s. 1(6).

Expenses

The tribunal may make appropriate orders for expenses. **8–11**
Motions for expenses should be made at the end of any hearing.[47]
In certain cases expenses may be reserved and the tribunal asked to
deal with them by written or oral representation after the decision
is issued.
The Lands Tribunal:

"Subject to the following provisions of this section, . . . may
order the costs of any proceedings before it incurred by any
party shall be paid by any other party and may tax and settle
the amount of the costs to be paid under any such order or
direct what manner they are to be taxed."[48]

Rule 33(1)[49] gives the tribunal a discretion to "deal in such
manner with expenses as in its discretion it thinks fit". The tribunal
may order either a specified sum to be paid in expenses or a
proportion of the expenses only.[50] The tribunal can order expenses
to be paid and taxed either by the Auditor of the Court of Session
at Court of Session scales or by the Auditor of a sheriff court
specified by the tribunal in accordance with the Sheriff Court Table
of Fees.[51]

Counsel's fees are allowed only if the tribunal has sanctioned the **8–12**
employment of counsel.[52] Similarly, the fair and reasonable fees of
an expert witness are allowed only where the tribunal has certified
the employment of such expert witnesses.

The tribunal may award an additional fee under the Court of **8–13**
Session rules or a percentage increase where expenses are awarded
at sheriff court scales.[53] The criteria to be applied in assessing
whether or not to award an additional fee or percentage uplift have
been summarised by the tribunal[54]:

"As was said in *C Bruce Miller and Co Ltd v City of Aberdeen
District Council*, 1992 SLT (Lands Tr) 95 where a 25 per cent

---

[47] *Guidance Notes for Prospective Applicants.*
[48] 1949 Act, s. 3(5).
[49] Lands Tribunal for Scotland Rules 1971.
[50] *ibid.* r. 33(2).
[51] *ibid.*
[52] r. 33(4); see *Cameron v. Stirling*, 1988 S.L.T. (Lands Tr.) 18 where sanction
refused.
[53] *Paramount Entertainments (Glasgow) Ltd v. Strathclyde R.C.*, 1990 S.L.T.
(Lands Tr.) 110 (Court of Session scales); *C. Bruce Miller & Co. Ltd v. City of
Aberdeen D.C.*, 1992 S.L.T. (Lands Tr.) (95% increase at sheriff court scales).
[54] *Harris v. Douglass*, 1993 S.L.T. (Lands Tr.) 56 at 60

increase in fees was allowed: 'In deciding whether an increase should be allowed and, if so, of what amount, the tribunal must apply certain criteria. The case must be one of importance or requiring special preparation. As was submitted on behalf of the acquiring authority, that must mean that it is of more than ordinary importance or that it requires more than normal preparation when compared with other cases of the same type which come before the tribunal. That is consistent with the decisions in *Feddon v R O Stuart (Plant) Ltd*, 1967 SLT (Notes) 24, and *Szaranek v Edmund Nuttall, Sons & Co (London) Ltd*, 1968 SLT (Notes) 48, in which the court was considering the similar, but perhaps less stringent, requirements of the rule regarding additional fees in judicial proceedings in the Court of Session. . . . In considering whether to allow such an increase, all of the seven factors listed must be taken into account, and an increase can only be properly allowed if, after balancing all of those factors, it appears that the responsibility undertaken by the solicitor in the conduct of the case is not adequately covered by the ordinary scale of fees: *see Paramount Entertainments (Glasgow) Ltd v Strathclyde Regional Council*, 1990 SLT (Lands Tr) 110'."

8–14   The general rule followed by the Lands Tribunal in an application for the variation or discharge of a land obligation is that there should be no expenses due to or by either party,[55] unless the benefited proprietor acts unreasonably in opposing the application. In *Harris v. Douglass* the tribunal commented[56]:

"In applications to this tribunal for variation or discharge of land obligations under s 1 (3) of the Conveyancing and Feudal Reform (Scotland) Act 1970, it has not been the tribunal's practice to award expenses against superiors for endeavouring to stand on their existing legal rights—except where they have acted unreasonably or vexatiously."

The reason behind this rule is that the burdened proprietor usually receives a substantial, and often financial benefit, from the variation or discharge of the land obligation and the superior or benefited proprietor, as contradictor, is of assistance to the tribunal in reaching their decision.[57]

Where there is a compensation claim in which the burdened proprietors are successful, the tribunal may follow the normal rule

---

[55] *British Steel plc v. Kaye*, 1991 S.L.T. (Lands Tr.) 7 at 9.
[56] 1993 S.L.T. (Lands Tr.) 56 at 59.
[57] See *Alison v. Dunbar*, January 19, 1984; LTS/LO/1983/25.

of no expenses due to or by either party in respect of the merits of the application, but award the burdened proprietors the expenses in relation to the compensation part of the claim, assessing the amount of time devoted to compensation and apportion the expenses accordingly.[58]

Expenses are sometimes not awarded against affected proprietors on the grounds that, "having received objections, and allowed the affected person to be heard", it is inappropriate to award expenses against them.[59]

Where an application was withdrawn, the tribunal found the applicants liable in expenses,[60] although this is not always the case.[61]

---

[58] *Leney v. Craig*, 1982 S.L.T. (Lands Tr.) 9 at 13; *Stewart v. Kasim*, June 22, 1995; LTS/LO/93/49.

[59] e.g. *Martin v. Kelly*, October 26, 1981; LTS/LO/1979/22.

[60] *Campbell v. Edinburgh Corporation*, 1972 S.L.T. (Lands Tr.) 38.

[61] *McGregor v. Eagle Star Insurance Co. Ltd*, July 1, 1981; LTS/LO/1980/28, where there was no need for the superior to have entered process.

CHAPTER 9

DIVERTING AND CLOSING RIGHTS OF WAY

General

9–01 The tribunal has no jurisdiction under the 1970 Act or otherwise to alter the route of or to close a public right of way upon the application of the landowner.

Local planning authorities have the power to agree the creation or to create, close or divert a public path[1] under Part III of the Countryside Act (Scotland) Act 1967 (as amended). Such an order requires to be confirmed by the Secretary of State unless, after notice is given, no representations or objections are made.[2] The Secretary of State may not confirm an order relating to land under, in, upon, over, along or across which there is apparatus belonging to or being used by any statutory undertakers for the purposes of their undertaking unless they consent, which consent is not to be unreasonably withheld.[3]

The orders require to be made in such form as may be prescribed.[4] An order must contain a map.[5] The orders or agreement require to contain a particular description, or a description by reference, of the lands affected.[6] Any agreement or order must be registered in the Register of Sasines or the Land Register as soon as possible after it is made or confirmed. Any such order is then enforceable by the local authority against singular successors in the land.[7]

---

[1] "Public path" means a way which is a footpath or bridle way or a combination of those (s. 30 of the 1967 Act).

[2] 1967 Act, Sched. 3, para 2(1A); see below, para. 9–07, regarding procedure.

[3] *ibid*. s. 39(6).

[4] See *ibid*. ss. 31(3), 34(3) and 35(6) and the Countryside (Scotland) Regulations 1982 (S.I. 1982 No. 1467) ("the 1982 Regulations").

[5] 1982 Regulations, regs 4–8.

[6] 1967 Act, s. 38(4). See *Rush v. Fife Regional Council*, 1994 S.L.T. 454.

[7] 1967 Act, s. 38(5). *Per* the proviso, an order cannot be enforced against a third party acquiring in good faith and for value and without notice of the order prior to the order being registered or any person deriving title from such a third person.

This power is without prejudice to any other statutory power to close or divert a road.[8] This chapter is not concerned with these other statutory powers or with the loss of a right of way by non-user for the prescriptive period.[9]

As this is an analogous power to that of the tribunal to vary or discharge a land obligation relating to access, it is now dealt with briefly, as the requirement to create, close or divert a public path may arise when a burdened proprietor seeks to vary or discharge a right of access which turns out to include a public path.

Diversion of public rights of way by consent

The public and the landowner may agree a diversion of the route **9–02** of a public right of way where the general public begin to use a different route and the landowner does not object or vice versa.[10] It is not necessary for the whole prescriptive period to pass for the new route to be established as the alternative route, but a shorter period of acquiescence—"it might be a year or less"—will be sufficient.[11] Where a public route is diverted, by consent, during the course of the prescriptive period, the two periods of use can be added together to establish the prescriptive period.[12]

Where a right of way is established by declarator as running between two points or by a general direction, the court has a discretion to fix the width and most convenient route having regard to the needs of the public and that of the landowner.[13] Where two routes had been established from a public road to a ford, starting about 187 yards apart and meeting near the ford, the court permitted one of the routes to be closed up.[14]

Creation of public paths

A local authority may enter into an agreement with any person **9–03** having the necessary power to create a public path over their land. Such an agreement, known as a "public path creation agreement", may be on such terms as to payment or otherwise as may be specified in the agreement and may provide for the creation of the

---

[8] 1967 Act, s. 38(2).

[9] See *Stair Memorial Encyclopaedia*, Vol. 18, paras 510 and 511.

[10] *Hozier v. Hawthorne* (1884) 11 R. 766; *Cadell v. Stevenson* (1900) 8 S.L.T. 8; *Kinloch v. Young*, 1911 S.C. (H.L.) 1.

[11] *Hozier v. Hawthorne*, above, *per* Lord Shand at 774.

[12] *Kinloch v. Young*, 1911 S.C. (H.L.) 1.

[13] *Mackintosh v. Moir* (1872) 10 M. 517. See Rankine, *Landownership in Scotland* (4th ed.), pp. 348–349.

[14] *Macdonald v. Farquharson* (1832) 10 S. 236.

public path subject to limitations or conditions affecting any public right of way thereover.[15]

Where it appears to a local authority that there is need for a public path over land in its area and it is satisfied that, having regard to the extent to which the path would add to the convenience or enjoyment of a substantial section of the public or the convenience of persons resident in the area and the effect which the creation of the path would have on the rights of persons interested in the land, account being taken of the provisions for compensation, it is expedient that a path should be created, may make a "public path creation order", if it appears impractical to reach agreement on a public path creation agreement. A right of way created by public path creation order may be either unconditional or subject to such limitations or conditions as may be specified in the order.[16]

The Secretary of State may confirm a public path creation order subject to such modification or conditions as he thinks fit.[17]

Closure of public path

9–04   Where it appears to a local planning authority that it is expedient that a public path should be closed on the ground that the path is not needed for public use, the authority may make a "public path extinguishment order", which is required to be submited to and confirmed by the Secretary of State.[18]

The Secretary of State may not confirm a public path extinguishment order unless he is satisfied that it is expedient so to do, having regard to the extent to which it appears to him that the path would be likely to be used by the public and having regard to the effect which the extinguishment of the right of way would have as respects land served by the path.[19]

Where the local planning authority or the Secretary of State is considering a public path extinguishment order concurrently with proceedings preliminary to the confirmation of a public path creation order or a public path diversion order, they may take into account the extent to which the public path creation or diversion order would provide an alternative path.[20]

Temporary circumstances preventing or diminishing the use of a path by the public are to be disregarded in considering whether or not to close a public path.[21]

---

[15] 1967 Act, s. 30(1) and (2).
[16] *ibid.* s. 31(1) and (2).
[17] *ibid.* s. 31(3).
[18] *ibid.* s. 34(1).
[19] *ibid.* s. 34(2).
[20] *ibid.* s. 34(5).
[21] *ibid.* s. 34(6).

Diversion of public path

Where an owner, tenant or occupier of land crossed by a public **9–05** path satisfies the planning authority that:

"for securing the efficient use of the land or of other land held therewith or providing a shorter or more convenient path across his land, it is expedient that the line of the path across his land, or part of that line, should be diverted (whether on to other of his or onto land of another owner, or occupier)"

the authority may make a "public path diversion order" creating a new path and closing the old path with effect from such date as they may specify.[22]

A right of way created by a public path diversion order may be either unconditional or subject to such limitations or conditions as may be specified in the order or in any confirmation by the Secretary of State, whether or not the right of way extinguished was subject to any limitations or conditions.[23]

Before making such an order, the authority may require the owner, tenant or occupier to enter into an agreement with them to defray, or to make such contribution as may be specified in the agreement towards, any compensation that may be payable under section 37, or which the local authority may incur in bringing the new path into a fit conditions for use by the public.[24]

The Secretary of State may not confirm a public path diversion order unless he is satisfied that the need for the diversion is expedient in terms of section 35(1) and that it will not be substantially less convenient to the public and that it is expedient to confirm the order having regard to the effect the diversion would have on (a) the public enjoyment of the path as a whole, (b) as respects other land served by the existing right of way and (c) any new right created would have as respects land over which the right is created and any land held therewith. The Secretary of State is to take into account the provisions for compensation under section 37 for the purposes of (b) and (c).[25]

Where a local authority proposes to make a public path diversion order, such that a different authority will be responsible for part of the path after diversion, the authority is required to consult the authority who will be responsible for that part prior to making the order.[26] Where a public path creation or extinguishment order

[22] 1967 Act, s. 35(1).
[23] *ibid*. s. 35(3).
[24] *ibid*. s. 35(4).
[25] *ibid*. s. 35(5).
[26] *ibid*. s. 36(4).

affects the land of more than one authority, the order may make provision requiring one of the authorities to defray or contribute towards the expenses incurred in consequence of the order by another of the authorities and may require the making authority to remain responsible for the costs of the diverted path.

Compensation

9–06 Where it is shown that the value of an interest of any person in land is depreciated, or that any person has suffered damage by being disturbed in the enjoyment of his land, in consequence of the coming into operation of a public path creation, diversion or extinguishment order, then the authority by whom the order was made shall pay to that person compensation equal to the amount of the depreciation or damage.[27]

Such a claim has to be made within six months from the coming into operation of the order in respect of which the claim was made.[28] The claim has to be made in writing and served on the authority by whom the order was made. It must contain a statement of the amount of compensation claimed and the particulars of the interest in land in respect of which the claim is made. The particulars must be sufficient to identify approximately the boundaries of the land and the nature of the claimant's title thereto.[29]

The right to compensation is limited to a person in right of land over which the public path runs or land in the same ownership, unless the owner of adjoining land could have taken legal action to prevent a voluntary agreement to the creation of the path by the owner of the land over which it runs.[30]

Any disputed claim for compensation falls to be determined by the Lands Tribunal for Scotland.[31] Compensation falls to be calculated in terms of rules 2 to 4 of section 12 of the Lands Compensation (Scotland) Act 1963 (as amended).[32]

There are special rules for heritable securities. Where there is a heritable security, the depreciation of the interest is calculated on the basis that the interest is not subject to a heritable security. The holder of the heritable security or anyone claiming under him may

---

[27] 1967 Act, s. 37(1).
[28] *ibid*. s. 37(2); 1982 Regulations, regs 18(2) and 20.
[29] *ibid*. s. 37(2); 1982 Regulations, regs 18(3) and 20.
[30] 1967 Act, s. 37(4).
[31] 1967 Act, s. 70(2).
[32] *ibid*. s. 70(4). See, *e.g.*, *Compulsory Purchase and Compensation* by Jeremy Rowan-Robinson (W. Green, 1990) for a consideration of the basis on which compensation may be calculated and claimed.

make the claim for compensation. The heritable creditor is not entitled to compensation in respect of his interest. Any compensation payable in respect of an interest is payable to the heritable security holder, who requires to treat it as a payment arising under a sale.[33]

Confirmation procedure

The procedure for submission of orders for confirmation and for   **9–07** confirmation are as prescribed.[34] Provision may be made for enabling procedures preliminary to the confirmation of a public path extinguishment order to be taken concurrently with proceedings preliminary to the confirmation of a public path creation order or a public path diversion order.[35]

Where there is no objection or representation following notice of the proposed order, no confirmation is required.[36]

Before any order is made, notice in the prescribed form[37] must be given, stating the general effect of the order and that, subject to paragraph 2(1) of Schedule 3 to the 1967 Act is being submitted for confirmation and naming a place in the area where a draft of the order and map may be inspected free of charge at all reasonable times. The order must specify the time, not being less than 28 days from the date of first publication, within which, and the manner in which, representations or objections with respect to the order may be made.[38]

Notices require to be published in at least one local newspaper circulating in the area. The notice has to be served on every owner, occupier and tenant (except tenants for a month or less and certain statutory tenants). The Secretary of State may direct that a notice is not served on an owner, occupier or tenant if it is not reasonably practical, but in that case a notice addressed to "the owners and any occupier" requires to be affixed to some conspicuous object on the land.[39]

In the case of a public path extinguishment or diversion order, a notice has to be served on every local authority and local planning authority whose area includes any land to which the order relates. A copy of the notice has to be displayed in a prominent position at the ends of so much of any path as is to be closed or diverted.[40]

---

[33] 1967 Act, s. 70(5).
[34] 1967 Act, Sched. 3, para. 3; 1982 Regulations, regs 12–17.
[35] 1967 Act, Sched. 3, para. 4.
[36] *ibid.* para. 2(1A) and (1).
[37] 1982 Regulations, reg 15 and Sched. 2 (Form).
[38] 1967 Act, Sched. 3, para. 1.
[39] *ibid.* Sched. 3, para. 1(3)(a) and (b).
[40] *ibid.* Sched. 3, para. 1(3)(b).

Where representations or objections are made following upon publication and service of notices, the draft order requires to go to the Secretary of State for possible confirmation.

If any representations or objections are made and then withdrawn, the Secretary of State may, if he thinks fit, confirm the order with or without modifications or conditions.[41]

Where representations or objections are not withdrawn, before confirming any order the Secretary of State requires either to cause a public inquiry to be held or to afford any person who made representations or objections an opportunity of being heard by a person appointed by the Secretary of State. After considering the report made by the person appointed to hold the inquiry or to hear the representations or objections, the Secretary of State may confirm the order with or without modifications or conditions.[42] Where the objection is made by any statutory undertaker on the ground that the order provides for the creation of a right of way over land used for the purpose of the undertaking or the curtilage of such land and the objection is not withdrawn, the order requires to be subject to special parliamentary procedure.[43]

Where the Secretary of State proposes to confirm an order with modifications that affect land outwith the land originally affected by the proposed order, the Secretary of State shall not confirm the order unless such notice as appears to him requisite is given of his proposal to modify the order and an opportunity is given for representations or objections and subsequent inquiry or opportunity to be hear is given.[44]

Publication of orders

9–08   As soon after an order has been made or confirmed, the authority or the Secretary of State requires to publish, in the same manner as notices of the draft order were given, a notice in the prescribed form describing the general effect of the order, stating that it has been confirmed and naming a place where a copy thereof may be inspected free of charge. Where notices of the proposed order were served, a copy of the confirmed order requires to be served on the same parties, if they have requested service of the confirmed order or displayed in the same manner.[45]

---

[41] 1967 Act, Sched. 3, para. 2(1).
[42] *ibid*. Sched. 3, para. 2(2).
[43] *ibid*. proviso. See para. 8 of Sched. 3 to the 1967 Act.
[44] 1967 Act, Sched. 3, para. 2(3).
[45] *ibid*. Sched. 3, para. 4.

Appeal procedures

Any appeal to the Court of Session has to be made within six **9–09**
weeks of the first publication of the confirmation of the order.
Any person aggrieved by an order, who desires to question the
validity thereof, or any provision contained therein, on the ground
that it was not within the powers of the 1967 Act or on any
ground that any requirement of the Act or of any regulations made
thereunder have not been complied with in relation thereto, may,
within six weeks from the date on which the notice of confirmation
was first published, make an application to the Court of Session.[46]
The Court of Session may by interim order suspend the operation of the order or any provision contained therein either
generally or so far as it affects any property of the application and,
if satisfied that the order, or any provision contained therein, is not
within the powers of the Act or that the interests of the applicant
have been substantially prejudiced by failure to comply with any
such requirement, may quash the order or any provision contained
therein, either generally or in so far as it affects any property of the
applicant.[47]
If the order is not appealed within six weeks, it may not be
questioned in any legal proceedings whatever.[48]

---

[46] 1967 Act, Sched. 3, para. 5. This appeal procedure and grounds of appeal are
virtually identical to appeal procedures against planning and compulsory decision.
[47] *ibid.* Sched. 3, para. 6.
[48] *ibid.* Sched. 3, para. 7. See *Pollock v. Secretary of State for Scotland*, 1993 S.L.T.
1173 for a consideration of the law relating to such an "ouster clause", where held
that failure to serve the relevant notices could not be challenged by judicial review
outwith the six-week period.

CHAPTER 10

RECTIFYING A LAND CERTIFICATE

General

10–01   While the power conferred by section 9 of the Land Registration (Scotland) Act 1979 to rectify a land certificate granted under section 5(2) of the Act is entirely different from the power to vary or discharge a land obligation under the 1970 Act, there are similarities which warrant a discussion of the issues raised in this book.

The rectification of a land certificate, particularly if it relates to a burden, has analogies with a variation or discharge of a land obligation. There is a right of appeal to the Lands Tribunal against decisions of the Keeper of the Registers.[1]

The land certificate

10–02   Where the Keeper has completed the registration of an interest in land with "any enforceable real right pertaining to the interest or subsisting real burden or condition affecting the interest"[2] in the Land Register, he is required to issue to the applicant a land certificate which is "a copy of the title sheet, authenticated by the seal of the register".[3]

The effect of registration is to vest in the person registered as entitled a real right in the land "subject only to the effect of any matter entered in the title sheet of that interest".[4]

The land certificate is accepted for all purposes as sufficient evidence of the contents of the title sheet of which the land certificate is a copy.[5]

---

[1] 1979 Act, s. 25; see below para. 10–13.
[2] 1979 Act, s. 6(1)(e).
[3] *ibid.* s. 5(2).
[4] *ibid.* s. 3(1) (a); see *MRS Hamilton Ltd v. Keeper of the Registers,* May 19, 1998; Lands Tribunal LTS/LR/1997/ 4–8.
[5] 1979 Act, s. 5(4).

The tribunal has said of the Keeper's duties to investigate the state of the title before registering that[6]:

"[I]t would be wrong to state the keeper's duty to investigate in absolute terms. One essential difference between the Scottish and English systems of land registration is that the Scottish system does not involve any inquiry into possible opposing interests. These can be clarified in due course on registration of the neighbouring interests, however, either by a qualification of indemnity or, if necessary, by rectification of the original interest under s. 9 (3)—provided this does not prejudice the proprietor in possession. In England, in contrast, the general practice is to describe properties by reference to general boundaries (i.e. the exact line is undetermined). It is also possible, however, to seek registration with fixed boundaries, but in that case the chief land registrar must notify adjoining proprietors and, if objections are taken to the proposed registration, exercise his judicial functions to adjudicate on any resulting dispute. There are no such provisions in Scotland, however, and the keeper has no power to seek documents or information from neighbours. The only occasion on which the keeper can advise a third party of an application for registration is in relation to foreshore, and this procedure is not to enable the keeper to investigate the matter further and then adjudicate upon it, but rather to give the Crown an opportunity of challenging the applicant's title—see s. 14 of the Act. If the Crown takes steps to do so, the keeper nonetheless must proceed with the registration but must exclude indemnity so far as the foreshore is concerned".

In relation to burdens the situation is different in that the **10–03** Keeper's duty extends to confirming that there is a subsisting real burden, *i.e.* one which appears on the face of the title, without having an obligation to ascertain that it is enforceable, unless he warrants enforceability. The tribunal explains this obligation thus[7]:

"Furthermore, the Act recognises that there must be a limit on the keeper's investigation in relation to his compilation of a burdens section. Section 6 (1) (e) of the Act, it should be noted, deals with two quite distinct matters; *enforceable* real rights on the one hand, and *subsisting* real burdens on the other. As regards the latter, under s. 12 (3) (g) of the Act

---

[6] *Brookfield Developments Ltd v. Keeper of the Registers of Scotland*, 1989 S.L.T. (Lands Tr.) 105 at 110.
[7] *ibid*. at 109F.

indemnity is excluded in the case of loss arising because a burden so entered proves to be unenforceable, unless the keeper expressly assumes responsibility for its enforceability. The use by the draftsman of these two different adjectives is in our view deliberate and is an acknowledgement that the keeper quite simply will not, on many occasions, know whether a burden is enforceable or not. In our view, "subsisting" in the context can only mean appearing on the face of the titles relating to the interest in question as still remaining in being. On many occasions the keeper may well be able to identify from the titles whether a burden is still enforceable or not. In some cases what appears on the face of it to be a subsisting burden may in fact, after inquiry, prove to be (un)enforceable; but we do not think that in carrying out his duties under s. 6 (1) of the Act the keeper has any duty to make inquiries of this nature, which in any event may not provide an answer."

Therefore in relation to burdens or land obligations, while these may appear on the face of the title, they are not necessarily enforceable. In an application under section 1 of the 1970 Act, the tribunal will treat such burdens as prima facie enforceable and therefore subject to their jurisdiction. If a party seeks to challenge the enforceability of a registered burden an application will have to be made to the court or the tribunal under section 25 of the 1979 Act for rectification of the register.

Rectification of the register[8]

10–04   Section 9 of the 1979 Act gives the Keeper certain powers to "rectify any inaccuracy" in the Land Register, subject to particular qualifications and subject to the rights to indemnification given by section 12. "(T)he provisions about rectification of the register contained in ss 9 and 12 of the Act are in some respects extremely obscure and difficult to understand".[9]

Section 9(1) provides that "the Keeper may . . . rectify any inaccuracy in the register". The word "may" is suggestive of an element of discretion. It has been held in England, where

---

[8] There are rectification provisions for the English Land Register in s. 82 of the Land Registration Act 1925, although being rather different the provisions and English case law have to be treated with caution.

[9] *Short's Trustee v. Keeper of the Registers of Scotland*, 1996 S.C. (H.L.) 14, *per* Lord Keith at 19G.

section 82(1) of the Land Registration Act provides that "The register may be rectified", that this is a discretionary power.[10] "Rectify any inaccuracy" has been given a wide meaning to include any incorrect or erroneous entry in or omission from the register. The tribunal has said that[11]:

> "The meaning of the word 'inaccuracy' appearing in s. 9 (1), as a result of which corrective insertions, amendments or cancellations may need to be made should, in our opinion, be construed widely so as to include any incorrect or erroneous entry in or omission from the register."

The fact that the Keeper might have properly carried out his administrative functions in preparing the burdens section "cannot, in our view, convert a burden which should have been excluded because it was in truth no longer subsisting into a subsisting one".[12]

The Keeper may, whether on being so requested or not, and shall on being ordered by the court[13] or the Lands Tribunal, rectify any inaccuracy in the register by inserting, amending or cancelling anything therein, subject to specific restrictions set out in section 9(3).[14]

Effectively the restriction provided by section 9(3) prevents the Keeper from rectifying the register if the proprietor in possession[15] would be prejudiced, except in the limited circumstances provided by the subsection. Section 9(3) provides:

> "(3) If rectification under subsection (1) above would prejudice a proprietor in possession—
> (a) the Keeper may exercise his power to rectify only where—
> (i) the purpose of the rectification is to note an overriding interest or to correct any information in the register relating to an overriding interest;

[10] *Claridge v. Tingley, Re Sea View Gardens* [1967] 1 W.L.R. 134, where the court suggested that if a proprietor stood by and allowed work to be done on the land, before applying for rectification, that might be a case to exercise the discretion against rectification.

[11] *Brookfield Developments Ltd v. Keeper of the Registers of Scotland*, 1989 S.L.T. (Lands Tr.) 105 at 109F.

[12] *ibid.* at 110K.

[13] Any court having jurisdiction in questions of heritable right: 1979 Act, s. 9(4)(a).

[14] 1979 Act, s. 9(1).

[15] The "proprietor in possession" means the person appearing as proprietor on the face of the Land Register: *Short's Trustee v. Keeper of the Registers of Scotland*, 1994 S.C. 122, *per* Lord Coulsfield at 128F. It is the "owner of land who is in possession"; it may apply to a proprietor in posesion, *e.g.* through a student daughter; it does not include the holder of a standard security unless decree of foreclosure has been obtained or someone merely in possession of some other legal interest: *Kaur v. Singh*, 1999 S.C. 180.

(ii) all persons whose interests in land are likely to be affected by the rectification have been informed by the Keeper of his intention to rectify and have consented in writing;

(iii) the inaccuracy has been caused wholly or substantially by the fraud or carelessness of the proprietor in possession[16]; or

(iv) the rectification relates to a matter in respect of which indemnity has been excluded under section 12(2) of this Act;

(b) the court or the Lands Tribunal for Scotland may order the Keeper to rectify only where sub-paragraph (i), (iii) or (iv) of paragraph (a) above applies or the rectification is consequential on the making of an order under section 8 of the Law Reform (Miscellaneous Provisions) (Scotland) Act 1985."

A rectification is permissible if the proprietor in possession will not be prejudiced. It may be a question of fact and/or law whether or not the proprietor in possession will be prejudiced. For example, the benefited proprietor of a real burden could have it removed from his title sheet if it was found to be no longer enforceable in law, or a servitude or other right could be entered on the title sheet if it had been acquired by prescription.[17] Such a proprietor would not be prejudiced because the right subject to the entry did, or as the case may be did not, exist in law irrespective of the title sheet. In *Re Chowood's Registered Land*[18] it was held that a rectification of the register would not put the applicant in a worse position than they were in before such rectification, because the other party had acquired rights to an area of land that was to be removed from the registered title under the Real Property Limitation Acts.

10–05   The court or the tribunal may order the Keeper to rectify the register only if grounds (i), (iii) or (iv) apply or the rectification is consequential on the making of an order under section 8 of the Law Reform (Miscellaneous Provisions) (Scotland) 1985.[19]

---

[16] See *Re Leighton's Conveyance* [1937] Ch. 149 (English Land Register rectified where daughter fraudulently obtained registration in her own name, when the title to the land was in her mother's name) and *Claridge v. Tingley, Re Sea View Gardens* [1967] 1 W.L.R. 134 which refers to a party lodging a "document which contains a misdescription of the property, then he has caused or substantially contributed to the mistake."; *Re 139 High Street, Deptford* [1951] 1 Ch. 884, where the applicant for registration made a mistake as to what was conveyed to him and therefore was held to have contributed to the mistake in the registration.

[17] See s. 3(2) of the 1979 Act: "Registration . . . shall be without prejudice to any other means of creating or affecting real rights or obligations under any enactment or rule of law."

[18] [1933] 1 Ch. 574.

[19] 1979 Act, s. 9(3)(b). Ground (ii) is not applicable because that is a rectification with the consent of all persons whose interests are likely to be affected.

Section 8 of the 1985 Act permits a rectification of a document only if the interests of defined third parties "would not be adversely affected to a material extent by the rectification", thus effectively imposing a similar test to that in section 9 of the 1979 Act.[20] Where a rectification is made in consequence of a section 8 order, the court "may order that the rectification shall have effect as from such later date as it may specify".[21]

Where the Keeper has examined the title deeds and entered a burden in the land register, the court or the tribunal may examine the title in detail to determine whether or not the burden is still a subsisting real burden or condition. If the court or tribunal determines that it is not still subsisting, subject to section 9(3)(b), the court or tribunal may order that the entry be corrected. Similarly, if a subsisting burden has been excluded the court or tribunal, subject to section 9(3)(b), may order the burden to be included.[22]

Where a disposition is reduced by the Court of Session, for example, on the ground that it was a gratuitous alienation by a sequestrated person, the Keeper may rectify the register, or be ordered to rectify the register, only if the limited provisions of section 9(3) apply. As Lord Keith said in *Short's Trustee v. Keeper of the Registers of Scotland*[23]:

> "So in my opinion the correct interpretation of the relevant provisions of ss 9 and 12 is that the remedy intended to be available to a person who has obtained the reduction of such a deed is either rectification of the register, if s 9 (3) (a) (ii) or (iii) applies, or if they do not then indemnity under s 12 (1) (b)."

Indemnification

Unless the Keeper has excluded the right to indemnification **10–06** under section 12(2) of the 1979 Act, there is a right to be indemnified, whether or not the Keeper refused to rectify the register or is not empowered to rectify it.[24]

---

[20] s. 9(1) of the Law Reform (Miscellaneous Provisions) (Scotland) Act 1985.
[21] Proviso to s. 9(3A) of the 1979 Act.
[22] *Brookfield Developments Ltd v. Keeper of the Registers of Scotland*, 1989 S.L.T. (Lands Tr.) 105, a case where the feu and superiority were consolidated and the question arose whether there remained any third party rights to enforce the burdens, that the Keeper had included. The tribunal held that, upon a proper construction of the title deeds, there were no third party rights and ordered the burdens to be struck out.
[23] 1996 S.C. (H.L.) 14, *per* Lord Keith at 22B.
[24] *Short's Trustee v. Keeper of the Registers of Scotland*, 1996 S.C. (H.L.) 14, *per* Lord Keith at 20G.

The first prerequisite of making a claim for indemnification is that loss must have been suffered and the second is that the loss must be attributed to one or more of the events (a) to (d) specified in section 12(1) of the 1979 Act.[25]

No form is prescribed for claiming indemnity. The claim must be made in writing to the Keeper and should quantify the loss, providing proof that it has resulted from one or more of the matters referred to in section 12(1) of the 1979 Act.[26]

Registration of title is designed to provide for a state guaranteed title and, as the circumstances under which the register may be rectified are limited, section 12(1) of the 1979 Act provides for indemnification by the Keeper for any "person who suffers loss as a result of":

> "(a) a rectification of the register made under section 9 of this Act;
>   (b) the refusal or omission of the Keeper to make such a rectification;
>   (c) the loss or destruction of any document while lodged with the Keeper;
>   (d) an error or omission in any land or charge certificate or in any information given by the Keeper in writing or in such other manner as may be prescribed by rules made under section 27 of this Act, shall be entitled to be indemnified by the Keeper in respect of that loss."

It should be noted that it is the "person who suffers loss", who is entitled to indemnification and it is this "interest" that was noted by the Lands Tribunal in *MRS Hamilton Ltd v. Keeper of the Registers*[27] as providing the right to make a claim.

The reason for this right to indemnification was explained in the Henry Report[28]:

> "On the other hand, under registration of title, which we advocate, all registered interests become indefeasible except in the rare case in which rectification of the register is allowed (see paragraphs 114 and 115); even in that case the state guarantee will ensure full compensation to the owner, and any other person who suffers loss by reason of any rectification, and any person who suffers loss because the register is not rectified will also be entitled to compensation."

---

[25] *Registration of Title Handbook* (HMSO, 1981), para. C.68.
[26] *ibid*.
[27] May 19, 1998; LTS/LR/1997/4–8.
[28] *Scheme for the Introduction and Operation of Registration of Title to Land in Scotland*, Cmnd 4137 (1969) ("the Henry Report"), para. 154.

The 1979 Act:

> "gives full effect to these principles. Rectification of the register is available only in a limited number of circumstances, and it is only just that a person clearly entitled to valuable rights who cannot bring himself within any of that limited number should receive compensation, unless there is good reason for denying it".[29]

Indemnity is also available:

> "where the keeper has refused or omitted to make a rectification (s 12 (1) (b)). Here a question arises whether the right arises where the keeper has refused to rectify because he has no power to do so under s 9 (3) (a) or only where he has such power but has failed to exercise it. Presumably the former is the correct view, because in the latter case the court could and would on application to it order him to rectify under s 9 (3) (b). It is, however, somewhat strange to speak of a person who has obtained the reduction or variation of a title under any of the enactments specified in s 12 (3) (b) but has failed to secure rectification of the register as having suffered loss which has arisen 'in respect of a title'. Although these enactments, other than the Divorce (Scotland) Act 1976, did not appear in the subparagraph as originally enacted, but were added by amendment, the point remained good on its original form. It is even stranger to speak of a person in whose favour an order under s 5 (2) of the Presumption of Death (Scotland) Act 1977 has been made as having suffered loss 'in consequence of the making' of the order (s 12 (3) (c)). The correct conclusion, in my opinion, is that the person in whose favour an order of the nature referred to in paras (b) and (c) has been made, is not, upon a proper construction of these paragraphs, a person who has suffered a loss of the nature thereby contemplated in the event of the keeper refusing to rectify the register so as to give effect to the order. Such a person has, however, undoubtedly suffered a loss through the keeper's refusal to rectify the register and is therefore entitled to an indemnity from him for it".[30]

---

[29] *Short's Trustee v. Keeper of the Registers of Scotland*, 1996 S.C. (H.L.) 14, *per* Lord Keith at 21C.
[30] *ibid. per* Lord Keith at 20G.

The Lands Tribunal,[31] in rejecting a submission that section 12(1)(d) did not relate to errors or omissions in the land certificate, explained section 12(1)(d) on the basis:

> "It may be that section 12(1)(d), like section 12(1)(c), was inserted to cover risks of clerical or administrative error, and that the risk of an inaccurate copy was, indeed, in mind, but we cannot accept that the provision as enacted is restricted to deficiencies in copying. It covers errors or omission in information given by the Keeper in writing and that must be error or omission assessed by reference to the true facts. A Land Certificate which does not include a burden which should have appeared on it, can be said to contain an omission even if the explanation for omission is that is was missed from the title sheet."

10–07   Section 12(3) provides for specific exclusions of indemnity.[32] These subheads "appear to cover a variety of miscellaneous circumstances and not to be related by a single unifying principle".[33] These are:

> "(3) There shall be no entitlement to indemnity under this section in respect of loss where—
> (a) the loss arises as a result of a title prevailing over that of the claimant in a case where—
> (i) the prevailing title is one in respect of which the right to indemnity has been partially excluded under subsection (2) above, and
> (ii) such exclusion has been cancelled but only on the prevailing title having been fortified by prescription;
> (b) the loss arises in respect of a title which has been reduced, whether or not under subsection (4) of section 34, or subsection (5) of section 36, of the Bankruptcy (Scotland) Act 1985 (or either of those subsections as applied by sections 615A and 615B of the Companies Act 1985, respectively), as a gratuitous alienation or fraudulent preference, or has been reduced or varied by an order under section 6(2) of the Divorce (Scotland) Act 1976 or by an order made by virtue of

---

[31] Lord Hamilton concurred in *MRS Hamilton Ltd v. Keeper of the Registers for Scotland*, Court of Session, Lord Hamilton, June 18, 1998 (not appealed on merits, but quantum still in issue).

[32] *Registration of Title Handbook* (HMSO, 1981), paras C.70–C.84 for a commentary on these exceptions.

[33] *Short's Trustee v. Keeper of the Registers of Scotland*, above, *per* Lord Coulsfield at 128E.

section 29 of the Matrimonial and Family Proceedings Act 1984 (orders relating to settlements and other dealings) or has been set aside or varied by an order under section 18(2) (orders relating to avoidance transactions) of the Family Law (Scotland) Act 1985;

(c) the loss arises in consequence of the making of a further order under section 5(2) of the Presumption of Death (Scotland) Act 1977 (effect on property rights of recall or variation of decree of declarator of presumed death);

(d) the loss arises as a result of any inaccuracy in the delineation of any boundaries shown in a title sheet, being an inaccuracy which could not have been rectified by reference to the Ordnance Map, unless the Keeper has expressly assumed responsibility for the accuracy of that delineation;

(e) the loss arises, in the case of land extending to 2 hectares or more the area of which falls to be entered in the title sheet of an interest in that land under section 6(1)(a) of this Act, as a result of the Keeper's failure to enter such area in the title sheet or, where he has so entered such area, as a result of any inaccuracy in the specification of that area in the title sheet;

(f) the loss arises in respect of an interest in mines and minerals and the title sheet of any interest in land which is or includes the surface land does not expressly disclose that the interest in mines and minerals is included in that interest in land;

(g) the loss arises from inability to enforce a real burden or condition entered in the register, unless the Keeper expressly assumes responsibility for the enforceability of that burden or condition;

(h) the loss arises in respect of an error or omission in the noting of an overriding interest; the loss is suffered by—

(i) a beneficiary under a trust in respect of any transaction entered into by its trustees or in respect of any title granted by them the validity of which is unchallengeable by virtue of section 2 of the Trusts (Scotland) Act 1961 (validity of certain transactions by trustees), or as the case may be, section 17 of the Succession (Scotland) Act 1964 (protection of persons acquiring title), or

(ii) a person in respect of any interest transferred to him by trustees in purported implement of trust purposes;

(k) the loss arises as a result of an error or omission in an office copy as to the effect of any subsisting adverse entry in the Register of Inhibitions and Adjudications affecting any person in respect of any registered interest in land, and that person's entitlement to that interest is neither disclosed in the register nor otherwise known to the Keeper;

(l) the claimant is the proprietor of the dominant tenement in a servitude, except insofar as the claim may relate to the validity of the constitution of that servitude;

(m) the claimant is a superior, a creditor in a ground annual or a landlord under a long lease and the claim relates to any information—

(i) contained in the feu writ, the contract of ground annual or the lease, as the case may be, and

(ii) omitted from the title sheet of the interest of the superior, creditor or landlord, (except insofar as the claim may relate to the constitution or amount of the feuduty, ground annual or rent and adequate information has been made available to the Keeper to enable him to make an entry in the register in respect of such constitution or amount or to the description of the land in respect of which the feuduty, ground annual or rent is payable);

(n) the claimant has by his fraudulent or careless act or omission caused the loss[34];

(o) the claim relates to the amount due under a heritable security;

(p) the loss arises from a rectification of the register consequential on the making of an order under section 8 of the Law Reform (Miscellaneous Provisions) (Scotland) Act 1985."

10–08   Lord Keith of Kinkel commented on section 12(3)(b) and (c) in *Short's Trustee*[35] suggesting that these sub-paragraphs do not in fact exclude indemnity. He said that:

"Paragraphs (b) and (c) of s 12 (3) appear to contemplate that a rectification of the register causing loss may have occurred as a result of an order of the court made under one or other of the specified enactments. But under s 9 (3) (a) (iii) no rectification can be made if it would prejudice the proprietor in possession, unless that proprietor has caused the inaccuracy through his fraud or carelessness. If that proprietor has suffered loss he must be prejudiced. If he would be

---

[34] See Lord Keith in *Short's Trustee v. Keeper of the Registers of Scotland*, above, at 20E–F: "possibly para (n) is intended to be a catch all provision". *MRS Hamilton Ltd v. Keeper of the Registers for Scotland*, Court of Session, Lord Hamilton, June 18, 1998. *Dougbar Properties Ltd v. Keeper of the Registers of Scotland*, Lord Macfadyen, February 9, 1999.

[35] *Short's Trustee v. Keeper of the Registers of Scotland*, above, at 20 B–F and 21 A–B.

prejudiced he would be unlikely to consent to a rectification under s 9 (3) (a) (ii), though that subparagraph certainly contemplates the possibility. In the great majority of cases where an order might be made under any of the enactments specified in s 12 (3) (b) or (c), particularly the matrimonial enactments and the Presumption of Death (Scotland) Act 1977, the prospect of the proprietor in possession having caused the so called inaccuracy by his fraud or carelessness must be extremely remote. On any view it follows that many orders of the court under these enactments would apparently be incapable of receiving effect by way of rectification of the Land Register. No doubt it is reasonable that a person who has caused an inaccuracy by his fraud or carelessness should not be entitled to an indemnity on rectification of it, but para (n) of s 12 (3) specifically excludes indemnity where 'the claimant has by his fraudulent or careless act or omission caused the loss'. The need for paras (b) and (c), so far as the proprietor in possession is concerned, is therefore not apparent, though possibly para (n) is intended to be a catch all provision covering a variety of situations. It may be that the draftsman had in mind possible cases where the proprietor in possession consented to rectification following an order for reduction or rectification, notwithstanding that he would be prejudiced and suffer loss. . . .

"The correct conclusion, in my opinion, is that the person in whose favour an order of the nature referred to in paras (b) and (c) has been made, is not, upon a proper construction of these paragraphs, a person who has suffered a loss of the nature thereby contemplated in the event of the Keeper refusing to rectify the register so as to give effect to the order. Such a person has, however, undoubtedly suffered a loss through the Keeper's refusal to rectify the register and is therefore entitled to an indemnity from him for it. . . .

"The inference is that Parliament did not intend that reduction of a deed constituting a title or midcouple should in general be an occasion for rectification of the register. The possibility of such a reduction was, however, within the contemplation of Parliament, as s 12 (3) (b) shows. The intention must therefore have been that the reduction should only lead to rectification of the register if the case fell within the limited parameters of s 9 (3) (a), particularly subpara (iii). It would be unjust if, in a case not falling within those parameters, the person in whose favour the reduction had been granted would have no right to indemnity following a necessary refusal to rectify the register. Nothing in paras (b) or (c) of s 12 (3) leads properly to the conclusion that he is intended to be excluded from the right."

10–08A   In *Dougbar Properties Ltd v. Keeper of the Registers of Scotland*[35a] Lord Macfadyen held that a proprietor of a registered interest in land can sustain a loss where the Land Register is rectified, even in circumstances where the proprietor knew that the Register contained an inaccuracy and might be rectified.

10–09   If a claimant to indemnity has by his fraudulent or careless act or omission contributed to the loss in respect of which he makes a claim, the amount of indemnity to which he would have been entitled, had he not contributed to his loss, shall be reduced proportionately to the extend to which he has so contributed.[36] This subsection should be read in conjunction with section 9(3)(iii) which permits the rectification of the register if "the inaccuracy has been caused wholly or substantially by the fraud of carelessness of the proprietor in possession" and with section 12(3)(n) which excludes indemnity where "the claimant has by his fraudulent or careless act or omission caused the loss".[37]

10–10   On settlement of any claim for indemnity under section 12, the Keeper is subrogated to all rights which would have been available to the claimant to recover the loss indemnified.[38] The Keeper may require a claimant, as a condition of payment of his claim, to grant, at the Keeper's expense, a formal assignation to the Keeper of any of the rights to which the Keeper is subrogated.[39]

Function of the Keeper

10–11   In the first instance it is for the Keeper to assess, whether or not a competent claim under section 12(1) has been made; to assess the quantification of the claim and to determine whether or not any of the exclusions or a contributory element should be applied.

If a party is dissatisfied with a determination by the Keeper of his claim or its quantification, then there is a right of appeal to the Lands Tribunal under section 25 of the 1979 Act or a right to take other court proceedings.

[35a] Court of Session, February 9, 1999.
[36] 1979 Act, s. 13(4).
[37] See below, para. 10–20.
[38] 1979 Act, s. 13(2).
[39] *ibid.* s. 13(3).

Expenses[40]

The Keeper is under an obligation to reimburse any expenditure **10–12**
reasonably incurred in pursuing a prima facie well-founded claim,
whether successful or not.[41] This obligation to reimburse arises
whether or not the claim is made with or without recourse to the
courts.

Section 13(1) of the 1979 Act provides:

> "Subject to any order by the Lands Tribunal for Scotland or
> the court for the payment of expenses in connection with any
> claim disposed of by the Lands Tribunal under section 25 of
> this Act or the court, the Keeper shall reimburse any expendi-
> ture reasonably and properly incurred by a person in pursuing
> a *prima facie* well-founded claim under section 12 of this Act,
> whether successful or not."

Subject to any order by the Lands Tribunal or court, it is for the
Keeper to assess what is "reasonably and properly incurred"
expenditure and to determine whether or not it was incurred "in
pursuing a *prima facie* well-founded claim". No statutory guidance
is given, although there is some resemblance to the basis of
charging in court proceedings where "Only such expenses as are
reasonable for conducting the cause in a proper manner shall be
allowed".[42]

Of section 13(1), Lord Hamilton has said[43]:

> "Section 13(1), on the other hand, does not in my view confer
> on the court of the tribunal any wider power in relation to
> expenses than they respectively have otherwise. The terms of
> the sub-section may be contrasted with statutory provisions
> which confer on a court a special power or duty in relation to
> expenses. Examples are section 154 of the Representation of
> the People Act 1983 and section 68(17) of the Corrupt and
> Illegal Practices Prevention Act 1883 (applied in *Hood v.
> Gordon* (1896) 23 R. 675, but now repealed). Moreover, it is
> not self evident that expenses of process on an agent and
> client basis are in all respect co-extensive with the expenditure
> referred to in section 13(1)."

MRS Hamilton Ltd, after the success at debate before the
Lands Tribunal, applied to the Keeper for an interim payment of

---

[40] *Registration of Title Handbook* (HMSO, 1981), para. C.86.
[41] 1979 Act, s. 13(1).
[42] Rules of the Court of Session, r. 42.10; see *Ahmed's Tr v. Ahmed (No. 1)*, 1993
S.L.T. 390.
[43] *MRS Hamilton Ltd v. Keeper of the Registers for Scotland*, Court of Session,
Lord Hamilton, June 18, 1998.

expenses under section 13(1). The Lands Tribunal had made an award of judicial expenses of the debate, without prejudice to any claim under section 13(1). The Keeper declined to consider the application until the proceedings were concluded. MRS Hamilton Ltd applied, in the Lands Tribunal appeal proceedings, by Single Bill to the Court of Session effectively for an order that the Keeper should reconsider that decision. In delivering the opinion of the court, Lord Coulsfield explained the scope of section 13(1), saying[44]:

> "In our view, it is clear that, as Lord Hamilton held, section 13(1) does not expand or add to the powers of the court in regard to making awards of expenses, interim or otherwise. The subsection does not, on its terms, confer any power on the court at all. What it does is to place an obligation on the Keeper to reimburse expenditure reasonably and properly incurred. Accordingly, the appropriate way of proceeding is to apply to the Keeper and, if necessary, to appeal against his decision under section 25 or proceed by judicial review. What the Keeper has to do, in our view, is to apply the statutory test to any application made to him, and decide on that basis whether to make reimbursement or not. The decision is not a discretionary one in the way that an ordinary decision on the expenses of a judicial proceeding would be: and the decision of the tribunal or the court on an appeal would similarly be a decision on the statutory basis. On the other hand, it appears to us that the Keeper must have some discretion as to whether he is in a position to deal with any given application made to him in relation to expenses incurred in pursuing a claim to indemnity under section 12, so long as the claim is not finally determined. There may well be cases in which some part, or the whole, of an application under section 13 is susceptible of determination even though a judicial proceeding is still in process, and there does not appear to be any reason in principle why an application should not, if appropriate in all the circumstances, be made by instalments. On the other hand there may equally be cases in which no decision can properly be taken until the judicial process is completed. If the Keeper takes an unreasonable view in deciding whether or not to deal with an application for reimbursement, his decision may, of course, be subject to review either through the appeal process or by judicial review. So far as the present case is concerned,

---

[44] *Keeper of the Registers of Scotland v. MRS Hamilton Ltd*, 1998 S.C. 116 at 119G.

therefore, the position seems to be simply this, that the subject matter of the motion before us is not a matter for this court to determine at this stage but that any application must be made to the Keeper, who must consider it and decide firstly whether he can appropriately deal with it at this stage and, secondly, if he can deal with it, whether he is under an obligation to reimburse the whole or any part of the claim.
We would only add two points. Firstly, we do not think that there is anything in section 13(1) to indicate that it was intended to function as some sort of legal aid provision. It may, in practice, give some benefit to a litigant, but it is not in our view designed to assist a litigant in obtaining finance for proceeding with a claim. It confers a legal right, which must be determined on the statutory terms. Secondly, we express no opinion on the question of the interrelation between awards of expenses and applications for reimbursement. The fact that there is provision that awards of reimbursement are subject to any orders of the court suggests that there may be an overlap between matters which can be dealt with by the court as expenses of process and claims for reimbursement under section 13(1). If so, a court applying the ordinary rules as to expenses following success might reach a different conclusion from that which would be reached by the Keeper under section 13(1). On the other hand, it might be arguable that a court or tribunal should take account of the terms of section 13(1) in deciding whether or not to make an award of expenses. However, any questions which may arise can only be resolved as the cases occur."

From this it can be seen that the scope and extent of section 13(1) remain far from clear.

Right of appeal

Section 25 provides: **10–13**

"(1) Subject to subsections (3) and (4) below, an appeal shall lie, on any question of fact or law arising from anything done or omitted to be done by the Keeper under this Act, to the Lands Tribunal for Scotland.
(2) Subject to subsections (3) and (4) below, subsection (1) is without prejudice to any right of recourse under any enactment other than this Act or under any rule of law."

It is important to note that the right of appeal is on any "question of fact or law". The jurisdiction of other courts (*e.g.* the Court of Session on judicial review) may exclude examination of the facts.

The scope of subsection (2) is far from clear. In *Short's Trustee v. Keeper of the Registers of Scotland*[45] the Keeper took a plea to the competency of the judicial review but, reserving his position, did not argue it as he wished a quick determination of the important question in issue. Lord Coulsfield said: "In view of the provisions of sec. 25(2), I do not think that the point of competency is so obvious that it must be *pars judicis* to determine it."

Acts or omissions of the Keeper have been challenged by judicial review[46] or by application to the Commercial Court of the Court of Session[47] and by appeal to the Lands Tribunal.[48]

Section 9(1), which refers to the Keeper rectifying the register following upon an order of the court[49] or of the Lands Tribunal, makes clear that other courts have this jurisdiction, at least in relation to instructing the Keeper to rectify the register.

MRS Hamilton Ltd cases

10–14   There have been two recent cases, both at the instance of *MRS Hamilton Ltd v. Keeper of the Registers of Scotland*[50] ("MRSH"), in which the scope of the indemnity given by section 12(1) has been examined in detail.

The facts

10–15   MRSH purchased the Blackwood Estate in 1994 from a Mr Douglas, who had acquired the estate from the Western European Building Corporation Ltd (WEBCO) in 1991. In the last century the Blackwood Estate had granted a number of 999 (or 975) year leases, of which MRSH became the landlord on the acquisition of the estate.

In the Court of Session action, MRSH claimed indemnification arising from the fact that in granting a land certificate in 1986 on

---

[45] 1994 S.C. 122, *per* Lord Coulsfield at 134G–135A; and the Lord President at 135E.

[46] *Short's Trustee v. Keeper of the Registers of Scotland*, 1996 S.C. (H.L.) 14.

[47] *MRS Hamilton Ltd v. Keeper of the Registers for Scotland*, Court of Session, Lord Hamilton, June 18, 1998.

[48] *ibid.* May 19, 1998; LTS/LR/1997/4–8; *Brookfield Developments Ltd v. Keeper of the Registers of Scotland*, 1989 S.L.T. (Lands Tr.) 105.

[49] s. 9(4) of the 1979 Act defines "court" as "any court having jurisdiction in questions of heritable right or title".

[50] *MRS Hamilton Ltd v. Keeper of the Registers for Scotland*, Court of Session, Lord Hamilton, June 18, 1998 (not appealed on merits, but quantum still in issue); *MRS Hamilton Ltd v. Keeper of the Registers for Scotland*, May 19, 1998; LTS/LR/1997/4–8 (Lord McGhie, President) (under appeal to the Court of Session).

the assignation of leased subjects, the Keeper had included within the land certificate an area of land about the same size again as the leased area (the back land) belonging to the Blackwood Estate, which was not subject to the lease. The Keeper did not exclude indemnity under section 12(2). The back land had been occupied by the lessee since about 1974. At the time of sale to MRSH neither Mr Douglas nor MRSH was aware of the error in the land certificate and it was averred that "the consideration given by (MRSH) to Mr Douglas was not affected by the error".

In the Lands Tribunal action MRSH claimed indemnification for the loss arising from the fact that the Keeper had failed to include within a number of land certificates issued on the assignation of leased subjects, the casualty provisions, which ought to have been included under section 6(1)(e) and (2). The casualty allowed for "a full year's rent" to be paid to the landlord on each assignation of the leased subjects. These land certificates were granted in 1986 and 1987 when WEBCO were the proprietors. There had been a number of subsequent assignations of these subjects during the proprietorship of both Mr Douglas and MRSH, for which causalities could not be claimed, because the casualty clauses had been omitted from the land register and land certificates. MRSH claimed indemnity under section 12(1)(b) and (d) of the 1979 Act.

In both cases the Keeper was unable to rectify the land certificate under section 9(1), because none of the factors in section 9(3) applied.

Both WEBCO and Mr Douglas had assigned to MRSH any claim that they might have had against the Keeper arising from these errors in the land certificates.

Reason for indemnity

Lord Hamilton explained the background to state indemnity **10–16** thus:

> "It is of importance to bear in mind the nature of the change to security of title which the 1979 Act brought about. In place of a system largely dependent on examination of deeds recorded in the Sasine Register, the Act introduced a state guaranteed system of registration of title. Persons became entitled to rely on the contents of the relative title sheet (as reflected in a land certificate or authenticated copy title sheet) as the measure of real rights in respect of interests in land. The possibility of inaccuracy in the registration process was recognised. Among other consequences of inaccuracy valuable 'true' rights might be lost. Against the prospect of loss

(including loss as a result of an unrectified inaccuracy) a system of state indemnity was provided unless in a particular case expressly excluded under section 12(2) by the Keeper on registration."

Person entitled to indemnification

10–17   The Keeper sought to argue that the right to make a claim for indemnity was restricted to the infeft proprietor at the time that the event which triggered a section 12(1) liability to indemnify arose, *i.e.* at the date of the Keeper's error or omission on first registration. This contention was rejected.

The primary contention in both cases was that MRSH had suffered no loss because MRSH had to take the title purchased as it stood and it was WEBCO or Mr Douglas who had been excluded from their land rights by the first registration and not MRSH. MRSH had suffered no diminution of their assets or its value.

Both Lord Hamilton and the Lands Tribunal held that it was the infeft proprietor at the time the error was discovered, and sought to have the error rectified, who was prima facie entitled to indemnification. In rejecting the Keeper's submission, and after explaining the background to the right to indemnity, Lord Hamilton said:

"Under the Sasine system a proprietor of land who discovered that possession had without agreement or permission been taken by another of that land or part of it was, unless a real right had been obtained by the possessor through positive prescription, entitled to take proceedings to remove the possessor. The entitlement to do so was vested in the proprietor for the time being, notwithstanding that possession had first been taken during the proprietorship of his immediate or a remoter predecessor in title. Had the Sasine system continued operation in Lanarkshire, the pursuer would have been entitled to secure such possession of the back land. As events have occurred, it is unable to do so. That is because the defender has refused to rectify the register so as to reflect the 'true' position, that refusal being the inevitable consequence where, as here, (1) indemnity was not excluded and (2) the affected person (*viz* the possessor or its successor in title) has not consented to rectification. In my view the disadvantage which the pursuer has suffered as a result of the events which have happened can properly be described as a 'loss' and is, at least *prima facie*, apt for indemnification under section 12. It is, in my view, an unduly narrow approach to the concept of loss for the purposes of that section to concentrate on the circumstance that the pursuer at *no* time during its ownership had a real right which included the right to vacant possession of the back land. That is to fail to recognise the genesis of the chain of events which led to the inability of the pursuer to secure such possession. Where it can be demonstrated (as the pursuer here offers to demonstrate) that no other ·person having had proprietorial rights in respect of the Blackwood Estate has been compensated for the diminution in the scope of those rights, the pursuer as the proprietor who first became aware of such diminution and has been refused rectification may properly be regarded as a person who, at least *prima facie*, has suffered loss as a result of that refusal. No doubt if it were to be demonstrated that financial account had already been taken of the prospect of such refusal (by adjustment of the purchase price paid by the pursuer or otherwise) its *prima facie* loss might be reduced or extinguished".

The Lands Tribunal reached a similar conclusion, saying:

"[I]t is important to look at the nature of the loss contemplated by the Act. In the first place it is plain that no provision is made for loss arising simply from omission or error in the title sheet as such. There is nothing in section 12 dealing with loss on first registration. On the contrary, title to claim indemnity appears to be given to the party faced with the consequences of any of the events there set out. With the possible exception of 12(1)(c) the subsection deals with events which would only occur sometime after first registration. The legislators must have been aware of the possibility of changes in title during such a period. It is loss to the party faced with one or other of the events specified which appears to be contemplated by the Act. Secondly, we have regard to the purpose to be served by the indemnity. The scheme for indemnity was necessary because the public benefit of certainty of the Register meant that parties had to lose the benefit of the right they had under the former Sasine system to go behind the recorded title. Under that system, if a party had better evidence to establish his rights, the adverse Sasine title would not necessarily prevail. Although the bases of loss set out under section 12(1) are varied, it seems clear that the right provided by section 12(1)(b), to be indemnified based on refusal to rectify is due to recognition that the claimants have lost their ability to rely on the rights they would have had under the rules of the Sasine system. The underlying basis of the present appellants' claim is that they have lost the rights they would otherwise have been able to rely on. This fits the scheme of the Act".

Right to assign claim against Keeper

10–18   In both cases MRSH had had assigned to them all WEBCO's and Mr Douglas's rights to claim against the Keeper. In the Court of Session action this was done on an *esto* basis, but in the Lands Tribunal certain of the casualty payment had fallen due prior to MRSH acquiring title.

The Keeper argued in both cases that there was no right to assign such claims and that in any event neither WEBCO nor Mr Douglas had sustained loss.

Lord Hamilton was reluctant to deal with the claim in the alternative, particularly without evidence, but expressed the view that if WEBCO was the party who lost the right to vacant possession of the back land, it would appear that it probably did not sustain loss, because it was not aware of the error in the land certificate and would appear to have received an undiminished price for the estate.

Both Lord Hamilton and the Lands Tribunal rejected a submission for the Keeper that "a claim for indemnity under section 12 was not of its nature assignable". Lord Hamilton said:

"There is no express exclusion of assignation of claims under section 12(1) of the 1979 Act and nothing in the words or schemes of the statute which by implication points to that result. The implication from the terms of the statute and from the common law background is, in my view, to the contrary. It would also be remarkable if claims did not pass by involuntary assignation (e.g. to a trustee in bankruptcy or to an executor-dative); I see no justification for excluding claims passing by voluntary assignation."

And the Lands Tribunal said:

"The rule is well established that incorporeal moveable rights are capable of assignation. We consider that there is nothing in the scheme of the 1979 Act which is reasonably capable of an inference that Parliament intended to exclude a right to assign indemnity. Plainly as a right to assign is normally implied, express provision is unnecessary and absence of express provision cannot lead to a contrary inference."

Prescription

In both actions, the Keeper argued that in any event the claims **10-19** had been extinguished by the short negative prescription under section 6 of the Prescription and Limitation (Scotland) Act 1973, because this was an obligation arising from a liability to make reparation. This contention was rejected, with the court and the tribunal holding that the long negative prescription applied to such claims.

Both Lord Hamilton and the Lands Tribunal, following *Miller v. City of Glasgow District Council*[51] and *Holt v. Dundee District Council*,[52] held that the obligation of the Keeper, which could arise without fault on his part, under section 12(1) was not an obligation of the kind referred to in Schedule 1(d) to the 1973 Act and was not an obligation to make reparation.

While the long negative prescription will therefore apply to claims for indemnity, the 10-year positive prescription under section 1 of the Prescription and Limitation (Scotland) Act 1973 may have the effect of excluding any loss by a claimant under section 12(1). If the 10-year prescriptive period has run to fortify what otherwise would have been a reducible title, it can be said that the claimant has in fact suffered no loss under the provisions of section 12(1).

Careless act or omission

In the Court of Session action, the Keeper sought exclusion of **10-20** indemnity, or in any event reduction of indemnity, on the ground that the proprietor had been careless by failing to realise that a person had encroached upon and occupied a larger area of land than he was entitled to occupy under the lease. Lord Hamilton said of sections 12(3)(n) and 13(4) of the 1979 Act that:

> "If in an operational area a proprietor so neglects his interests that substantial encroachment or other intrusion followed by protracted possession is effected by his neighbour, a situation may well be created on the ground which causes or contributed to an inaccuracy entering the register. In such circumstances that proprietor's failure to act may, in my view, constitute a careless omission for the purposes of the 1979 Act."

With hesitation, Lord Hamilton allowed proof of averments relating to an extended possession from 1974, the nature and extent of

---

[51] 1988 S.C. 440.
[52] 1990 S.L.T. (Lands Tr.) 30.

the encroachment amounting to about double the leased area and other related matters.[53]

10-21   In *Dougbar Properties Ltd v. Keeper of the Registers*[54] Lord Macfadyen held that knowledge that the Register was inaccurate and might be rectified was not sufficient on its own to be a careless act or omission. It is necessary to identify the act or omission which, in light of that knowledge, could be characterised as careless. The mere fact of continuing with a transaction, where there is knowledge of the inaccuracy, is not necessarily careless. Failure to draw the Keeper's attention to the inaccuracy at the time of registration of the proprietor's title is not a careless omission. Lord Macfadyen rejected the Keeper's contention that Dougbar should not be entitled to indemnification in respect of a loss that they knew from the outset they might suffer.

---

[53] Subsequently the Keeper conceded the merits of the case, leaving only quantum to be settled by the court.
[54] Court of Session, February 9, 1999.

APPENDICES

CONVEYANCING AND FEUDAL REFORM (SCOTLAND) ACT 1970

(1970 c. 35)

An Act to provide as respects Scotland for the variation and discharge of certain obligations relating to land; to facilitate the allocation of feu-duties and ground annuals; reduce the period of positive prescription of 20 years to 10 years; to provide for a new form of heritable security; to make certain amendments to the existing law relating to heritable securities; to make certain other amendments to the law relating to conveyancing; to abolish the rights of pre-emption of heritors in respect of glebes; to amend the Lands Tribunal Act 1949; and for connected purposes.

[29th May 1970]

PART I

FEUDAL REFORM

Variation and discharge of land obligations

Variation and discharge of land obligations

¹**1.**—(1) The provisions of this section and of section 2 of this Act shall, without prejudice to any other method of variation or discharge, apply for the variation or discharge of any land obligation, however constituted, and whether subsisting at the commencement of this Act or constituted thereafter:

Provided that the provisions of the said sections shall not apply in relation to an obligation specified or referred to in Schedule 1 to this Act.

(2) For the purposes of this section and of section 2 of this Act, a land obligation is an obligation relating to land which is enforceable by a proprietor of an interest in land, by virtue of his being

187

such proprietor, and which is binding upon a proprietor of another interest in that land, or of an interest in other land, by virtue of his being such proprietor.

For the purposes mentioned in this subsection, an obligation includes a future or contingent obligation, an obligation to defray or contribute towards some cost, an obligation to refrain from doing something, and an obligation to permit or suffer something to be done or maintained.

(3) Subject to the provisions of this section and of section 2 of this Act, the Lands Tribunal, on the application of any person who, in relation to a land obligation, is a burdened proprietor, may from time to time by order vary or discharge the obligation wholly or partially in relation to the interest in land in respect of which the application is made, on being satisfied that in all the circumstances,

  (a) by reason of changes in the character of the land affected by the obligation or of the neighbourhood thereof or other circumstances which the Tribunal may deem material, the obligation is or has become unreasonable or inappropriate; or

  (b) the obligation is unduly burdensome compared with any benefit resulting or which would result from its performance; or

  (c) the existence of the obligation impedes some reasonable use of the land.

(4) An order varying or discharging a land obligation under this section may direct the applicant to pay, to any person who in relation to that obligation is a benefited proprietor, such sum as the Lands Tribunal may think it just to award under one, but not both, of the following heads—

  (i) a sum to compensate for any substantial loss or disadvantage suffered by the proprietor as such benefited proprietor in consequence of the variation or discharge; or

  (ii) a sum to make up for any effect which the obligation produced, at the time when it was imposed, in reducing the consideration then paid or made payable for the interest in land affected by it:

but the Tribunal may refuse to vary or discharge land obligation on the ground specified in subsection (3)(c) of this section if they are of the opinion that due to exceptional circumstances related to amenity or otherwise, money would not be an adequate compensation for any loss or disadvantage which a benefited proprietor would suffer from the variation or discharge.

(5) The power conferred by this section to vary or discharge an obligation includes power to add or substitute any such provision (not being an award of money otherwise than by way of compensation under subsection (4) of this section) as appears to the Lands Tribunal to be reasonable as the result of the variation or discharge of the obligation and as may be accepted by the applicant; and the Tribunal may accordingly refuse to vary or discharge the obligation without some such provision.

(6) On the taking effect of an order under this section varying or discharging to any extent a land obligation, any irritant or resolutive clause or other condition relating to the enforcement of the obligation shall, in relation to any act or omission occurring after the date of such taking effect, be effective (if at all) only in so far as it would have been effective if the obligation had to that extent been varied or discharged by the person entitled to enforce the obligation; and any such added or substituted provision as is referred to in subsection (5) of this section shall be enforceable in the same manner as the obligation to the variation or discharge of which it relates.

AMENDMENT
1. Excluded by the Ancient Monuments and Archaeological Areas Act 1979 (c. 46), s. 17(7).

. . . . . .

Provisions supplementary to section 1

¹2.—(1) On an application under section 1 of this Act, the Lands Tribunal shall give such notice thereof, whether by way of advertisement or otherwise, as may be prescribed, to the persons who, in relation to the obligation which is the subject of the application, appear to them to be either benefited or burdened proprietors, and to such other person as the Tribunal may think fit.

(2) In an application to the Lands Tribunal under section 1 of this Act, any person who, in relation to the obligation which is the subject of the application, is either a burdened or a benefited proprietor, shall be entitled, within such time as may be prescribed, to oppose or make representations in relation to the application, and the Tribunal shall allow any such person, and may allow any other person who appears to them to be affected by the obligation or by its proposed variation or discharge, to be heard in relation to the application.

(3) An order made under section 1 of this Act shall take effect in accordance with such rules as may be prescribed.

²(4) Where an extract of an order made under section 1 of this Act which has taken effect is duly recorded, it shall be binding on all persons having interest.

(5) Where a land obligation is first created, whether before or after the commencement of this Act, in a conveyance, deed, instrument or writing, no application shall be brought under section 1 of this Act in relation thereto until the expiry of two years after the date of its creation.

(6) For the purposes of this section and of section 1 of this Act,

"benefited proprietor", in relation to a land obligation; means a proprietor of an interest in land who is entitled, by virtue of his being such proprietor, to enforce the obligation; and "burdened proprietor", in relation to such an obligation; means a proprietor of an interest in land upon whom, by virtue of his being such proprietor, the obligation is binding; and—

(i) the benefited proprietor or the burdened proprietor of an interest in land held by two or more persons jointly or in common means either all those persons or any of them;

(ii) the benefited proprietor or the burdened proprietor of an interest in land which is subject to a heritable security constituted by *ex facie* absolute disposition or assignation includes the person who, if the debt were discharged, would be entitled to be vested in that interest;

"interest in land" means any estate or interest in land which is capable of being owned or held as a separate interest and to which a title may be recorded in the Register of Sasines; "land obligation" has the meaning assigned to it in section 1(2) of this Act.

(7) Section 189 of the Housing (Scotland) Act 1966 (power of sheriff to authorise conversion of house into separate dwellings) shall cease to have effect.

AMENDMENTS

1. Excluded by the Ancient Monuments and Archaeological Areas Act 1979 (c. 46), s. 17(7).

2. As amended by the Land Tenure Reform (Scotland) Act 1974 (c. 38), s. 19.

Provisions for contracting out of sections 1 to 6 to be void

Provisions for contracting out of sections 1 to 6 void

7. Any agreement or other provision, however constituted, shall be void in so far as it purports to exclude or limit the operation of any enactment contained in sections 1 to 6 of this Act.

LAW OF PROPERTY ACT 1925

(1925 c. 20)

An Act to consolidate the enactments relating to Conveyancing and the Law of Property in England and Wales.

[9th April 1925]

. . . . . .

PART II

. . . . . .

Power to discharge or modify restrictive covenants affecting land

84.—(1) The Lands Tribunal shall (without prejudice to any concurrent jurisdiction of the court) have power from time to time, on the application of any person interested in any freehold land affected by any restriction arising under covenant or otherwise as to the user thereof or the building thereon, by order wholly or partially to discharge or modify any such restriction on being satisfied—

(a) that by reason of changes in the character of the property or the neighbourhood or other circumstances of the case which the Lands Tribunal may deem material, the restriction ought to be deemed obsolete, or
　²(aa) that in a case falling within subsection (1A) below the continued existence thereof would impede some reasonable user of the land for public or private purposes or, as the case may be, would unless modified so impede such user; or

(b) that the persons of full age and capacity for the time being or from time to time entitled to the benefit of the restriction, whether in respect of estates in fee simple or any lesser estates or interests in the property to which the benefit of the restriction is annexed, have agreed, either expressly or by implication, by their acts or omissions, to the same being discharged or modified; or

(c) that the proposed discharge or modification will not injure the persons entitled to the benefit of the restriction:

and an order discharging or modifying a restriction under this subsection may direct the applicant to pay to any person entitled to the benefit of the restriction such sum by way of consideration as the Tribunal may think it just to award under one, but not both, of the following heads, that is to say, either—

(i) a sum to make up for any loss or disadvantage suffered by that person in consequence of the discharge or modification; or

(ii) a sum to make up for any effect which the restriction had, at the time when it was imposed, in reducing the consideration then received for the land affected by it.

²(1A) Subsection (1)(aa) above authorises the discharge or modification of a restriction by reference to its impeding some reasonable user of land in any case in which the Lands Tribunal is satisfied that the restriction, in impeding that user, either—

(a) does not secure to persons entitled to the benefit of it any practical benefits of substantial value or advantage to them; or

(b) is contrary to the public interest;

and that money will be an adequate compensation for the loss or disadvantage (if any) which any such person will suffer from the discharge or modification.

²(1B) In determining whether a case is one falling within subsection (lA) above, and in determining whether (in any such case or otherwise) a restriction ought to be discharged or modified, the Lands Tribunal shall take into account the development plan and any declared or ascertainable pattern for the grant or refusal of planning permissions in the relevant areas, as well as the period at which and context in which the restriction was created or imposed and any other material circumstances.

²(1C) It is hereby declared that the power conferred by this section to modify a restriction includes power to add such further provisions restricting the user of or the building on the land affected as appear to the Lands Tribunal to be reasonable in view of the relaxation of the existing provisions, and as may be accepted by the applicant; and the Lands Tribunal may accordingly refuse to modify a restriction without some such addition.

[1](2) The court shall have power on the application of any person interested—

    (a) To declare whether or not in any particular case any freehold land is or would in any given event be affected by a restriction imposed by any instrument; or

    (b) To declare what, upon the true construction of any instrument purporting to impose a restriction, is the nature and extent of the restriction thereby imposed and whether the same is or would in any given event be enforceable and if so by whom.

Neither subsections (7) and (11) of this section nor, unless the contrary is expressed, any later enactment providing for this section not to apply to any restrictions shall affect the operation of this subsection or the operation for purposes of this subsection of any other provisions of this section.

[1](3) The Lands Tribunal shall, before making any order under this section direct such enquiries, if any, to be made of any government department or local authority, and such notices, if any, whether by way of advertisement or otherwise, to be given to such of the persons who appear to be entitled to the benefit of the restriction intended to be discharged, modified, or dealt with as, having regard to any enquiries notices or other proceedings previously made, given or taken, the Lands Tribunal may think fit.

[2](3A) On an application to the Lands Tribunal under this section the Lands Tribunal shall give any necessary directions as to the persons who are or are not to be admitted (as appearing to be entitled to the benefit of the restriction) to oppose the application, and no appeal shall lie against any such direction; but rules under the Lands Tribunal Act 1949 shall make provision whereby, in cases in which there arises on such an application (whether or not in connection with the admission of persons to oppose) any such question as is referred to in subsection (2)(a) or (b) of this section, the proceedings on the application can and, if the rules so provide, shall be suspended to enable the decision of the court to be obtained on that question by an application under that subsection, or by means of a case stated by the Lands Tribunal, or otherwise, as may be provided by those rules or by rules of court

    (4) . . .

[3](5) Any order made under this section shall be binding on all persons, whether ascertained or of full age or capacity or not, then entitled or thereafter capable of becoming entitled to the benefit of any restriction, which is thereby discharged, modified, or dealt with, and whether such persons are parties to the proceedings or have been served with notice or not.

[1](6) An order may be made under this section notwithstanding that any instrument which is alleged to impose the restriction intended to be discharged, modified, or dealt with, may not have been produced to the court or the Lands Tribunal, and the court or the Lands Tribunal may act on such evidence of that instrument as it may think sufficient.

(7) This section applies to restrictions whether subsisting at the commencement of this Act or imposed thereafter, but this section does not apply where the restriction was imposed on the occasion of a disposition made gratuitously or for a nominal consideration for public purposes.

[1](8) This section applies whether the land affected by the restrictions is registered or not, but, in the case of registered land, the Land Registrar shall give effect on the register to any order under this section in accordance with the Land Registration Act, 1925.

[1](9) Where any proceedings by action or otherwise are taken to enforce a restrictive covenant, any person against whom the proceedings are taken, may in such proceedings apply to the court for an order giving leave to apply to the Lands Tribunal under this section, and staying the proceedings in the meantime.

(10) . . .

[1](11) This section does not apply to restrictions imposed by the Commissioners of Works under any statutory power for the protection of any Royal Park or Garden or to restrictions of a like character imposed upon the occasion of any enfranchisement effected before the commencement of this Act in any manor vested in His Majesty in right of the Crown or the Duchy of Lancaster, nor subject to subsection (11A) below to restrictions created or imposed—

(a) for Naval, Military or Air Force purposes,

[4](b) for civil aviation purposes under the powers of the Air Navigation Act 1920, of section 19 or 23 of the Civil Aviation Act 1949 or of section 30 or 41 of the Civil Aviation Act 1982.

[2](11A) Subsection (11) of this section—

(a) shall exclude the application of this section to a restriction falling within subsection (11)(a) and not created or imposed in connection with the use of any land as an aerodrome, only so long as the restriction is enforceable by or on behalf of the Crown; and

(b) shall exclude the application of this section to a restriction falling within subsection (11)(b), or created or imposed in connection with the use of any land as an aerodrome, only so long as the restriction is enforceable by or on behalf of the Crown or any public or international authority.

⁵(12) Where a term of more than forty years is created in land (whether before or after the commencement of this Act) this section shall, after the expiration of twenty-five years of the term, apply to restrictions affecting such leasehold land in like manner as it would have applied had the land been freehold:

Provided that this subsection shall not apply to mining leases.

(13) . . .

AMENDMENTS
¹ Amended by the Law of Property Act 1969 (c. 59), s. 28.
² Inserted by the Law of Property Act 1969 (c. 59), s. 28.
³ Amended by the Lands Tribunal Act 1949 (c. 42), Sched. 2.
⁴ Amended by the Civil Aviation Act 1982 (c. 16), Sched. 15.
⁵ Amended by the Landlord and Tenant Act 1954 (c. 56), s. 52(1).

LANDS TRIBUNAL ACT 1949

(12 & 13 Geo. 6, c. 42)

An Act to establish new tribunals to determine in place of official arbitrators and others certain questions relating to compensation for the compulsory acquisition of land and other matters, . . . and for purposes connected therewith.

[14th July 1949]

NOTE

See the Law Reform (Miscellaneous Provisions) (Scotland) Act 1980 (c. 55), s. 18 as to interest on sums awarded as compensations by the Lands Tribunal for Scotland.

Establishment and jurisdiction of Lands Tribunal

¹**1.**—(1) There shall be set up, to exercise the jurisdiction hereafter mentioned in this Act, the following tribunals, namely—

   (a) tribunal for Scotland, to be called "the Lands Tribunal for Scotland"; and
   (b) a tribunal for the remainder of the United Kingdom, to be called "the Lands Tribunal".

(2) Except in so far as the context otherwise requires, references in this Act to the Lands Tribunal shall be taken, in relation to Scotland, as references to the Lands Tribunal for Scotland.

·   ·   ·   ·   ·   ·

AMENDMENT

¹As applied in relation to the Lands Tribunal for Scotland by subs. (8): extended by the Coast Protection Act (c. 74), s. 24.

Members, officers and expenses of Lands Tribunal

¹**2.**—(1) The Lands Tribunal shall consist of a President and such number of other members as the Lord President of the Court of

Session may determine, to be appointed by the Lord President of the Court of Session.

²(2) The President shall be a person appearing to the Lord President of the Court Session to be suitably qualified by the holding of judicial office or by experience as an advocate or solicitor, and of the other members of the Lands Tribunal such number as the Lord President of the Court of Session may determine shall be persons so qualified, and the others shall be persons who have had experience in the valuation of land appointed after consultation with the chairman of the Scottish Branch of the Royal institution of Chartered Surveyors.

(3) In the case of the temporary absence or inability to act of the President, the Lord President of the Court of Session may appoint another member of the Lands Tribunal to act as deputy for the President, and a member so appointed shall, when so acting, have all the functions of the President.

(4) If a member of the Lands Tribunal becomes, in the opinion of the Lord President of the Court of Session unfit to continue in office or incapable of performing his duties, the Lord President of the Court of Session shall forthwith declare his office to be vacant and shall notify the fact in such manner as he thinks fit, and thereupon the office shall become vacant.

. . . . . .

AMENDMENTS

¹ As applied in relation to the Lands Tribunal for Scotland by subs. (9).

² Substituted for s. 2(9)(b) and (c) by the Conveyancing and Feudal Reform (Scotland) Act 1970 (c. 35), s. 50.

Procedure, appeals, costs and fees

¹3.—(1) Subject to the provisions of this Act, the jurisdiction of the Lands Tribunal may be exercised by any one or more of its members, and references in this Act to the Lands Tribunal shall be construed accordingly.

(2) The member or members who is or are to deal with any case shall be selected as follows:—

(a) the President may select a member or members to deal with a particular case or class or group of cases; or

(b) the President may select for a class or group of cases members amongst whom a member or members to deal with any particular case shall be selected, and the selection from amongst those members of a member or members to deal with a particular case shall then be made either by the President or, if he so directs, by one of those members appointed by the President to be their chairman.

This subsection shall apply to the selection of a member of the Lands Tribunal for the purposes of subsection (6) of section 1 of this Act as if the case were one to be dealt with by the Lands Tribunal.

(3) Where a case is dealt with by two or more members of the Tribunal—

(a) if the President is one of them he shall preside at the hearing and, if he is not, one of them shall be nominated to preside at the hearing by the person selecting them to deal with the case;

(b) a decision shall be taken, in the event of a difference between the members dealing with the case, by the votes of the majority and, in the event of an equality of votes, the person presiding at the hearing shall be entitled to a second or casting vote.

. . . . . .

(5) Subject to the following provisions of this section, the Lands Tribunal may order that the costs of an proceedings before it incurred by any party shall be paid by any other party and may tax or settle the amount of any costs to be paid under any such order or direct in what manner they are to be taxed.

²(6) Subject to the provisions of this Act, rules may be made for regulating proceedings before the Lands Tribunal and, subject to the approval of the Treasury, the fees chargeable in respect of those proceedings, and may in particular—

(a) make provision—

(i) as to the form in which any decision of the Tribunal is to be given and as to the amendment of any such decision in pursuance of any directions which may be given by the court dealing with an appeal under this section;

(ii) as to the time within which any proceedings before the Tribunal are to be instituted;

(iii) as to the evidence which may be required or admitted in any such proceedings;

(b) provide for the Tribunal to be assisted by assessors when dealing with cases calling for special knowledge and, subject to the approval of the Treasury, for making payments to the assessors as part of the expenses of the Tribunal;

(c) provide for requiring persons to attend to give evidence and produce documents, and for authorising the administration of oaths to witnesses, and for granting to any person such recovery of documents as might be granted by the Court of Session.

³(6A) It is hereby declared that this section authorises the making of rules which allow the Tribunal to determine cases without an oral hearing.

³(6B) The rules shall require that the determination without an oral hearing of any disputed claim for compensation which—

(a) is payable in respect of a compulsory acquisition of land, or

(b) depends directly or indirectly on the value of any land,

shall require the consent of the person making the claim.

³(6C) Where the Tribunal determine a case without an oral hearing, subsection (3) of this section shall apply subject to such modifications as may be prescribed by the rules.

. . . . . .

(10) Rules made under this section shall provide for preserving, so far as appears to the rule-making authority to be practicable, the effect of things done before the commencement of this Act in or for the purposes of the exercise of any jurisdiction transferred by this Act to the Lands Tribunal, and those rules may exclude the operation of this Act, in whole or in part, in relation to any proceedings pending at the commencement of this Act.

(11) Subject to the following subsection—

. . . . . .

(b) the rule-making authority for the purposes of this Act shall be the Lord Advocate.

⁴(12) In relation to the Lands Tribunal for Scotland, the following provisions shall have effect—

. . . . . .

⁵(c) any person who without reasonable excuse fails to comply with any requirement imposed by rules under this section

in accordance with paragraph (c) of subsection (6) of this section shall be guilty of an offence and liable on summary conviction to a fine not exceeding level 3 on the standard scale or imprisonment for a term not exceeding three months or both;

(d) any extract of an order of the Tribunal may be recorded for execution in the Books of Council and Session and shall be enforceable accordingly;

. . . . . .

AMENDMENTS

[1] As applied in relation to the Lands Tribunal for Scotland by subs. (12)(a)(b) and (e).

[2] As amended by the Local Government, Planning and Land Act 1980, Sched. 33.

[3] Inserted by the Local Government, Planning and Land Act 1980, Sched. 33.

[4] As amended by the Conveyancing and Feudal Reform (Scotland) Act 1970, s. 50(2), the Tribunals and Inquiries Act 1971, Sched. 3, S.I. 1972 No. 2002, and the Land Tenure Reform (Scotland) Act 1974, s. 19.

[5] As amended by virtue of the Criminal Procedure (Scotland) Act 1975, ss 289F and 289G.

TRIBUNALS AND INQUIRIES ACT 1992

(1992 c. 53)

An Act to consolidate the Tribunals and Inquiries Act 1971 and certain other enactments relating to tribunals and inquiries.

[16th July 1992]

. . . . . .

Appeals from certain tribunals

[1]**11.**—[2](1) Subject to subsection (2), if any party to proceedings before any tribunal specified in paragraph 8, 15(a), (d) or (e), 16, 18, 24, 26, 31, 33(b), 37, 40A, 44 or 45 of Schedule 1 is dissatisfied in point of law with a decision of the tribunal he may, according as rules of court may provide, either appeal from the tribunal to the High Court or require the tribunal to state and sign a case for the opinion of the High Court.

[3](2) This section shall not apply in relation to proceedings before employment tribunals which arise under or by virtue of any of the enactments mentioned in section 21(1) of the Employment Tribunals Act 1996.

(3) Rules of court made with respect to all or any of the tribunals referred to in subsection (1) may provide for authorising or requiring a tribunal, in the course of proceedings before it, to state, in the form of a special case for the decision of the High Court, any question of law arising in the proceedings; and a decision of the High Court on a case stated by virtue of this subsection shall be deemed to be a judgment of the Court within the meaning of section 16 of the Supreme Court Act 1981 (jurisdiction of Court of Appeal to hear and determine appeals from judgments of the High Court).

(4) In relation to proceedings in the High Court or the Court of Appeal brought by virtue of this section, the power to make rules of court shall include power to make rules prescribing the powers of the High Court or the Court of Appeal with respect to—

(a) the giving of any decision which might have been given by the tribunal;

(b) the remitting of the matter with the opinion or direction of the court for re-hearing and determination by the tribunal;

(c) the giving of directions to the tribunal;

and different provisions may be made for different tribunals.

(5) An appeal to the Court of Appeal shall not be brought by virtue of this section except with the leave of the High Court or the Court of Appeal.

(6) Subsection (1) shall apply to a decision of the Secretary of State on an appeal under section 41 of the Consumer Credit Act 1974 from a determination of the Director General of Fair Trading as it applies to a decision of any of the tribunals mentioned in that subsection, but with the substitution for the reference to a party to proceedings of a reference to any person who had a right to appeal to the Secretary of State (whether or not he has exercised that right); and accordingly references in subsections (1) and (4) to a tribunal shall be construed, in relation to such an appeal, as references to the Secretary of State.

(7) The following provisions shall have effect for the application of this section to Scotland—

(a) in relation to any proceedings in Scotland of any of the tribunals referred to in the preceding provisions of this section, or on an appeal under section 41 of the Consumer Credit Act 1974 by a company registered in Scotland or by any other person whose principal or prospective principal place of business in the United Kingdom is in Scotland this section shall have effect with the following modifications—

(i) for references to the High Court or the Court of Appeal there shall be substituted references to the Court of Session,

(ii) in subsection (3) for "in the form of a special case for the decision of the High Court" there shall be substituted "a case for the opinion of the Court of Session on" and the words from "and a decision" to the end of the subsection shall be omitted, and

(iii) subsection (5) shall be omitted,

(b) this section shall apply, with the modifications specified in paragraph (a)—

(i) to proceedings before any such tribunal as is specified in paragraph 51, 56(b), 59 or 63 of Schedule 1, and

(ii) subject to paragraph (c) below, to proceedings before the Lands Tribunal for Scotland,

as it applies to proceedings before the tribunals referred to in subsection (1);

(c) subsection (1) shall not apply in relation to proceedings before the Lands Tribunal for Scotland which arise under section 1(3A) of the Lands Tribunal Act 1949 (jurisdiction of the tribunal in valuation matters);

(d) an appeal shall lie, with the leave of the Court of Session or the House of Lords, from any decision of the Court of Session under this section, and such leave may be given on such terms as to costs or otherwise as the Court of Session or the House of Lords may determine.

(8) In relation to any proceedings in Northern Ireland of any of the tribunals referred to in subsection (1) and in relation to a decision of the Secretary of State on an appeal under section 41 of the Consumer Credit Act 1974 by a company registered in Northern Ireland or by any other person whose principal or prospective principal place of business in the United Kingdom is in Northern Ireland, this section shall have effect with the following modifications—

(a) in subsection (3), for the words from the beginning to "provide" there shall be substituted "Rules may be made under section 55 of the Judicature (Northern Ireland) Act 1978 providing", and for "section 16 of the Supreme Court Act 1981" there shall be substituted "section 35 of the Judicature (Northern Ireland) Act 1978";

(b) in subsection (4), for "the power to make rules of court shall include power to make rules" there shall be substituted "rules may be made under section 55 of the Judicature (Northern Ireland) Act 1978";

(c) at the beginning of subsection (5), there shall be inserted "Rules made under section 55 of the Judicature (Northern Ireland) Act 1978, relating to such proceedings as are mentioned in subsection (4), shall provide that the appeal shall be heard, or as the case may be, the decision of the High Court shall be given, by a single judge, but".

(9) Her Majesty may by Order in Council direct that all or any of the provisions of this section, so far as it relates to proceedings in the Isle of Man or any of the Channel Islands of the tribunal specified in paragraph 45 of Schedule 1, shall extend to the Isle of Man or to any of the Channel Islands subject to such modifications as may be specified in the Order.

(10) In this section "decision" includes any direction or order, and references to the giving of a decision shall be construed accordingly.

AMENDMENTS

[1] As amended by the Sea Fish (Conservation) Act 1992 (c. 60), s. 9(2). Excluded by the Employment Agencies Act 1973 (c. 35), s. 3D(2), inserted by the Deregulation and Contracting Out Act 1994 (c. 40), Sched. 10, para. 1(3) (effective January 3, 1995).

[2] As amended by the Education Act 1993 (c. 35), s. 181(2).

[3] As amended by the Employment Tribunals Act 1996 (c. 17), Sched. 1, para. 9, the Employment Rights Act 1996 (c. 18), Sched. 1, para. 57 and the Employment Rights (Dispute Resolution) Act 1998 (c. 8), s. 1.

APPENDIX V

COUNTRYSIDE (SCOTLAND) ACT 1967

(1967 c. 86)

[1]An Act to make provision for the better enjoyment of the Scottish countryside, . . . for the improvement of recreational and other facilities; to extend the powers of local planning authorities as respects land in their districts; to make financial provision with respect to the matters aforesaid; and for connected purposes.

[27th October 1967]

NOTE

[1] Certain functions of planning authorities transferred by the Local Government and Planning (Scotland) Act 1982, s.9, Sched. 1, Pt I. As amended by the Natural Heritage (Scotland) Act 1991, s.14 (all references to "the Commission" substituted by "Scottish Natural Heritage").

. . . . . .

PART III

PUBLIC PATHS AND LONG-DISTANCE ROUTES

Creation of public paths

Creation of public paths by agreement

30.—[1](1) A general or district planning authority shall have power to enter into an agreement with any person having the necessary power in that behalf for the creation by that person of a public path over land in their area.

(2) An agreement made under the foregoing subsection (in this Act referred to as a "public path creation agreement") shall be on such terms as to payment or otherwise as may be specified in the

agreement, and may, if it is so agreed, provide for the creation of the public path subject to limitations or conditions affecting any public right of way thereover.

(3) In this Part of this Act "public path" means a way which is a footpath or bridleway or a combination of those.

AMENDMENT
[1] As amended by the Local Government and Planning (Scotland) Act 1982, s. 9, Sched. 1, Pt I, Pt II, para. 10.

Compulsory powers for creation of public paths

31.—(1) Where it appears to a general or district planning authority that there is need for a public path over land in their area and they are satisfied that, having regard to—

(a) the extent to which the path would add to the convenience or enjoyment of a substantial section of the public, or to the convenience of persons resident in the area, and

(b) the effect which the creation of the path would have on the rights of persons interested in the land, account being taken of the provisions as to compensation contained in section 37 below,

it is expedient that the path should be created, the authority, if it appears to them impracticable to create the path by means of a public path creation agreement may by order (in this Act referred to as a "public path creation order") made by them and, subject to paragraph 2(1A) of Schedule 3 to this Act, submitted to and confirmed by the Secretary of State create a public path.

[2](2) A right of way created by a public path creation order may be either unconditional or subject to such limitations or conditions as may be specified in the order, and the Secretary of State may, in a case where his confirmation of the order is required, confirm it subject to such modifications or conditions as he thinks fit.

(3) A public path creation order shall be in such form as may be prescribed and shall contain a map, on such scale as may be prescribed, defining the land over which a public path is thereby created.

(4) The provisions in that behalf of Schedule 3 to this Act shall apply to the making, confirmation, validity and date of operation of public path creation orders.

AMENDMENTS
[1] As amended by the Local Government and Planning (Scotland) Act 1982, s. 9, Sched. 1, Pt I, Pt II, para. 11 and Sched. 3, para. 8.

² As amended by the Local Government and Planning (Scotland) Act 1982, Sched. 3, para. 8.

Exercise of powers under ss. 30 and 31

32.—(1) [Repealed by the Countryside (Scotland) Act 1981, Sched. 2.]

¹(2) Where a proposed public path lies partly within and partly outside the area of a general or district planning authority, the powers conferred by the two last foregoing sections on the authority shall extend to the whole of the path as if it lay wholly within their area:

Provided that, in relation to so much of the path as lies outside the area of the authority, the said powers shall not be exercisable as respects any part thereof in the area of any other general or district planning authority except with the consent of that authority.

(3) [Repealed by the Countryside (Scotland) Act 1981, Sched. 2.]

AMENDMENT
¹ As amended by the Local Government and Planning (Scotland) Act 1982, s. 9, Sched. 1, Pt I, Pt II, para. 12.

Making up and maintenance of public paths

33.—(1) On the creation of a public path in pursuance of a public path creation agreement, or on the coming into operation of a public path creation order or public path diversion order, the general or district planning authority shall carry out such work as appears to them to be necessary to bring it into a fit condition for use by the public as a public path in conformity with the terms and conditions of the said agreement or order, as the case may be, and shall maintain it in such condition.

(2)–(4) [Repealed by the Countryside (Scotland) Act 1981, Sched. 2.]

AMENDMENT
¹ As amended by the Local Government and Planning (Scotland) Act 1982, s. 9, Sched. 1, Pt I, Pt II, para. 13.

Closure of public paths

34.—¹(1) Where it appears to a general or district planning authority as respects a public path in their area that it is expedient that the path should be closed on the ground that the path is not needed for public use, the authority may by order (in this Act referred to as a "public path extinguishment order") made by them and, subject to paragraph 2(1A) of Schedule 3 to this Act, submitted to and confirmed by the Secretary of State extinguish the right of way over the path.

(2) The Secretary of State shall not confirm a public path extinguishment order unless he is satisfied that it is expedient so to do having regard to the extent to which it appears to him that the path would, apart from the order, be likely to be used by the public, and having regard to the effect which the extinguishment of the right of way would have as respects land served by the path, account being taken of the provisions as to compensation contained in section 37 below.

(3) A public path extinguishment order shall be in such form as may be prescribed and shall contain a map, on such scale as may be prescribed, defining the land over which the right of way is thereby extinguished.

(4) Schedule 3 to this Act shall have effect as to the making, confirmation, validity and date of operation of public path extinguishment orders.

²(5) where in accordance with regulations made under paragraph 3 of the said Schedule proceedings preliminary to the making or confirmation of a public path extinguishment order are taken concurrently with proceedings preliminary to the making or confirmation of a public path creation order or of a public path diversion order then, in considering—

(a) under subsection (1) above whether the path to which the public path extinguishment order relates is needed for public use, or

(b) under subsection (2) above to what extent that path would apart from the order be likely to be used by the public.

the local planning authority or the Secretary of State, as the case may be, may have regard to the extent to which the public path creation order or the public path diversion order would provide an alternative path.

(6) For the purposes of subsections (1) and (2) above, any temporary circumstances preventing or diminishing the use of a path by the public shall be disregarded.

AMENDMENTS

¹ As amended by the Local Government and Planning (Scotland) Act 1982, s. 9, Sched. 1, Pt I, Pt II, para. 14 and Sched. 3, para. 9.

² As amended by the Local Government and Planning (Scotland) Act 1982, Sched. 3, para. 9 and Sched. 4, Pt I.

Diversion of public paths

35.—[1](1) Where an owner, tenant or occupier of land crossed by a public path satisfies the general or district planning authority in whose area the land is situated that for securing the efficient use of the land or of other land held therewith or providing a shorter or more convenient path across his land, it is expedient that the line of the path across his land, or part of that line, should be diverted (whether on to other land or his or on to land of another owner, tenant or occupier), the authority may by order (in this Act referred to as a "public path diversion order") made by them and, subject to paragraph 2(1A) of Schedule 3 to this Act, submitted to and confirmed by the Secretary of State—

  (a) create, as from such date as may be specified in the order, any such new public path as appears to the authority requisite for effecting the diversion, and

  (b) extinguish as from such date as may be so specified in accordance with the provisions of the next following subsection, the right of way over so much of the path as appears to the authority requisite as aforesaid.

(2) Where it appears to the authority that work requires to be done to provide necessary facilities for the convenient use of any such new public path as is mentioned in subsection (1)(a) above, the date specified under subsection (1)(b) above shall be later than the date specified under subsection (1)(a) above by such time as appears to the authority requisite for enabling the work to be carried out.

[2](3) A right of way created by a public path diversion order may either be unconditional or may (whether or not the right of way extinguished by the order was subject to limitations or conditions of any description) be subject to such limitations or conditions as may be specified in the order, and the Secretary of State may, in a case where his confirmation of the order is required, confirm it subject to such modifications or conditions as he thinks fit.

(4) Before determining to make a public path diversion order on the representation of an owner, tenant or occupier, the authority may require him to enter into an agreement with them to defray, or to make such contribution as may be specified in the agreement towards—

  (a) any compensation which may become payable under section 37 below;

  [3](b) any expenses which any general or district planning authority may incur in bringing the new site of the path into a fit condition for use by the public.

(5) The Secretary of State shall not confirm a public path diversion order unless he is satisfied that the diversion to be effected thereby is expedient as mentioned in subsection (1) above, and further that the path will not be substantially less convenient to the public in consequence of the diversion and that it is expedient to confirm the order having regard to the effect which—

(a) the diversion would have on public enjoyment of the path as a whole,

(b) the coming into operation of the order would have as respects other land served by the existing right of way, and

(c) any new right of way created by the order would have as respects the land over which the right is so created and any land held therewith.

so, however, that for the purposes of paragraphs (b) and (c) of this subsection the Secretary of State shall take into account the provisions as to compensation of section 37 below.

(6) A public path diversion order shall be in such form as may be prescribed and shall contain a map, on such scale as may be prescribed, showing the existing site of so much of the line of the path as is to be diverted by the order and the new site to which it is to be diverted, and indicating whether a new right of way is created by the order over the whole of the new site or whether some part thereof is already comprised in a public path and, in the latter case, defining the part thereof so comprised.

(7) Schedule 3 to this Act shall have effect as to the making, confirmation, validity and date of operation of public path diversion orders.

AMENDMENTS

[1] As amended by the Local Government and Planning (Scotland) Act 1982, s. 9, Sched. I, Pt I, Pt II, para. 15 and Sched. 3, para. 10.

[2] As amended by the Local Government and Planning (Scotland) Act 1982, Sched. 3, para. 10.

[3] As amended by the Local Government and Planning (Scotland) Act 1982, s. 9, Sched. 1, Pt I, Pt II, para. 15.

Exercise of powers under sections 34 and 35

36.—[1](1) Subject to the provisions of this section, section 32(2) above shall apply in the exercise of the powers conferred by the two last foregoing sections in relation to any public path as it applies in the exercise of the powers referred to in the said subsection.

(2), (3) [Repealed by the Countryside (Scotland) Act 1981, Sched. 2.]

(4) An authority proposing to make a public path diversion order such that the authority who will be responsible for a part of the path after the diversion will be a different body from the authority who before the diversion are so responsible shall, before making the order, consult the authority who will be responsible for that part.

AMENDMENT

[1] As amended by the Countryside (Scotland) Act 1981, Sched. 1, para. 2 and Sched. 2.

Compensation for creation, diversion and closure of public paths

37.—(1) Subject to the following provisions of this section, if, on a claim made in accordance with this section, it is shown that the value of an interest of any person in land is depreciated, or that any person has suffered damage by being disturbed in his enjoyment of land, in consequence of the coming into operation of a public path creation order, a public path diversion order or a public path extinguishment order, the authority by whom the order was made shall pay to that person compensation equal to the amount of the depreciation or damage.

(2) A claim for compensation under this section shall be made within such time and in such manner as may be prescribed and shall be made to the authority by whom the order was made.

(3) [Repealed by the Countryside (Scotland) Act 1981, Sched. 2.]

(4) Nothing in this section shall confer on any person, in respect of a right of way created by a public path creation order or a public path diversion order, a right to compensation for depreciation of the value of an interest in land, or for disturbance in his enjoyment of land, not being in either case land over which the right of way was created or land held therewith, unless the creation of the right of way would have been actionable at his instance if it had been effected otherwise than in the exercise of statutory powers.

Supplementary provisions as to creation, closure and diversion of public paths

38.—(1) Sections 34 to 36 above shall apply in relation to all public rights of way, whether created before or after the commencement of this Act.

(2) The provisions of sections 34 to 36 above shall not prejudice any power conferred by any other enactment to close or divert a road, and shall not otherwise affect the operation of any enactment relating to the extinguishment, suspension, diversion or variation of rights of way.

[1](3) A public path creation order, a public path extinguishment order or a public path diversion order affecting in any way the area of more than one general or district planning authority may contain provisions requiring one of the authorities to defray, or contribute towards, expenses incurred in consequence of the order by another of the authorities; and a public path diversion order diverting a part of the line of a path from a site in the area of one such local planning authority to a site in the area of another may provide that the first mentioned authority shall continue to be responsible for the maintenance of that part of the path after the diversion.

(4) Every public path creation agreement, public path creation order, public path extinguishment order and public path diversion order shall contain a particular description of the lands affected or a description by reference of those lands in the manner provided by section 61 of the Conveyancing (Scotland) Act 1874.

(5) As soon as may be after any such agreement as is referred to in the last foregoing subsection is made, or after any such order is confirmed, the local planning authority shall cause it to be recorded in the Register of Sasines, and when so recorded, it shall be enforceable at the instance of the local planning authority against persons deriving title to the land from the person so entitled when the agreement or order was made:

Provided that any such agreement or order shall not be so enforceable against a third party who shall have in good faith and for value acquired right (whether completed by infeftment or not) to the land prior to the agreement or order being recorded as aforesaid, or against any person deriving title from such third party.

[2](6) The Secretary of State shall not make or confirm a public path creation order, a public path extinguishment order or a public path diversion order relating to a right of way over land under, in, upon, over, along or across which there is any apparatus belonging to or used by any statutory undertakers for the purpose of their undertaking unless the undertakers have consented to the making or confirmation of the order, as the case may be; and any such consent may be given subject to the condition that there are included in the order such provisions for the protection of the undertakers as they may reasonably require.

The consent of statutory undertakers to any such order shall not be reasonably withheld, and any question arising under this subsection whether the withholding of a consent is unreasonable or whether any requirement is reasonable shall be determined by the appropriate Minister within the meaning of section 217 of the Town and Country Planning (Scotland) Act 1997.

³(7) Where in pursuance of a public path extinguishment order or a public path diversion order a public path is closed or diverted and, immediately before the date on which the order comes into force, there was under, in, upon, over, along or across the path any telecommunication apparatus kept installed for the purposes of a telecommunications code system, the operator of that system shall have the same powers in respect of the telecommunication apparatus as if the order had not come into force; but any person entitled to land over which the path subsisted shall be entitled to require the alteration of the apparatus.

⁴(8) Paragraph 1(2) of the telecommunications code (alteration of apparatus to include moving, removal or replacement of apparatus) shall apply for the purposes of the preceding provisions of this section as it applies for the purposes of that code.

⁴(9) Paragraph 21 of the telecommunications code (restriction on removal of apparatus) shall apply in relation to any entitlement conferred by this section to require the alteration moving or replacement of any telecommunication apparatus as it applies in relation to an entitlement to require the removal of any such apparatus.

AMENDMENTS

¹ As amended by the Local Government and Planning (Scotland) Act 1982, s. 9, Sched. 1, Pt I, Pt II, para. 16.

² As amended by the Planning (Consequential Provisions) (Scotland) Act 1997, Sched. 2, para. 15.

³ As amended by the Telecommunications Act 1984, Sched. 4, para. 46.

⁴ Inserted by the Telecommunications Act 1984, Sched. 4. para. 46.

. . . . . .

Supplementary provisions as to compensation under ss. 20, 37 and 62

70.—(1) The following provisions shall have effect in respect of compensation under sections 20, 37 and 62 of this Act.

(2) Any dispute arising on a claim for any such compensation shall be determined by the Lands Tribunal for Scotland, but until sections 1 to 3 of the Lands Tribunal Act 1949 come into force as regards Scotland, any such dispute shall be determined by an official arbiter appointed under Part I of the Land Compensation (Scotland) Act 1963.

¹(3) Subject to the provisions of this section the said Act of 1963, so far as appropriate, shall apply in relation to any question of

disputed compensation referred to in subsection (1) above as it applies to any such question referred to in section 2(1) of that Act, with the substitution for references to the acquiring authority of references to the body from whom the compensation in question is claimed.

(4) Rules 2 to 4 of the rules contained in section 12 of the said Act of 1963 (rules for assessing compensation) shall apply to the calculation of any compensation referred to in subsection (1) above, in so far as it is calculated by reference to the depreciation of the value of an interest in land.

(5) In the case of an interest in land subject to a heritable security—

  (a) compensation referred to in subsection (1) above in respect of the depreciation of that interest shall be calculated as if the interest were not subject to the heritable security;

  (b) a claim or application for the payment of any such compensation, or an application for the recording of a claim in respect of the interest under section 22(1) of this Act, may be made by any person who when the order giving rise to the compensation was made was the heritable creditor, or by any person claiming under such a person, but without prejudice to the making of a claim or application by any other person;

  (c) a heritable creditor shall not be entitled to any such compensation in respect of his interest as such; and

  (d) any compensation payable in respect of the interest subject to the heritable security shall be paid to the heritable creditor or, where there is more than one heritable creditor, to the creditor whose heritable security has priority over any other heritable securities secured on the land, and shall in either case be applied by him as if it were proceeds of sale.

(6) In this section "heritable security" has the same meaning as in the Conveyancing (Scotland) Act 1924 except that it includes a security constituted by ex facie absolute disposition or assignation, and "heritable creditor" shall be construed accordingly.

AMENDMENT

[1] As amended by the Natural Heritage (Scotland) Act 1991, Sched. 10, para. 4.

· · · · · ·

Sections 14, 31, 34 and 35   ¹SCHEDULE 3

PROVISIONS AS TO MAKING CONFIRMATION, COMING INTO OPERATION AND VALIDITY OF CERTAIN ORDERS

NOTE

¹Extended by the Post Office Act 1969, Sched. 4, para. 93(1)(*xxvii*) and the Civil Aviation Act 1982, Sched. 2, para. 4.

PART I

Provisions for making and confirming access orders and certain orders relating to public paths

1.—¹(1) Before a body makes an access order, a public path creation order, a public path extinguishment order or a public path diversion order it shall give notice in the prescribed form—

²(a) stating the general effect of the order and that it is about to be made and, subject to paragraph 2(lA) of this Schedule, submitted for confirmation.

³(b) naming a place in the area in which the land to which the order relates is situated where a draft of the order and of the map referred to therein may be inspected free of charge at all reasonable hours, and

³(c) specifying the time (not being less than twenty-eight days from the date of the first publication of the notice) within which, and the manner in which, representations or objections with respect to the draft order may be made.

(2) [Repealed by the Local Government and Planning (Scotland) Act 1982, Sched. 4, Pt I.]

³,⁴(3)The notices to be given under sub-paragraph (1) above shall be given—

(a) in the case of an access order or a public path creation order, by publication in at least one local newspaper circulating in the area in which the land to which the order relates is situated, and by serving a like notice on every owner, occupier and tenant (except tenants for a month or any period less than a month and statutory tenants within the meaning of the Rent (Scotland) Act 1971 of any of that land, so however that—

  (i) except in the case of an owner, occupier or tenant being a local authority, local planning authority or statutory undertaker, the Secretary of State may in any particular case direct that it shall not be necessary to serve notice as aforesaid if in his opinion it is not reasonably practicable to do so, but

  (ii) if the Secretary of State so directs in the case of any land, then in addition to publication the notice shall be addressed to "the owners and any occupiers" of the land (describing it) and a copy or copies of it shall be affixed to some conspicuous object or objects on the land;

(b) in the case of a public path extinguishment order or a public path diversion order, by publication and the service of notices as mentioned in head (a) of this sub-paragraph and also—

(i) by serving such a notice as is therein mentioned on every local authority and local planning authority whose area includes any of the land to which the order relates, and

(ii) by causing a copy of the notice to be displayed in a prominent position at the ends of so much of any public path as is to be closed or diverted by virtue of the order.

Notes

[1] As amended by the Natural Heritage (Scotland) Act 1991, Sched. 10, para. 4.

[2] Substituted by the Local Government and Planning (Scotland) Act 1982, Sched. 3, para. 11.

[3] As amended by the Local Government and Planning (Scotland) Act 1982, Sched. 3, para. 11.

[4] As amended by virtue of the Interpretation Act 1978, s. 17(2)(a).

2.—[1](1A) If an authority have given notice under paragraph 1(1) above as regards a public path creation order, a public path extinguishment order or a public path diversion order, and no representations or objections are duly made in terms of paragraph 1(1)(c) of this Schedule or if any so made are withdrawn, then, subject to the provisions of Part II of this Schedule, the order shall on being made by them have effect without their having to submit it to the Secretary of State and without his confirmation.

[2](1) In the case of an order other than one which has effect under sub-paragraph (IA) above, if no representations or objections are duly made in terms of sub-paragraph (1)(c) of paragraph 1 of this Schedule, or if any so made are withdrawn, the Secretary of State may, if he thinks fit, confirm the order with or without modifications or conditions.

[2](2) If any representation or objection duly made is not withdrawn, the Secretary of State shall, before confirming the order, either—

(a) cause a local inquiry to be held, or

(b) afford to any person by whom any representation or objection has been duly made and not withdrawn an opportunity of being heard by a person appointed by him for the purpose.

and, after considering the report of the person appointed to hold the inquiry or to hear representations or objections, may confirm the order with or without modifications or conditions:

Provided that, where objection is made by statutory undertakers to a public path creation order or a public path diversion order, on the ground that the order provides for the creation of a right of way over land covered by works used for the purposes of their undertaking or the curtilage of such land, and the objection is not withdrawn, the order shall be subject to special parliamentary procedure.

[2](3) Notwithstanding anything in the foregoing provisions of this paragraph, the Secretary of State shall not confirm an order so as to affect land not affected by the order as submitted to him except after—

(a) giving such notice as appears to him requisite of his proposal so to modify the order, specifying the time (not being less than twenty-eight days from the date of the first publication of the notice) within which, and the manner in which, representations or objections with respect to the proposal may be made,

    (b) holding a local inquiry or affording to any person by whom any representation or objection has been duly made and not withdrawn an opportunity of being heard by a person appointed by him for the purpose, and

    (c) considering the report of the person appointed to hold the inquiry or to hear representations or objections, as the case may be,

and, where objection is made by statutory undertakers to a public path creation order or a public path diversion order, on the ground that the order as modified would provide for the creation of a right of way over land covered by works used for the purposes of their undertaking or the curtilage of such land, and the objection is not withdrawn, the order shall be subject to special parliamentary procedure.

Notes

  [1] Added by the Local Government and Planning (Scotland) Act 1982, Sched. 3, para. 11.

  [2] As amended by the Local Government and Planning (Scotland) Act 1982, Sched. 3, para. 11 and Sched. 4, Pt I.

3.—(1) Subject to the provisions of this Part of this Schedule, the procedure on the submission and confirmation of orders to which this Schedule applies shall be such as may be prescribed.

(2) Provision may be prescribed for enabling proceedings preliminary to the confirmation of a public path extinguishment order to be taken concurrently with proceedings preliminary to the confirmation of a public path creation, or a public path diversion order.

PART II

Validity and date of operation of orders to which this Schedule applies

[1]4. As soon as may be after an order to which this Schedule applies has been confirmed by the Secretary of State or, in the case of an order which has effect under paragraph 2(1A) of this Schedule, has been made by an authority, the authority by whom the order was made, shall publish, in the manner required in relation to the class of order in question by paragraph 1(3) of this Schedule, a notice in the prescribed form describing the general effect of the order, stating that it has been confirmed or made, and naming a place where a copy thereof as confirmed or made may be inspected free of charge at all reasonable hours, and—

    (a) where under the said sub-paragraph (3) notice was required to be served, shall serve a like notice and a copy of the order as confirmed or made on any persons on whom notices were required to be served under that sub-paragraph; and

    (b) where under the said sub-paragraph (3) a notice was required to be displayed, shall cause a like notice to be displayed in the like manner as the notice required to be displayed under that sub-paragraph:

Provided that no such notice or copy need be served on a person unless he has sent to the authority a request in that behalf specifying an address for service.

NOTE
[1] As amended by the Local Government and Planning (Scotland) Act 1982, Sched. 3, para. 11 and Sched. 4, Pt. I.

5. If a person aggrieved by an order to which this Schedule applies desires to question the validity thereof, or of any provision contained therein, on the ground that it is not within the powers of this Act or on the ground that any requirement of this Act or of regulations made thereunder has not been complied with in relation thereto, he may, within six weeks from the date on which the notice required by the last foregoing paragraph is first published, make an application for the purpose to the Court of Session.

6. On any such application as aforesaid, the Court—

(a) may by interim order suspend the operation of the order, or of any provision contained therein, either generally or in so far as it affects any property of the applicant, until the final determination of the proceedings; and

(b) if satisfied that the order, or any provision contained therein, is not within the powers of this Act or that the interests of the applicant have been substantially prejudiced by failure to comply with any such requirement as aforesaid, may quash the order or any provision contained therein, either generally or in so far as it affects any property of the applicant.

7. Subject to the provisions of the last foregoing paragraph, an order to which this Schedule applies shall not, either before or after it has been made or confirmed, be questioned in any legal proceedings whatever, and shall become operative on the date on which the notice required by paragraph 4 above is first published, or on such later date as may be specified in the order.

8. In relation to any order to which this Schedule applies, being an order which is subject to special parliamentary procedure, the foregoing provisions of this Schedule shall have effect subject to the following modifications—

(a) if the order is confirmed by Act of Parliament under section six of the Statutory Orders (Special Procedure) Act 1945, paragraphs 5 to 7 shall not apply; and

(b) in any other case, paragraph 5 shall have effect as if, for the reference therein to the date on which the notice required by paragraph 4 is first published, there were substituted a reference to the date on which the order becomes operative under the said Act of 1945, and paragraph 7 shall have effect as if the words from "and shall become operative" to the end of the paragraph were omitted.

LAND REGISTRATION (SCOTLAND) ACT 1979

(1979 c. 33)

An Act to provide a system of registration of interests in land in Scotland in place of the recording of deeds in the Register of Sasines; and for indemnification in respect of registered interests in land; to simplify certain deeds relating to land and to provide as to the effect of certain other such deeds; to enable tenants-at-will to acquire their landlords' interests in the tenancies; to provide for the fixing of fees payable to the Keeper of the Registers of Scotland; and for connected purposes.

[4th April 1979]

. . . . . .

Rectification of the register

9.—(1) Subject to subsection (3) below, the Keeper may, whether on being so requested or not, and shall, on being so ordered by the court or the Lands Tribunal for Scotland, rectify any inaccuracy in the register by inserting, amending or cancelling anything therein.

(2) Subject to subsection (3)(b) below, the powers of the court and of the Lands Tribunal for Scotland to deal with questions of heritable right or title shall include power to make orders for the purposes of subsection (1) above.

(3) If rectification under subsection (1) above would prejudice a proprietor in possession—

    (a) the Keeper may exercise his power to rectify only where—

        (i) the purpose of the rectification is to note an overriding interest or to correct any information in the register relating to an overriding interest;

        (ii) all persons whose interests in land are likely to be affected by the rectification have been informed by the

Keeper of his intention to rectify and have consented in writing;

(iii) the inaccuracy has been caused wholly or substantially by the fraud or carelessness of the proprietor in possession; or

(iv) the rectification relates to a matter in respect of which indemnity has been excluded under section 12(2) of this Act;

[1](b) the court or the Lands Tribunal for Scotland may order the Keeper to rectify only where sub-paragraph (i), (iii) or (iv) of paragraph (a) above applies or the rectification is consequential on the making of an order under section 8 of the Law Reform (Miscellaneous Provisions) (Scotland) Act 1985.

[2](3A) Where a rectification of an entry in the register is consequential on the making of an order under section 8 of the said Act of 1985, the entry shall have effect as rectified as from the date when the entry was made:

Provided that the court, for the purpose of protecting the interests of a person to whom section 9 of that Act applies, may order that the rectification shall have effect as from such later date as it may specify.

[3](4) In this section—

(a) "the court" means any court having jurisdiction in questions of heritable right or title;

(b) "overriding interest" does not include the interest of

(i) a lessee under a lease which is not a long lease and

(ii) a non-entitled spouse within the meaning of section 6 of the Matrimonial Homes (Family Protection) (Scotland) Act 1981.

AMENDMENTS

[1] As amended by the Law Reform (Miscellaneous Provisions) (Scotland) Act 1985 (c. 73), Sched. 2, para. 21, with effect from December 10, 1985.

[2] Inserted by the Law Reform (Miscellaneous Provisions) (Scotland) Act 1985 (c. 73), Sched. 2, para. 21, with effect from December 10, 1985.

[3] As amended by the Matrimonial Homes (Family Protection) (Scotland) Act 1981 (c. 59), s. 6(4).

.   .   .   .   .   .

Part II

Indemnity in Respect of Registered Interests in Land

Indemnity in respect of loss

12.—(1) Subject to the provisions of this section, a person who suffers loss as a result of—

(a) a rectification of the register made under section 9 of this Act;

(b) the refusal or omission of the Keeper to make such a rectification;

(c) the loss or destruction of any document while lodged with the Keeper;

(d) an error or omission in any land or charge certificate or in any information given by the Keeper in writing or in such other manner as may be prescribed by rules made under section 27 of this Act,

shall be entitled to be indemnified by the Keeper in respect of that loss.

(2) Subject to section 14 of this Act, the Keeper may on registration in respect of an interest in land exclude, in whole or in part, any right to indemnity under this section in respect of anything appearing in, or omitted from, the title sheet of that interest.

(3) There shall be no entitlement to indemnity under this section in respect of loss where—

(a) the loss arises as a result of a title prevailing over that of the claimant in a case where—

(i) the prevailing title is one in respect of which the right to indemnity has been partially excluded under subsection (2) above, and

(ii) such exclusion has been cancelled but only on the prevailing title having been fortified by prescription;

¹(b) the loss arises in respect of a title which has been reduced, whether or not under subsection (4) of section 34, or subsection (5) of section 36, of the Bankruptcy (Scotland) Act 1985 (or either of those subsections as applied by sections 615A and 615B of the Companies Act 1985,

respectively), as a gratuitous alienation or fraudulent preference, or has been reduced or varied by an order under section 6(2) of the Divorce (Scotland) Act 1976 or by an order made by virtue of section 29 of the Matrimonial and Family Proceedings Act 1984 (orders relating to settlements and other dealings) or has been set aside or varied by an order under section 18(2) (orders relating to avoidance transactions) of the Family Law (Scotland) Act 1985;

(c) the loss arises in consequence of the making of a further order under section 5(2) of the Presumption of Death (Scotland) Act 1977 (effect on property rights of recall or variation of decree of declarator of presumed death);

(d) the loss arises as a result of any inaccuracy in the delineation of any boundaries shown in a title sheet, being an inaccuracy which could not have been rectified by reference to the Ordnance Map, unless the Keeper has expressly assumed responsibility for the accuracy of that delineation;

(e) the loss arises, in the case of land extending to 2 hectares or more the area of which falls to be entered in the title sheet of an interest in that land under section 6(1)(a) of this Act, as a result of the Keeper's failure to enter such area in the title sheet or, where he has so entered such area, as a result of any inaccuracy in the specification of that area in the title sheet;

(f) the loss arises in respect of an interest in mines and minerals and the title sheet of any interest in land which is or includes the surface land does not expressly disclose that the interest in mines and minerals is included in that interest in land;

(h) the loss arises from inability to enforce a real burden or condition entered in the register, unless the Keeper expressly assumes responsibility for the enforceability of that burden or condition;

(h) the loss arises in respect of an error or omission in the noting of an overriding interest;

(j) the loss is suffered by—

(i) a beneficiary under a trust in respect of any transaction entered into by its trustees or in respect of any title granted by them the validity of which is unchallengeable by virtue of section 2 of the Trusts (Scotland) Act 1961 (validity of certain transactions by trustees), or as the case may be, section 17 of the Succession (Scotland) Act 1964 (protection of persons acquiring title), or

(ii) a person in respect of any interest transferred to him by trustees in purported implement of trust purposes;

(k) the loss arises as a result of an error or omission in an office copy as to the effect of any subsisting adverse entry in the Register of Inhibitions and Adjudications affecting any person in respect of any registered interest in land, and that person's entitlement to that interest is neither disclosed in the register nor otherwise known to the Keeper;

(l) the claimant is the proprietor of the dominant tenement in a servitude, except insofar as the claim may relate to the validity of the constitution of that servitude;

(m) the claimant is a superior, a creditor in a ground annual or a Landlord under a long lease and the claim relates to any information—

(i) contained in the feu writ, the contract of ground annual or the lease, as the case may be, and

(ii) omitted from the title sheet of the interest of the superior, creditor or landlord,

(except insofar as the claim may relate to the constitution or amount of the feuduty, ground annual or rent and adequate information has been made available to the Keeper to enable him to make an entry in the register in respect of such constitution or amount or to the description of the land in respect of which the feuduty, ground annual or rent is payable);

(n) the claimant has by his fraudulent or careless act or omission caused the loss;

(o) the claim relates to the amount due under a heritable security;

²(p) the loss arises from a rectification of the register consequential on the making of an order under section 8 of the Law Reform (Miscellaneous Provisions) (Scotland) Act 1985.

(4) A refusal or omission by the Keeper to enter into a title sheet—

(a) any over-feuduty or over-rent exigible in respect of a registrable interest;

(b) any right alleged to be a real right on the ground that by virtue of section 6 of this Act he has no duty to do so since it is unenforceable,

shall not by itself prevent a claim to indemnity under this section.

AMENDMENTS

[1] As amended by the Matrimonial and Family Proceedings Act 1984 (c. 42), Sched. 1, para. 28, the Bankruptcy (Scotland) Act 1985 (c. 66), Sched. 7, para. 15 and the Family Law (Scotland) Act 1985 (c. 37), Sched. 1, para. 10.

[2] Inserted by the Law Reform (Miscellaneous Provisions) (Scotland) Act 1985 (c. 73), Sched. 2, para. 22.

Provisions supplementary to section 12

13.—(1) Subject to any order by the Lands Tribunal for Scotland or the court for the payment of expenses in connection with any claim disposed of by the Lands Tribunal under section 25 of this Act or the court, the Keeper shall reimburse any expenditure reasonably and properly incurred by a person in pursuing a *prima facie* well-founded claim under section 12 of this Act, whether successful or not.

(2) On settlement of any claim to indemnity under the said section 12, the Keeper shall be subrogated to all rights which would have been available to the claimant to recover the loss indemnified.

(3) The Keeper may require a claimant, as a condition of payment of his claim, to grant, at the Keeper's expense, a formal assignation to the Keeper of the rights mentioned in subsection (2) above.

(4) If a claimant to indemnity has by his fraudulent or careless act or omission contributed to the loss in respect of which he claims indemnity, the amount of the indemnity to which he would have been entitled had he not so contributed to his loss shall be reduced proportionately to the extent to which he has so contributed.

. . . . . .

Appeals

25.—(1) Subject to subsections (3) and (4) below, an appeal shall lie, on any question of fact or law arising from anything done or omitted to be done by the Keeper under this Act, to the Lands Tribunal for Scotland.

(2) Subject to subsections (3) and (4) below subsection (1) above is without prejudice to any right of recourse under any enactment other than this Act or under any rule of law.

(3) Nothing in subsection (1) above shall enable the taking of an appeal if it is, under the law relating to *res judicata*, excluded as a result of the exercise of any right of recourse by virtue of subsection (2) above; and nothing in subsection (2) above shall enable the exercise of any right of recourse if it is so excluded as a result of the taking of an appeal under subsection (1) above.

(4) No appeal shall lie under this section, nor shall there be any right of recourse by virtue of this section in respect of a decision of the Keeper under section 2(1)(b) or 11(1) of this Act.

LANDS TRIBUNAL FOR SCOTLAND RULES 1971

(S.I. 1971 No. 218)

[8th February 1971]

In exercise of the powers conferred upon me by section 3 of the Lands Tribunal Act 1949 as amended by section 50 of the Conveyancing and Feudal Reform (Scotland) Act 1970, and of all other powers enabling me in that behalf, and after consultation with the Council on Tribunals, and with the approval of the Treasury in regard to the fees prescribed by these rules in respect of proceedings before the Tribunal, I hereby make the following rules—

PRELIMINARY

Citation and commencement
1. These rules may be cited as the Lands Tribunal for Scotland Rules 1971 and shall come into operation on 1st March 1971.

Interpretation
2.—(1) In these rules, unless the context otherwise requires—

"the Act of 1949" means the Lands Tribunal Act 1949;
"the Act of 1963" means the Land Compensation (Scotland) Act 1963;
"the Act of 1970" means the Conveyancing and Feudal Reform (Scotland) Act 1970;
"benefited proprietor", "burdened proprietor", "interest in land" and "land obligation" have the meanings assigned to them by section 2(6) of the Act of 1970;
"*cumulo* feuduty" and "feu" have the meanings assigned to them by section 3(2) of the Act of 1970;
"General Commissioners" have the same meaning as in the Taxes Management Act 1970;

227

"notice of allocation", "proprietor", and "superior" have the meanings assigned to them by section 5(7) of the Act of 1970; "the President" means the President of the Lands Tribunal for Scotland, or the member appointed under the provisions of the Act of 1949 to act for the time being as deputy for the President;

"Special Commissioners" have the same meaning as in the Taxes Management Act 1970;

"the Tribunal" means the Lands Tribunal for Scotland.

(2) A form referred to by number means the form so numbered in Schedule 1 to these rules.

(3) In these rules any reference to any enactment shall be construed as a reference to that enactment as amended by or under any other enactment.

(4) The Interpretation Act 1889 shall apply for the interpretation of these rules as it applies for the interpretation of an Act of Parliament.

PART I

APPLICATIONS UNDER SECTION 1 OF THE CONVEYANCING AND FEUDAL REFORM (SCOTLAND) ACT 1970

Method of making application

3. Any burdened proprietor who wishes to make an application under section 1 of the Act of 1970 (variation and discharge of land and obligations) shall send to the Tribunal an application in or as nearly as may be in accordance with Form 1.

Giving of notices

4.—[1](1) On receipt of an application the Tribunal shall

(a) give notice thereof in writing to the persons who appear to it to either benefited or burdened proprietors having an interest the subject of the application;

Provided that if the Tribunal is satisfied that any such proprietor cannot by reasonable inquiry be identified or found notice may be given by advertisement or by such other method as the Tribunal thinks fit; and

(b) give notice in writing or by advertisement or by such other method as the Tribunal thinks fit to any other persons whom it considers should receive notice.

(2) The notice shall require those benefited and burdened proprietors who wish to oppose or to make representations in

relation to the application to send intimation thereof in writing to the Tribunal and to the applicant within such time, not being less than 14 days from the date of the notice, as may be specified. Such intimation shall contain a concise statement of the facts and contentions on which it is intended to rely. The Tribunal shall send copies of any such intimations to those other persons whom at that stage it considers should receive a copy.

(3) The notice shall also intimate that subject to the Tribunal's discretion other persons to whom notice has been given under paragraph (1) of this rule may be heard in relation to the application.

AMENDMENT
[1] As amended by S.I. 1985 No. 581.

Provisions as to orders
5.—[1](1) Subject to the provisions of paragraphs (2) and (3) of this rule, an order made by the Tribunal varying or discharging a land obligation shall take effect on the occurrence of whichever of the following events last occurs after the Tribunal has made the order, that is to say—

(a) the expiry of a period of 21 days after the date when the order was made by the Tribunal;
(b) the disposal by the Court of Session of a case stated by the Tribunal on appeal to that court or, if there is an appeal to the House of Lords, the disposal of the case by the House of Lords;
(c) the abandonment or other termination of the proceedings on a case so stated without a decision having been given;
(d) the abandonment or other termination of an appeal against the decision of the Court of Session in a case so stated or the expiry of the time for bringing any such appeal without it having been brought; or
(e) the variation by the Tribunal of the order in compliance with any directions given by the Court of Session or the House of Lords in proceedings relating to such a case;

Provided, that where the application is unopposed or all persons who have opposed or made representations in respect of the application have informed the Tribunal that they consent to the order taking effect immediately, and it is so certified in the order, such order shall take effect on the date on which it is made by the Tribunal.

(2) Where a land obligation is varied or discharged subject to the payment of any compensation awarded by the Tribunal, the order

of the Tribunal shall not, so far as it affects such variation or discharge, take effect until the Tribunal has endorsed the order to the effect either that the compensation has been paid or that all persons to whom any compensation has been awarded but who have not received payment of it have agreed to the order taking effect.

(3) The Tribunal may direct that the compensation shall be paid or satisfied within a specified time and that, unless it is so paid or satisfied, the order shall be void on the expiration of the time so specified.

AMENDMENT
¹ Substituted by S.I. 1977 No. 432.

. . . . . .

PART VI

GENERAL

Method of making application
19.—Except where these rules otherwise provide any question which is to be determined by or referred to the Tribunal shall be brought before it by way of written application and a copy of the application shall be sent by the Tribunal to each of the other parties to the proceedings and to such other persons whom it considers should receive a copy. In a case in which the Tribunal is acting as arbiter under a reference by consent the notice of reference shall be in or as nearly as may be in accordance with Form 3.

Procedure
20. Subject to the provisions of these rules and to any direction given by the President the Tribunal may—

    (a) regulate its procedure as it thinks fit; and
    (b) amend in such way as it thinks fit any of the forms in Schedule 1 to these rules.

Sittings of Tribunal
21.—(1) Sittings of the Tribunal shall be on such dates and at such times and places as the President may from time to time determine and, not less than twenty-one days or such shorter

period as the parties agree to before the date of a hearing, the Tribunal shall—

    (a) give notice in writing to the parties to the proceedings and
    (b) give notice by such method as it may determine (whether by way of advertisement or otherwise) to any other persons whom it considers have an interest in the proceedings

of the date, time and place of the hearing.

(2) The Tribunal shall sit in public except that when it is acting as arbiter under a reference by consent the proceedings shall be heard in private if the parties to the reference so request.

Representation

22. In any proceedings before the Tribunal any party to the proceedings may appear and may be heard in person or be represented by counsel or solicitor or, with the leave of the Tribunal, by any other person.

Administration of oaths

23. The Tribunal may administer oaths to witnesses in due form.

Default of appearance

24. If, after due notice of a hearing has been given to a party, that party or his representative fails to appear at the hearing, the Tribunal may dispose of the application in the absence of that party or his representative or may adjourn the hearing:

Provided that where the Tribunal has so disposed of the application, the Tribunal, on an application made by that party within seven days of the disposal, may if it is satisfied that there was sufficient reason for such absence, set aside its decision on such terms as to expenses or otherwise as it thinks fit.

Evidence

[1]**24A.** Evidence before the Tribunal may be given orally or, if the parties to the proceedings consent or the Tribunal so orders, by affidavit, but the Tribunal may at any stage of the proceedings require the personal attendance of any deponent for examination and cross-examination.

AMENDMENT
[1] Inserted by S.I. 1985 No. 581.

Power to require further particulars and attendance of witnesses and to order recovery of documents

25.—[1](1) The Tribunal may on the motion of any party to the proceedings or *ex proprio motu* by notice in writing—

(a) require a party to furnish in writing further particulars of his case;

(b) order a record to be made up;

(c) grant to a party such commission and diligence for the recovery of documents, or provide such other means of recovery thereof, as could be granted or provided by the Court of Session in a cause before them, such recovery being effected, where a commission and diligence has been granted, by execution thereof or in that or any other case in any manner in which recovery could be provided for by the Court of Session in such a cause; and

(d) require the attendance of any person as a witness or require the production of any document relating to the question to be determined;

and may appoint the time at or within which or the place at which any act required in pursuance of this rule is to be done:
Provided that—

(i) No person shall be required in obedience to such a requirement to attend at any place which is more than 10 miles from the place where he resides unless the necessary expenses are paid or tendered to him by the party at whose instance his attendance has been required or by the Tribunal as the case may be; and

(ii) nothing in this provision shall empower the Tribunal to require any person to produce any book or document or to answer any question which he would be entitled, on the ground of privilege or confidentiality, to refuse to produce or to answer if the proceedings were proceedings in a court of law.

²(2) The Tribunal may also by notice in writing order any party who intends, at a proof or hearing,

(a) to use or put in evidence any documents, or

(b) to rely for valuation purposes on properties comparable to those to which the proceedings relate to produce the documents, or, as the case may be, to supply, in such form as may be required by the Tribunal, a list of the properties, on such date before the proof or the hearing as the Tribunal may specify.

³(3) Any notice given under head (c) or head (d) of paragraph (1) or under paragraph (2) of this Rule shall contain a reference to the provisions of section 3(12)(c) of the Act of 1949 (by which any person who, without reasonable excuse, fails to comply with any

such notice shall be liable on summary conviction to a fine not exceeding [level 3 on the standard scale] or to imprisonment for a term not exceeding three months or to both such fine and imprisonment).

AMENDMENTS
[1] As amended by S.I. 1977 No 432.
[2] As substituted by S.I. 1977 No 432.

Provision for other parties
26. Subject to the provisions of these rules the Tribunal, on the application of any person who appears to it to have an interest in the proceedings, may allow that person to become a party to the proceedings.

Withdrawal of party
27. The Tribunal may, on such terms as to expenses or otherwise as it thinks fit, consent to any party withdrawing from the proceedings.

Extension of time and adjournment of hearing
28. The Tribunal may on such terms as to expenses or otherwise as it thinks fit—

(a) extend any time appointed by, or specified by it in terms of, these rules notwithstanding that that time may have expired;
(b) postpone, or adjourn, any hearing.

Assessors
29.—(1) If it appears to the President that any case before the Tribunal calls for special knowledge and that it would be desirable for the Tribunal to sit with an Assessor or Assessors, he may direct that the Tribunal shall hear the case with the aid of such Assessor or Assessors as the President may, after consulting such persons, if any, as he may think fit, appoint.

(2) The remuneration to be paid to any Assessor appointed under this rule shall be such as the President may, with the approval of the Treasury determine.

Notices
30. Any notice or other document required or authorised to be given to any person for the purpose of these rules shall be deemed to have been duly given if sent by post by means of the recorded

delivery service or registered post or delivered to that person at his ordinary address or to the address specified by him for intimation under these rules:

Provided that, when difficulty is experienced in effecting such intimation for any reason, the Tribunal, on being satisfied that all practicable steps have been taken in an effort to intimate, may dispense with intimation upon such person or may take such other steps as it thinks fit.

Power to dispose of case without a hearing

[1]**31.** Notwithstanding the provisions of these rules the Tribunal, with the consent of all parties whom it considers to have an interest in the application (including any application relating to a disputed claim for compensation to which section 3(6B) of the 1949 Act as enacted by paragraph 3(1) of Schedule 10 to the Community Land Act 1975 applies), may dispose of any application before it without a hearing.

AMENDMENT

[1] As amended by S.I. 1977 No. 432.

Decision of Tribunal

[1]**32.**—(1) The decision of the Tribunal in any proceedings shall be given in writing, and shall include a statement of the Tribunal's reasons for its decision.

Provided that a decision given on an application under section 4 of the Act of 1970 shall include a statement of the Tribunal's reasons for giving the decision only if a party to the proceedings requests that the Tribunal should do so.

(2) Where an amount awarded or value determined by the Tribunal is dependent upon the decision of the Tribunal on a question of law which is in dispute in the proceedings, the Tribunal shall ascertain, and shall state in its decision the alternative amount or value (if any) which it would have awarded or determined if it had decided otherwise on the question of law.

(3) The Tribunal shall send a copy of the decision to all parties to the proceedings.

(4) An accidental or arithmetical error in any decision of the Tribunal may be corrected by the Tribunal if, before making the correction, they have given notice of their intention to make it to all those who were parties to the proceedings.

(5) When a correction is made under the last foregoing paragraph, or for the purpose of giving effect to any decision of the Court of Session in a case stated for their opinion, the Tribunal

shall give notice that it has been made to all the parties to the proceedings by sending to each of them a copy of the decision as corrected.

AMENDMENT
[1] As amended by S.I. 1977 No. 432.

Expenses
[1]**33.**—(1) Except in cases to which the provisions of section 11 of the Act of 1963 apply or proceedings referred to in paragraph (6) of this rule, the Tribunal shall deal in such manner with expenses as in its discretion it thinks fit.

(2) The Tribunal may order that a party shall pay to another party either a specific sum in respect of the expenses incurred by that other party or such proportion of these expenses as the Tribunal thinks fit.

(3) In default of agreement between the parties as to the amount of the expenses, the expenses shall be taxed, in the discretion of the Tribunal, either by the Auditor of the Court of Session according to the fees payable in the Court of Session or by the Auditor of the Sheriff Court specified by the Tribunal according to the Sheriff Court Table of Fees.

(4) Counsel's fees and the fees for instruction of counsel shall be allowed as an item of a party's expenses only where the Tribunal has sanctioned the employment of counsel.

(5) Additional expenses at such rate as the Auditor taxing the expenses considers fair and reasonable shall be allowed for the employment of expert witnesses only where the Tribunal has certified the employment of such expert witnesses.

(6) In proceedings under Part VC of these rules the Tribunal shall not have power to order payment of expenses and the foregoing provisions of this rule shall not apply.

AMENDMENT
[1] As amended by S.I. 1985 No. 581.

Fees
[1]**34.**—(1) The fees specified in Schedule 2 to these rules shall be payable to the Tribunal in respect of the matters mentioned in the said Schedule:
Provided that the Tribunal may waive the whole or part of the fees payable by a party where it considers that the financial circumstances of the party are such that undue hardship would be caused by payment of the said fees.

(2) The hearing fee shall, unless the Tribunal otherwise directs, be payable by the party by whom the proceedings were instituted (without prejudice to his right to recover the amount of the fee from any other party by virtue of any order as to expenses).

AMENDMENT
¹ As amended by S.I. 1977 No. 432.

Transitional provisions
35. Where, before the date on which sections 1 to 4 of the Act of 1949 come into operation in Scotland, proceedings have been commenced for the determination of any question, dispute or other matter which, by virtue of the coming into operation in Scotland of the said sections, is required to be referred to and determined by the Tribunal then—

(a) where the hearing has not begun at that date, anything done for the purpose of determining such question, dispute or other matter shall be treated, so far as practicable, as if it had been done for the purpose of an application under these rules and shall be dealt with by the Tribunal in accordance with the provisions of these rules; and

(b) where the hearing has begun the hearing, unless the parties agree otherwise, shall proceed in accordance with the procedure in force immediately before the coming into operation in Scotland of the said sections.

Revocations
36.—(1) The rules specified in Schedule 3 to these rules are hereby revoked as from the date when sections 1 to 4 of the Act of 1949 come into operation in Scotland.

(2) Section 38 of the Interpretation Act 1889 shall apply as if these rules were an Act of Parliament and as if the rules revoked by these rules were Acts of Parliament repealed by an Act of Parliament.

Rule 3   SCHEDULE 1

¹FORM I

Application under Section 1 of the Conveyancing and Fedual Reform (Scotland) Act 1970

NOTE

¹As amended by S.I. 1977 No. 432.

To: The Lands Tribunal for Scotland
    (*address*)

1. I/We, AB (*name and address of applicant*), proprietor of the subjects known as† which subjects are under burden of the land obligation of which particulars are set out in paragraph 2 below, hereby apply for the land obligation* [to be discharged wholly] [to be discharged to the extent of (*here specify*)] to be varied by (*here specify*)]. The circumstances rendering necessary the application are set out in paragraph 3 below. The statutory basis of the application is set out in paragraph 4 below.

2. Particulars of Land Obligation—

   (a) Nature of land obligation.
   (b) Land burdened by land obligation.
   (c) Manner and date of creation of land obligation.
   (d) Persons entitled to benefit of the land obligation (*here state names and addresses of benefited proprietors*).

3. Details of Application (*here give a concise statement of the circumstances which have led to the application*).

4. Statutory basis of application (*here specify which of the circumstances referred to in section 1 (3) of the Conveyancing and Feudal Reform (Scotland) Act 1970 is/are considered relevant*).

                              Signed
                              Date
                              (*To be signed by the burdened proprietor or by his Solicitor, who will add his designation and the words Agent of the said AB.*)

† *Here distinguish the subjects sufficiently precisely to enable them to be identified.*
* *Strike out the words not applicable.*

NOTES FOR THE INFORMATION OF APPLICANTS

1. It will be in the applicant's own interest to enclose with this application a copy of the conveyance, deed, instrument or writing under which the land obligation was created, a large-scale plan of the location identifying adjacent properties and any grant of planning permission which has been obtained for any proposed development, with any plans relating to it.

2. At any hearing relating to this application you will be required to adhere to the case set out above unless the Tribunal considers that the introduction of new material would not prejudice the interests of other parties.

3. Section 1(3) of the Conveyancing and Feudal Reform (Scotland) Act 1970 reads as follows—

"Subject to the provisions of this section and of section 2 of this Act, the Lands Tribunal, on the application of any person who, in relation to a land obligation, is a burdened proprietor, may from time to time by order vary or discharge the obligation wholly or partially in relation to the interest in land in respect of which the application is made, on being satisfied that in all the circumstances,

(a) by reason of changes in the character of the land affected by the obligation or of the neighbourhood thereof or other circumstances which the Tribunal may deem material, the obligation is or has become unreasonable or inappropriate; or
(b) the obligation is unduly burdensome compared with any benefit resulting or which would result from its performance; or
(c) the existence of the obligation impedes some reasonable use of the land."

FORM 1

Before completing this form, please read the [Notes for the Information of Applicants]

APPLICATION UNDER SECTION 1 OF THE
CONVEYANCING AND FEUDIAL REFORM
(SCOTLAND) ACT 1970

To: The Lands Tribunal for Scotland   [alternative address for
    1 Grosvenor Crescent   Members of Rutland Exchange
    Edinburgh   Box 259
    EH12 5ER   Rutland Exchange
                                 Edinburgh]

1. *I/We, ...
....
....

proprietor(s)* of the subjects known as
....
....
....

which subjects are under burden of the land
obligation(s)* of which particulars are set out in
paragraph 2, hereby apply for the land obliga-
tion(s)*

    *to be discharged wholly

    *to be discharged to the

    extent of ....
....

    *to be varied by ....
....

Right column notes:
Name and address
of Applicant(s)*

Here distinguish the
subjects sufficiently
to enable them to be
identified

The circumstances rendering necessary the application are set out in paragraph 3.
The statutory basis of the application is set out in paragraph 4.

Strike out words or letters not applicable.

239

2. <u>Particulars of Land Obligation(s)</u>

a. Nature of land obligation(s)
  (Here quote details of the obligation(s) from the title deed(s))

b. Land burdened by land obligation(s)
  (Here give a full description which should include a conveyancing description)

c. Manner and date of creation of land obligation(s)
  (Here state details of the deed(s) creating the obligation(s))

d. Persons entitled to benefit of land obligation(s)
  (Here state name(s) and address(es) of the benefited proprietor(s))

3. <u>Details of Application</u>

  (Here give a concise statement of the circumstances which have led to the application)

4. <u>Statutory basis of application</u>

Here specify which of the circumstances referred to in section 1(3) of the Conveyancing and Feudal Reform (Scotland) Act 1970 is/are considered relevant

Date . . . .

Signed . . . .

. . . .

To be signed by the burdened proprietor(s) or his/their Solicitor who should add his designation and the words "Agent of . . . . (name of applicant(s))"

NOTES FOR THE INFORMATION OF APPLICANTS

1. (a) The applicant should enclose with this application a copy of the conveyance, deed, instrument or writing under which the land obligation(s) was/were created, together with a copy of the applicant's title, a large scale plan of the location identifying adjacent properties and any grant of planning permission which has been obtained for any proposed development, with any plans relating to it. It will be in the applicant's own interest to identify the proprietors of the adjacent properties.

    (b) An application fee is payable and payment should accompany this application. Full details of current fees can be obtained from the Clerk to the Tribunal but it should be noted that fees are payable for any hearing which is arranged and also for an order granting the application. The cost of an advertisement is also recoverable from an applicant—advertisements are invariably required in applications involving missing superiors, alcohol and major developments which may have widespread implications.

2. At any hearing (usually held near the subjects) relating to this application you will be required to adhere to the case set out above unless the Tribunal consider that the introduction of new material would not prejudice the interests of other parties.

3. Section 1(3) of the 1970 Act reads as follows:—
    "Subject to the provisions of this section and of section 2 of this Act, the Lands Tribunal, on the application of any person who, in relation to a land obligation, is a burdened proprietor, may from time to time by order vary or discharge the obligation wholly or partially in relation to the interest in land in respect of which the application is made, on being satisfied that in all the circumstances,

    (a) by reason of changes in the character of the land affected by the obligation or of the neighbourhood thereof or other circumstances which the Tribunal may deem material, the obligation is or has become unreasonable or inappropriate; or

    (b) the obligation is unduly burdensome compared with any benefit resulting or which would result from its performances; or

    (c) the existence of the obligation impedes some reasonable use of the land."

4. Section 1(4) of the 1970 Act provides that the Tribunal may direct a successful applicant to pay compensation to a benefited proprietor.

5. The Tribunal have discretion to deal with claims for expenses as they think fit.

RULES OF THE COURT OF SESSION

(S.I. 1994 No. 1443)

[5th September 1994]

CHAPTER 41

. . . . . .

PART II

APPEALS BY STATED CASE ETC.

Application and interpretation of this Part

41.4. Subject to the provisions of the enactment providing for appeal and to Parts III to X, this Part shall regulate the procedure in—

(a) an appeal by stated case, special case, case, reference or submission against the decision of a tribunal;

(b) a case stated by an arbiter;

(c) all statutory proceedings for obtaining the opinion of the court on a question before the issue of a decision by a tribunal or by appeal against such a decision; and

(d) a case required to be stated by a tribunal referred to in subsection (1), as modified by subsection (7), of section 11 of the Tribunals and Inquiries Act 1992.

Applications for case

41.5.—(1) An application for a case for the opinion of the court on any questions shall be made by minute setting out the question on which the case is applied for.

(2) A minute under paragraph (1) shall be sent to the clerk of the tribunal—

(a) where the application must be made before the issue of the decision of the tribunal, at any time before the issue of the decision; or

[1](b) where the application may be made—

(i) after the issue of the decision of the tribunal, or
(ii) in a cause in which a statement of the reasons for the decision was given later than the issue of the decision, after the issue of that statement,

within the period mentioned in paragraph (3).

[2](3) The period referred to in paragraph (2)(b) is—

(a) the period prescribed by the enactment under which the appeal is made; or
(b) where no such period is prescribed, within 14 days after the issue of the decision or statement of reasons, as the case may be.

AMENDMENTS
[1] As amended by Act of Sederunt (Rules of the Court of Session Amendment No. 3) (Miscellaneous) 1996 (S.I. 1996 No. 1756), para. 2.
[2] As inserted by *ibid.*

Additional questions by other parties
41.6.—(1) On receipt of an application under rule 41.5 (applications for case), the clerk of the tribunal shall send a copy of the minute to every other party.

(2) Within 14 days after the date on which the clerk of the tribunal complied with paragraph (1), any other party may lodge with the clerk a minute setting out any additional question he proposes for the case; and on so doing he shall send a copy of it to every other party.

Consideration of application by tribunal
41.7.—(1) Within 21 days after the expiry of the period allowed for lodging a minute under rule 41.6 (2) (additional questions by other parties), the tribunal shall—

(a) decide to state a case on the basis of the questions set out in the application for a case under rule 41.5(1) and any minute under rule 41.6(2);
(b) where it is of the opinion that the proposed question—

(i) does not arise,
(ii) does not require to be decided for the purposes of the appeal, or
(iii) is frivolous, refuse to state a case on that question; or

(c) where the application under rule 41.5(1) is made before the facts have been ascertained and the tribunal is of the opinion that it is necessary or expedient that the facts should be ascertained before the application is disposed of, defer further consideration of the application until the facts have been ascertained by it.

(2) Where the tribunal has deferred a decision under paragraph (1)(c), it shall, within 14 days after it has ascertained the facts, decide whether to state or refuse to state a case.

(3) Where the tribunal makes a decision under paragraph (1) or (2), the clerk of the tribunal shall intimate that decision to each party.

(4) Where the tribunal has refused to state a case on any question, there shall be sent to the applicant with the intimation under paragraph (3)—

(a) a certificate specifying—

(i) the date of the decision of the tribunal; and
(ii) the reasons for refusal; and

(b) where the refusal has been made after the facts have been ascertained, a note of the proposed findings-in-fact on which the tribunal proposes to base its decision; or

(c) where the refusal has been made before the facts have been ascertained, a note of, or sufficient reference to, the averments of the parties in the appeal on which the refusal is based.

Procedure for ordaining tribunal to state a case

41.8.—(1) Where the tribunal has refused to state a case on any question, the party whose application has been refused may, within 14 days after the date on which intimation of such refusal was made under rule 41.7(3), lodge in the General Department—

(a) an application by note to the Inner House for an order to require the other party to show cause why a case should not be stated;

(b) the certificate and any note issued under rule 41.7(4); and

(c) a process in accordance with rule 4.4 (steps of process).

(2) A note under paragraph (1)(a) shall—

(a) state briefly the grounds on which the application is made; and

(b) specify the order and any incidental order sought.

(3) An application under paragraph (1) shall be put out in the Single Bills before the Inner House on the first available day after

the date on which the note under paragraph (1)(a) was lodged for an order for service of the note on—

(a) the tribunal; and
(b) every other party.

(4) After the period for lodging answers has expired, the Inner House shall, on a motion by the noter, without hearing parties—

(a) appoint the note to the Summar Roll for hearing; or
(b) direct that the note be heard in the Single Bills.

(5) The noter shall intimate the decision of the Inner House on the note to the tribunal.

Preparation and issue of the case
41.9.—(1) Where the tribunal has decided, or is ordered under rule 41.8, to state a case, the tribunal shall, within 14 days after the date of intimation of its decision to the parties; cause the case to be prepared in Form 41.9 and copies of it to be submitted in draft to each party.

(2) The case shall—

(a) specify the relevant provision of the enactment under which it is prepared;
(b) state in numbered paragraphs the facts and circumstances out of which the case arises, as agreed or found, or as the case may be, the decision of the tribunal and the reasons for the decision; and
(c) set out the question for answer by the court.

(3) Within 21 days after the date on which the draft case is submitted under paragraph (1), each party shall—

(a) return a copy of it to the clerk of the tribunal with a note of any amendments which he seeks to have made; and
(b) intimate such amendments to every other party.

(4) Within 28 days after the expiry of the period for return of the case under paragraph (3), the tribunal—

(a) shall adjust and settle the case; and
(b) may, when doing so, add such further or additional findings-in-fact and such additional questions as it thinks necessary for the disposal of the subject-matter of the case.

(5) Where the tribunal does not accept any amendment sought by a party, it shall append to the case a note of—

(a) the terms of the amendment proposed by the party and any statement by that party in support of the proposal; and

(b) its reasons for rejecting the proposed amendment.

(6) When the case has been settled by the tribunal, the case shall be authenticated by the clerk of the tribunal who shall send it to the party, or first party, who applied for it.

Intimation of intention to proceed

41.10.—(1) The party to whom the case has been sent under rule 41.9(6) or paragraph (3) of this rule shall, within 14 days after the date of receipt of it—

    (a) intimate to every other party a notice stating whether or not he intends to proceed with the case; and

    (b) send a copy of the case to every other party.

(2) Where the party to whom the case has been sent under rule 41.9(6) does not intend to proceed with it, he shall, on intimating that fact to every other party under paragraph (1), send the case back to the clerk of the tribunal.

(3) On receipt of the case sent back under paragraph (1), the clerk of the tribunal shall send it to any other party who had applied for a case.

Lodging of case in court

41.11.—(1) The party who applied for the case shall, within the period mentioned in paragraph (2)—

    (a) lodge in the General Department—

        (i) the case; and

        (ii) a process in accordance with rule 4.4 (steps of process) including any productions to he referred to in the appeal;

    (b) on giving written intimation to every other party of the lodging of the case, send four copies of the case to every other party; and

    (c) endorse and sign a certificate on the case that the requirements of rule 4.6 (intimation of steps of process) have been complied with.

(2) The period referred to in paragraph (1) shall be—

    (a) the period prescribed by the enactment under or by virtue of which the appeal is brought; or

    (b) where no such period is prescribed, within 28 days after the date on which the case was received by him from the clerk of the tribunal by virtue of rule 41.9(6) or 41.10(3), as the case may be.

Abandonment of appeal
41.12.—(1) If a party—

(a) fails to comply with a requirement of rule 41.11(1) (lodging of case in court), and

(b) does not apply to be reponed under rule 41.13 (reponing against deemed abandonment), he shall be deemed to have abandoned his appeal.

(2) Where a party is deemed to have abandoned his appeal under paragraph (1) and another party has also applied for a case and has had no opportunity of proceeding with his appeal, the party deemed to have abandoned his appeal shall—

(a) intimate to that other party that his appeal is abandoned, and

(b) send the case to that other party;

and that other party shall be entitled to proceed in accordance with rule 41.11.

(3) In the application of rule 41.11 to a party entitled to proceed by virtue of paragraph (2) of this rule, for the words "on which the case" to "rule 41.9(6) or 41.10(3), as the case may be" in paragraph (2)(b) of that rule, there shall be substituted the words "of intimation of abandonment under rule 41.12(2)".

Reponing against deemed abandonment
41.13. A party may apply by motion to the Inner House within 7 days after the expiry of the period specified in rule 41.11(2) (period for lodging of case in court), to be reponed against a failure to comply with a requirement of rule 41.11(1).

Procedure on abandonment
41.14.—(1) On the abandonment of the appeal by all parties entitled to proceed, the case shall be sent to the Deputy Principal Clerk.

(2) On receiving a case sent to him under paragraph (1), the Deputy Principal clerk shall—

(a) endorse the case with a certificate in Form 41.14; and

(b) transmit the case to the clerk of the tribunal.

(3) where a case has been transmitted under paragraph (2), the tribunal shall, on a motion being made to it to that effect—

(a) dispose of the cause; and

(b) where one party only has applied for a stated case, find him liable for payment to the other party in the appeal of

the expenses of the abandoned appeal as taxed by the
Auditor of the Court of Session.

Motions for hearing of appeals
41.15.—(1) On lodging a case under rule 41.11 (lodging of case
in court), the party lodging it shall apply by motion to the Inner
House for an order for a hearing.

(2) The Inner House shall, on a motion under paragraph (1),
without hearing parties—

    (a) appoint the cause to the Summar Roll for hearing; or
    (b) direct that the cause be heard in the Single Bills.

Amendment or re-statement of case
41.16. The Inner House may, at any time before the final
determination of the case—

    (a) allow the case to be amended with the consent of the
        parties; or
    (b) remit the case for restatement, or further statement, in
        whole or in part by the tribunal.

Remit to reporter
41.17.—(1) Where, in order to determine the case, any inquiry
into matters of fact may be made, the Inner House may remit to a
reporter, the Lord Ordinary or one of its own number to take
evidence and to report to the court.

(2) On completion of a report made under paragraph (1), the
reporter shall send his report and three copies of it, and a copy of
it for each party, to the Deputy Principal Clerk.

(3) On receipt of such a report, the Deputy Principal clerk
shall—

    (a) cause the report to be lodged in process; and
    (b) given written intimation to each party that this has been
        done and that he may uplift a copy of the report from
        process.

(4) After the lodging of such a report, any party may apply by
motion for an order in respect of the report or for further
procedure.

. . . . . .

PART VIII

STATED CASES UNDER SECTION 11(3) OF THE TRIBUNALS AND
INQUIRIES ACT 1992

Case stated by tribunal at its own instance
41.39.—(1) A tribunal referred to in subsection (1), as modified
by subsection (7), of section 11 of the Tribunals and Inquiries Act
1992 may, at its own instance, state a case for the opinion of the
court on any question arising in the course of proceedings before
it.

(2) Part II (appeals by stated case etc.) shall apply to a case
stated under paragraph (1) subject to the following provisions of
this Part.

Modifications of Part II to appeals under this Part
41.40.—(1) The following rules shall apply to a case to which this
Part applies subject to the following provisions of this rule—

rule 41.9 (preparation and issue of the case),
rule 41.11 (lodging of case in court),
rule 41.15 (motions for hearing of appeals).

(2) For paragraph (1) of rule 41.9 there shall be substituted the
following paragraph—

"(1) Where the tribunal decides to state a case at its own
instance, it shall intimate that decision to each party.".

(3) For paragraph (6) of rule 41.9 there shall be substituted the
following paragraphs—

"(6) When the case has been settled by the tribunal, the case
shall be authenticated by the clerk of the tribunal who shall—

(a) send a copy of the case to each party; and
(b) transmit to the Deputy Principal Clerk the case with a
certificate endorsed on it and signed by him certifying that
sub-paragraph (a) has been complied with.

(7) The Deputy Principal Clerk shall endorse the case with the
date on which he received it from the clerk of the tribunal and
return it to the clerk.".

(4) For rule 41.11 there shall be substituted the following rule:

"**41.11.**—Not earlier than seven days and not later than 14
days after the date on which the case was received by the
Deputy Principal Clerk, the clerk of the tribunal shall—

(a) lodge in the General Department—

    (i) the case; and

    (ii) a process in accordance with rule 4.4 (steps of process) including any productions to be referred to in the appeal;

(b) on giving written intimation to every other party of the lodging of the case, send five copies of the case to every such party; and

(c) endorse and sign a certificate on the case that the requirements of rule 4.6 (intimation of steps of process) have been complied with.".

(5) Rule 41.15 shall apply to the clerk of the tribunal in a cause to which this Part applies as it applies to the party lodging a case under rule 41.11.

RULES OF THE COURT OF SESSION

(S.I. 1994 No. 1443)

[5th September 1994]

CHAPTER 41

. . . . . .

PART III

APPEALS IN FORM 41.19

Application of this Part
41.18. Subject to the provisions of the enactment providing for appeal, this Part applies to an appeal against a decision of a tribunal other than an appeal to which Part II (appeals by stated case etc.) applies.

Form of appeal
41.19.—(1) An appeal to which this Part applies shall be made in Form 41.19 presented to the Inner House.
(2) An appeal referred to in paragraph (1) shall—

(a) specify the relevant provision of the enactment under the authority of which the appeal is brought;
(b) specify the decision complained of, the date on which the decision was made and on which it was intimated to the appellant, and any other necessary particulars;
(c) where the appeal is against only a part of such a decision, specify or distinguish that part;
(d) set out the decision appealed against or refer to the decision (a copy of which shall be appended to the appeal);

(e) state, in brief numbered propositions, the grounds of appeal; and

(f) set out in a schedule the names and addresses of the respondents in the appeal and the name and address, so far as known to the appellant, of any other person who may have an interest in the appeal.

Lodging of appeal in court

41.20.—[1](1) Subject to paragraphs (2) and (3) the appeal shall be lodged in the General Department—

(a) within the period prescribed by the enactment under which it is brought; or

(b) where no such period is prescribed, within 42 days after—

(i) the date on which the decision appealed against was intimated to the appellant; or

(ii) where the tribunal issued a statement of reasons for its decision later than the decision, the date of intimation of that statement of reasons to the appellant.

[2](2) Where leave to appeal to the court has been granted by the tribunal under any of the following enactments, the appeal shall be lodged in the General Department within 42 days after the date on which the decision to grant leave was intimated to the appellant—

(a) section 25 of the Child Support Act 1991 (appeal from decision of a commissioner on a question of law with leave of the commissioner);

(b) section 24 of the Social Security Administration Act 1992 (appeal from decision of a commissioner on a question of law with leave of the commissioner); and

(c) section 9 of the Asylum and Immigration Appeals Act 1993 (appeal on a question of law from a final determination of an immigration appeals tribunal with leave of the tribunal).

[3](3) Where an application for leave to appeal was made to the court within the period specified in paragraph (1)(b) but that period has expired before leave has been granted, the appeal may be lodged within 7 days after the date on which that leave was granted.

(2) There shall be lodged with the appeal under paragraph (1)—

(a) a process in accordance with rule 4.4 (steps of process), unless an application has already been made to the court for leave to appeal;

(b) where appropriate, evidence that leave to appeal has been granted by the tribunal;

(c) the documents mentioned in rule 41.2(6)(c) and (d) (copies of decisions of tribunal) unless already lodged; and

(d) such other documents founded on by the appellant so far as in his possession or within his control.

AMENDMENTS

[1] As amended by Act of Sederunt (Rules of the Court of Session Amendment No. 3) (Miscellaneous) 1996 (S.I. 1996 No. 1756), para. 2.

[2] As inserted by *ibid.*

[3] As inserted by *ibid.*

Orders for service and answers

41.21.—(1)The appeal shall, without a motion being enrolled—

(a) during session, appear in the Single Bills on the first available day after being lodged for an order for—

(i) service of the appeal on the respondent and such other person as the court thinks fit; and

(ii) any person on whom the appeal has been served, to lodge answers, if so advised, within the period of notice; and

(b) during vacation, be brought before the vacation judge for such an order.

(2) In the application of paragraph (1) to an appeal under section 9(5) of the Transport Act 1985 (appeal from decision of the Secretary of State), the order for service under that paragraph shall include a requirement to serve the appeal on—

(a) the Secretary of State; and

(b) every person who had, or if aggrieved would have had, a right to appeal to the Secretary of State, whether or not he has exercised that right.

[1](3) In the application of paragraph (1) to an appeal under section 25(1) of the Child Support Act 1991 (appeal from Child Support Commissioner) or section 24(1) of the Social Security Administration Act 1992 (appeal from Social Security Commissioner), the order for service under that paragraph shall include a requirement to serve the appeal on—

(a) the Secretary of State for Social Security and the Chief Child Support Officer or the Chief Adjudication Officer, as the case may be; and

(b) if it appears to the court that a person has been appointed by the Secretary of State to pursue a claim for benefit to which the appeal relates, that person.

(4) In the application of paragraph (1) to an appeal from a tribunal referred to in subsection (1), as modified by subsection (7), of section 11 of the Tribunals and Inquiries Act 1992, the order for service pronounced under that paragraph shall include a requirement to serve the appeal on every other party to the proceedings before the tribunal and on the clerk of the tribunal.

(5) In the application of paragraph (1) to an appeal to which subsection (6), as modified by subsection (7), of section 11 of the Tribunal and Inquiries Act 1992 (which relates to an appeal from a decision under section 41 of the Consumer Credit Act 1974 applies—

(a) the order for service under that paragraph shall include a requirement to serve the appeal on—

(i) the Secretary of State; and
(ii) where the appeal is by a licencee under a group licence against compulsory variation, suspension or revocation of that licence, the original applicant, if any; and

(b) the court may remit to the Secretary of State for him to provide the court with such further information as the court may require.

AMENDMENT
¹ As amended by Act of Sederunt (Rules of the Court of Session Amendment No. 3) (Miscellaneous) 1996 (S.I. 1996 No. 1756), para. 2.

Motion for further procedure
41.42—(1) Within 14 days after the expiry of the period allowed for lodging answers to an appeal, whether or not answers have been lodged, the appellant shall apply by motion to the Inner House for—

(a) such order for further procedure as is sought; or
(b) an order for a hearing.

(2) The inner House shall, on a motion under paragraph (1)—

(a) in relation to a motion under paragraph (1)(a), make such order as it thinks fit; or
(b) in relation to a motion under paragraph (1)(b) without hearing parties—

(i) appoint the cause to the Summar roll for hearing; or
(ii) direct that the cause be heard in the Single Bills.

FORM 41.19

Form of appeal in appeal under statute to the Court of Session

APPEAL

to

THE COURT OF SESSION

under

(*State provision in enactment under which appeal is made*)

by

[A.B.] (*designation and address*)
Appellant

against

A decision [*or as the case may be*] of (*name of tribunal*)
dated (*date*) communicated to the appellant on (*date*)

The decision [*or as the case may be*] of (*name of tribunal*) dated (*date*) is in the following terms [*or where a lengthy or reasoned decision is appealed against*, is appended to this appeal].

The appellant appeals against the foregoing decision [*or as the case may be*] on the following grounds.

GROUNDS OF APPEAL

(*State the grounds of appeal in numbered paragraphs*)

(*Signed*)

Appellant
[*or* Solicitor [*or* Agent] for appellant]

APPENDIX

(*Here set out lengthy or reasoned decision appealed against.*)

RULES OF THE COURT OF SESSION

(S.I. 1994 No. 1443)

[5th September 1994]

. . . . . .

Applications for commission and diligence for recovery of documents or for orders under section 1 of the Act of 1972[1]

35.2.—(1) An application by a party for—

(a) a commission and diligence for the recovery of a document, or

(b) an order under section 1 of the Act of 1972,

shall be made by motion.

(2) At the time of enrolling a motion under paragraph (1), a specification of—

(a) the document or other property sought to be inspected, photographed preserved, taken into custody, detained, produced, recovered, sampled or experimented on or with, as the case may be, or

(b) the matter in respect of which information is sought as to the identity of a person who might be a witness or a defender,

shall be lodged in process.

(3) A copy of the specification lodged under paragraph (2) and the motion made under paragraph (1) shall be intimated by the applicant to—

(a) every other party;

(b) in respect of an application for an order under section 1(1) of the Act of 1972, any third party haver; and

(c) where necessary, the Lord Advocate.

(4) Where the Lord Ordinary grants a motion made under paragraph (1), in whole or in part, in an action before calling of the

summons, he may order the applicant to find such caution or give such other security as he thinks fit.

(5) The decision of the Lord Ordinary on a motion under paragraph (1) in an action before calling of the summons shall be final and not subject to review.

(6) The Lord Advocate may appear at the hearing of any motion under paragraph (1).

AMENDMENT
[1]Administration of Justice (Scotland) Act 1972.

THE COUNTRYSIDE (SCOTLAND) REGULATIONS 1982

(S.I. 1982 No. 1467)

[16th November 1982]

In exercise of the powers conferred . . . by sections 14(3), 22, 26(1), 31(3), 34(3), 35(6), 37(2), 62(8) and 78(1) of, and paragraphs 1(1), 3 and 4 of Schedule 3 to, the Countryside (Scotland) Act 1967 and of all other powers enabling . . . make the following regulations—

PART I

Citation, Commencement, Interpretation and Revocation

1. These regulations may be cited as the Countryside (Scotland) Regulations 1982 and shall come into operation on 16th November 1982.

2.—(1) In these regulations, unless the context otherwise requires, the following expressions have the meanings hereby assigned to them respectively, that is to say—

"the Act" means the Countryside (Scotland) Act 1967;
"a public path creation order" means an order made under section 31;
"a public path diversion order" means an order made under section 35;
"a public path extinguishment order" means an order made under section 34;
"a public path order" means a public path creation order, a public path diversion order or a public path extinguishment order, and includes an order revoking or varying any such order.

(2) Any reference in these regulations to a section bearing a number is a reference to the section bearing that number in the Act.

3. The Countryside (Scotland) Regulations 1975 are hereby revoked.

PART II

ACCESS TO OPEN COUNTRY

4. This Part of these regulations shall apply to the following maps—

(a) any map required to be contained in an access order made under section 14 (hereinafter referred to as an "access order map");

(b) any map required to be prepared under section 26 (hereinafter referred to as a "rights of public access map").

5. Any maps to which this Part of these regulations apply shall be on a scale not less than the scale shown opposite the description of that map in the following tables—

Description of Map	Minimum Scale of Map
Access order map	1:10,000 or 1:10,560 where 1:10,000 is not available.
Rights of public access map	1:25,000 or 1:50,000 where 1:25,000 is not available.

6. Every access order map shall define the land comprised in the order by means of a green edging, and in addition, so far as it appears practicable to the authority making the order, shall identify—

(a) any land so comprised, which is subject to restrictions on access by virtue of the order, by means of green edging and green dots overall;

(b) any land so comprised, which at the time when the order is made is excepted land, by means of green vertical hatching edged green.

7.—(1) Every right of public access map shall identify land of any of the descriptions specified in Column 1 of the following table by means of the symbol specified opposite that description in Column 2 of the said table (enclosing an identification number if appropriate) on the said map—

Column 1	Column 2
Land subject to an access agreement	□
Land subject to an access order	○
Land acquired and held under section 24	▲
Land acquired and held under section 25	◇

(2) Every right of public access map shall, in addition, so far as appears practicable to the authority required to prepare the map, define—

   (a) any land comprised in an access agreement or order, which is subject to restrictions on access by virtue of the agreement or order, by means of a green edging and green dots overall;

   (b) any land so comprised, which is for the time being excepted land, by means of green vertical hatching edged, green;

   (c) any land comprised in land acquired and held under section 24 or 25, from which, for the purpose of avoiding danger to the public or to persons employed thereon or for any other reason, the public are excluded, by means of green cross hatching edged green.

8. Inset maps on a larger scale than the minimum specified in regulation 5 hereof may be included in any map to which this Part of these regulations applies for the purpose of more particularly defining any part of any land and in the case of conflict between the map and the inset map the latter shall prevail.

Part III

Form of Public Path Orders

9. A public path order shall be in the appropriate form (or substantially in the appropriate form) set out in Schedule I hereto with such modifications as the circumstances may require.

10. The map required to be contained in a public path order shall be on a scale of not less than 1:2,500 provided that the Secretary of State may in any particular case authorise a smaller scale.

11. In the case of any conflict between the map and the particulars contained in the schedule to the public path order, the schedule shall prevail.

PART IV

PROCEDURE FOR MAKING OF ORDERS

12. An order submitted to the Secretary of State for confirmation shall be accompanied by—

(a) two copies of the order;

(b) a copy of any notice given before submission as required by Schedule 3 to the Act;

(c) a statement by the order-making authority of the grounds on which they consider the order should be confirmed;

(d) a copy of all representations and objections to the order; and

(e) in any case in which the Act requires the authority to obtain the consent of any other authority before the order is made, a certificate to the effect that such consent has been obtained.

13. After an order has been confirmed, or has taken effect by virtue of paragraph 2(1A) of Schedule 3 to the Act, the authority by whom the order was made shall, as soon as the requirements of paragraph 4 of Schedule 3 to the Act have been complied with, furnish the Secretary of State with a certificate to that effect.

14. Any proceedings required to be taken under the Act preliminary to the confirmation of a public path extinguishment order may be taken concurrently with any such proceedings preliminary to the confirmation of a public path creation order or a public path diversion order.

15. Any notice required to be given, published, served, affixed or displayed under Schedule 3 to the Act by an authority by whom an order is made shall be in the appropriate form (or substantially in the appropriate form) of Forms Numbers 1, 2, 3 and 4 set out in Schedule 2 hereto with such modifications as the circumstances may require.

16. Any notice or other document to be served on an owner, occupier or tenant in accordance with paragraphs 1(3), 2(3) or 4 of Schedule 3 to the Act shall at the beginning of such notice or document have clearly and legibly inscribed upon it in the following form, the words:

**IMPORTANT—THIS COMMUNICATION MAY
AFFECT YOUR PROPERTY**

and where the notice or document is sent otherwise than by prepaid registered letter or by the recorded delivery service the cover under which it is sent shall in addition be endorsed in like manner.

17. In this Part of these regulations the expression "order" means a public path or an access order made under section 14 and includes any order varying or revoking any such order.

PART V

CLAIMS FOR COMPENSATION

18.—(1) An application to record a claim to be entitled to an interest in land in respect of which compensation will become payable under section 20 in consequence of the coming into operation of an access order shall be in writing and shall be served on the planning authority by whom the access order was served by delivering it at the office of the authority addressed to the authority or by sending it by registered letter or by the recorded delivery service addressed as aforesaid.

(2) The time within which any such application shall be served shall be a period of six months from the coming into operation of the order in respect of which such claim is made.

(3) Any such application shall be accompanied by particulars of the interest in land in respect of which the claim is made, being particulars sufficient to identify approximately the boundaries of the land, and of the nature of the claimant's title thereto.

(4)(a) Every planning authority shall keep a register of the claims in respect of which application is made to them in accordance with this regulation containing the following information—

    (i) the name and address of the claimant;

    (ii) the date of the application to record the claim;

    (iii) particulars of the interest in land in respect of which the claim is made and of the nature of the claimant's title thereto and the order in respect of which the claim is made.

(b) Such register shall be kept at the office of the planning authority and shall be available for inspection by the public at all reasonable hours.

(5) Particulars of every such claim as is mentioned in paragraph (1) of this regulation in respect of which an application is served

within the time and in the manner prescribed by this regulation shall be entered by the planning authority in the register within seven days of the serving of the application and entry thereof in the register shall be notified by the planning authority to the claimant in writing as soon as practicable after the entry has been recorded.

19.—(1) An application for the payment of compensation under section 20 in respect of a claim recorded in accordance with the immediately preceding regulation hereof shall be in writing and shall be served on the planning authority by whom the claim was recorded in like manner as prescribed for an application to record a claim in the immediately preceding regulation hereof.

(2) The time within which any such application shall be served shall be a period of six months after the end of the period after which compensation may be claimed under section 21.

(3) Any such application shall include a statement of the amount of compensation claimed and particulars of the applicant's title to receive the compensation claimed and shall be accompanied by sufficient documentary evidence of the applicant's title to the interest in land in respect of which compensation is claimed.

(4) The rate of interest payable on any compensation payable under section 20 shall be the rate payable in terms of regulations made under section 40(1) of the Land Compensation (Scotland) Act 1963.

20. A claim for compensation under section 37 in consequence of the coming into operation of a public path order shall be in writing and shall be served on the authority by whom the order was made in like manner and within the like time as prescribed in regulation 18(2) hereof and shall include a statement of the amount of compensation claimed and the like particulars as prescribed in regulation 18(3) hereof.

21.—(1) A claim for compensation under section 62 in consequence of any work done under the powers conferred by section 61 shall be in writing and shall be served on the body by whom the work was carried out by delivering it at the office of the body addressed to the body or by sending it by registered letter or by the recorded delivery service addressed as aforesaid.

(2) The time within which any such claim shall be served shall be a period of six months from the date of completion of the work in respect of which the claim is made.

(3) Any such claim shall include a statement of the amount of compensation claimed and the like particulars as prescribed in regulation 18(3) hereof.

SCHEDULE 1   Regulation 9

Form No. 1   FORMS OF PUBLIC PATH ORDERS
                              PUBLIC PATH CREATION ORDER
                              COUNTRYSIDE (SCOTLAND) ACT 1967
                              (*Name of order-making authority*)
                              (*Title of order*)

Whereas it appears to the (*name of order-making authority*) that there is need for a [footpath] [bridleway] over the land to which this order relates;

And whereas the (*name of order-making authority*) are satisfied, having regard to the extent to which the [path] [way] would add to the [[convenience] [enjoyment] of a substantial section of the public] [convenience of persons resident in the area] and the effect which the creation of the [path] [way] would have on the rights of persons interested in the land (account being taken as to the compensation provisions of section 37 of the Countryside (Scotland) Act 1967 (hereinafter referred to as "the Act")), that it is expedient that the [path] [way] should be created;

And whereas it has proved impracticable to the (*name of order-making authority*) to create the [path] [way] by means of a public path creation agreement within the meaning of the Act;

[And whereas (*name of consenting authority or authorities*) have consented under Section 32(2) of the Act to the making of this order;]

Now therefore (*name of order-making authority*) in exercise of the powers conferred on them by section 31 of the Act and of all other powers enabling them in that behalf hereby make the following order—

1. There shall be at the expiration of   days from the date of [confirmation of this order by the Secretary of State] [the making of this order by (*name of order-making authority*)] a [footpath] [bridleway] over the land described in [Part 1 of] the Schedule hereto and shown coloured [purple] [green] on the map executed as relative to this order.

[2. Notwithstanding anything contained in this order (*name of statutory under-taker*) shall have the following rights over the land referred to in paragraph 1 hereof namely—   .]

[3. The rights conferred on the public by this order shall be subject to the limitations and conditions specified in Part II of said Schedule.]

[4. (*Provisions regarding expenses in terms of section 38(3) of the Act*).]

5. This order may be cited as the (*name of order-making authority and name of or reference to path or way*) Public Path Creation Order 19   .

Date

                              (*Authenticate in the manner
                              appropriate to the order-making
                              authority.*)

SCHEDULE

[PART I]

DESCRIPTION OF LAND

(Describe land in manner specified in section 38(4) of the Act)

[PART II]

LIMITATIONS AND CONDITIONS

Part of [footpath] [bridleway] to which limitations and conditions specified opposite are to apply	*Limitations and Conditions*
(Describe part of same)	*(Specify the same)]*

Note: Omit the words in square brackets where inappropriate.

Form No. 2   PUBLIC PATH EXTINGUISHMENT ORDER
COUNTRYSIDE (SCOTLAND) ACT 1967
(Name of order-making authority)
(Title of order)

Whereas it appears to the *(name of order-making authority)* that the [footpath] [bridleway] to which this order relates is not needed for public use [having regard to the extent to which *(here specify the relevant Public Path Creation/Diversion Order)* would provide an alternative [path] [way]];

[And whereas *(name of consenting authority or authorities)* have consented under Section 32(2) as read with Section 36(1) of the Countryside (Scotland) Act 1967 to the making of this order;]

Now therefore the *(name at order-making authority)* in exercise of the powers conferred on them by section 34 of the Countryside (Scotland) Act 1967 and of all other powers enabling them in that behalf hereby make the following order—

1. The public right of way over the land described in the Schedule hereto and shown coloured brown on the map executed as relative to this order shall be extinguished at the expiration of   days from the date of [confirmation of this order by the Secretary of State] (the making of the order by the *(name of order-making authority)*].

[2. Notwithstanding anything contained in this order *(name of statutory undertaker)* shall have the following rights over the land referred to in paragraph 1 hereof, namely—   .]

[3. *(Provisions regarding expenses in terms of section 38(3) of the Countryside (Scotland) Act 1967).*]

4. This order may be cited as the *(name of order-making authority and name of or reference to path or way)* Public Path Extinguishment Order 19 .

Date

(Authenticate in the manner appropriate to the order-making authority.)

SCHEDULE

DESCRIPTION OF LAND

(*Describe in manner specified in section 38(4) of the Act*)

Note: Omit the words in square brackets where inappropriate.

Form No. 3   PUBLIC PATH DIVERSION ORDER
COUNTRYSIDE (SCOTLAND) ACT 1967
(*Name of order-making authority*)
(*Title of order*)

Whereas (*name and designation*) is the [owner] [tenant] [occupier] of land crossed by the [footpath] [bridleway] referred to in paragraph 1 of this order and has satisfied (*name of order-making authority*) that [for securing the efficient use [of that land] [of other land held therewith]] [for providing a [shorter] [more convenient] [path] [way]] it is expedient that the line of the [path] [way] should be diverted;

[And whereas the (*name of consenting authority or authorities*) have consented under section 32(2) as read with section 36(1) of the Countryside (Scotland) Act 1967 to the making of this order) [and] [(*name of authority*) have been consulted in pursuance of section 36(4) of the Act];]

Now therefore the (*name of order-making authority*) in exercise of the powers conferred on them by section 35 of the Countryside (Scotland) Act 1967 and of all other powers enabling them in that behalf hereby make the following order—

1. The public right of way over the land described in Part 1 of the Schedule [1] hereto and shown coloured brown on the map executed as relative to this order shall be extinguished at the expiration of   days from the date of [confirmation of this Order by the Secretary of State] [the making of this order by (*name of order-making authority*)].

[2. Notwithstanding anything contained in paragraph 1 of this order (*name of statutory undertaker*) shall have the following rights over the land referred to in the said paragraph, namely—   .]

3. There shall be at the expiration of   days from the date of [confirmation of this order by the Secretary of State] [the making of the order by (*name of order-making authority*)] a [footpath] [bridleway] over the land described in Part II of the said Schedule [1] and shown coloured [purple] [green] on the said map.

[4. The rights conferred on the public by this order shall be subject to the limitations and conditions specified in schedule 2 hereto.]

[5. (*Provisions regarding expenses or responsibility for maintenance in terms of section 38(3) of the Countryside (Scotland) Act 1967*).]

6. This order may be cited as the (*name of authority and name of or reference to path or way*) Public Path Diversion Order 19 .

Date

(*Authenticate in the manner appropriate to the order-making authority*)

SCHEDULE [1]

PART I

DESCRIPTION OF LAND AFFECTED BY EXISTING PATH OR WAY
(*Describe in manner specified in section 38(4) of the Act*)

PART II

DESCRIPTION OF LAND AFFECTED BY NEW PATH OR WAY
(*Describe in manner specified in section 38(4) of the Act*)

[SCHEDULE 2]

LIMITATIONS AND CONDITIONS

Part of [footpath] [bridleway] to which limitations and conditions specified opposite are to apply *(Describe part of same)*	*Limitations and Conditions*
	(Specify the same)]

Note: Omit the words in square brackets where inappropriate.

SCHEDULE 2   Regulation 15

FORMS OF NOTICES

Form No. 1   NOTICE OF PROPOSED PUBLIC PATH ORDER
COUNTRYSIDE (SCOTLAND) ACT 1967
(*Name of order-making authority*)
(*Title of Order*)

*To (*insert name and address of owner, occupier or tenant, as the case may be*).

Notice is hereby given that the above order is about to be made and submitted to the Secretary of State for confirmation, except that, in accordance with the provisions of paragraph 2(1A) or Schedule 3 to the above Act, if no representations or objections are duly made to the (*name of order-making authority*) or, if any so made are withdrawn, the order shall on being made take effect without it having to be submitted to the Secretary of State and without his confirmation.

The effect of the order as proposed will be to [create a [footpath] [bridleway] from   to   ] [extinguish the public right of way from   to   ] [divert the public right of way from to   to a line from   to] [[revoke] [vary] the   Order 19 , so as to].

A draft of the order and of the map referred to therein together with the statement of the reasons for the making of the order has been deposited at and may be inspected free of charge there during office hours.

*If you wish to have sent to you in due course any notice to the effect that the order has come into operation and a copy of the order as operative you should write to the (*name and address of order-making authority*) giving your name and address to which these documents may be sent.

Compensation for depreciation or damage in consequence of the coming into operation of the order is payable in accordance with sections 37 and 70 of the above Act.

Any representation or objection with respect to the draft of the order may be sent in writing to (*name and address of order-making authority*) before and should state the grounds on which it is made.

Date

(*Signature and designation of proper officer*)

*Notes: *Insert only in a notice to be served.*
Omit the words in square brackets where inappropriate.

Form No. 2   NOTICE OF PROPOSED ACCESS ORDER
COUNTRYSIDE (SCOTLAND) ACT 1967
(*Name of order-making authority*)
(*Title of order*)

*To (*insert name and address of owner, occupier or tenant, as the case may be*).

Notice is hereby given that the above order made on the (*date*) is about to be submitted to the Secretary of State for Scotland for confirmation.

The effect of the order if confirmed without modification will be to enable the public to have access for open-air recreation to certain areas of open country in the Parish of

A copy of the order and of the map referred to therein together with the statement of the reasons for the making of the order has been deposited at   and may be inspected free of charge during office hours.

*If you wish to have sent to you in due course any notice to the effect that the order has been confirmed and a copy of the order as confirmed you should write to the (*name and address of order-making authority*) giving your name and the address to which those documents may be sent.

Compensation for depreciation or damage in consequence of the coming into operation of the order is payable in accordance with sections 20, 21, 22, 23 and 70 of the above Act.

Any representation or objection with respect to the order may be sent in writing to the Secretary, Scottish Development Department, New St. Andrew's House, St. James Centre, Edinburgh EH1 3SZ, before   and should state the grounds on which it is made.

Date

(*Signature and designation of proper officer.*)

*Note: *Insert only in a notice to be served.*

Form No. 3 NOTICE OF COMING INTO OPERATION OF PUBLIC PATH ORDER
COUNTRYSIDE (SCOTLAND) ACT 1967
(*Name of order-making authority*)
(*Title of Order*)

*To (*insert name and address of owner, occupier or tenant, as the case may be*).

Notice is hereby given that on the (*date*), the [Secretary of State for Scotland confirmed [with modifications] the above order.] [(*order-making authority*) made the above order which takes effect by virtue of the provisions of paragraph 2(1A) of Schedule 3 to the above Act.]

The effect of the order [as confirmed] is to [create a [footpath] [bridleway] from
        to   ] [extinguish the public right of way
from   to   ] [divert the public right of way from
        to   to a line from   to
] [[revoke] [vary] the   Order 19 , so as to
].

A copy of the order [as confirmed] and of the map referred to therein has been deposited at   and may be inspected there free of charge during office hours.

*Any person who wishes to claim compensation for depreciation or damage in consequence of the coming into operation of the order in accordance with sections 37 and 70 of the above Act should do so within the time and manner prescribed by the Countryside (Scotland) Regulations 1982 (S.I. 1982/1467), a copy of which may be purchased from Her Majesty's Stationery Office, 13a Castle Street, Edinburgh EH2 3AR. The Regulations are also available for inspection at the offices of (*order-making authority*).

The order becomes operative as from (*date*), but any person aggrieved by the order or desiring to question the validity thereof, or of any provision contained therein, on the grounds that it is not within the powers of the above Act or on the ground that any requirement of that Act or of regulations made thereunder has not been complied with in relation thereto, may, within six weeks from the date on which this notice is first published, make an application for the purpose to the Court of Session.

Date

                (*Signature and designation of
                proper officer*)

*Notes: *Insert only in a notice to be served.
      Omit the words in square brackets where inappropriate.*

Form No. 4   Notice of Coming into Operation of Access Order
             Countryside (Scotland) Act 1967
             (*Name of order-making authority*)
                (*Title of order*)

*To (*insert name and address of owner, occupier or tenant, as the case may be*).

Notice is hereby given that on the (*date*) the Secretary of State for Scotland [confirmed [with modifications]] the above order.

The effect of the order as confirmed is to enable the public to have access for open-air recreation to certain areas of open country in the Parish(es) of

A copy of the order as confirmed and of the map referred to therein has been deposited at   and may be inspected free of charge during office hours.

*Any person who wishes to claim compensation for depreciation or damage in consequence of the coming into operation of the order in accordance with sections 20, 21, 22, 23 and 70 of the above Act should do so within the time and in the manner prescribed by the Countryside (Scotland) Regulations 1982 (S.I. 1982/1467), a copy of which may be obtained from Her Majesty's Stationery Office, 13a Castle Street, Edinburgh. The Regulations are also available for inspection at the offices of (*order-making authority*).

The order becomes operative as from (*date*), but any person aggrieved by the order or desiring to question the validity thereof, or of any provision contained therein, on the ground that it is not within the powers of the above Act or on the ground that any requirement of that Act or of regulations made thereunder has not been complied with in relation thereto, may, within six weeks from the date on which this notice is first published, make an application for the purpose to the Court of Session.

Date

(*Signature and designation of
proper officer*).

Notes: *Insert only in a notice to be served.*
      Omit the words in square brackets where inappropriate.

INDEX